THE
FINAL
DIAGNOSIS

THE
FINAL
DIAGNOSIS

Cynric Temple-Camp

HarperCollins*Publishers*

HarperCollins*Publishers*
Australia • Brazil • Canada • France • Germany • Holland • India
Italy • Japan • Mexico • New Zealand • Poland • Spain • Sweden
Switzerland • United Kingdom • United States of America

First published in 2024
by HarperCollinsPublishers (New Zealand) Limited
Unit D1, 63 Apollo Drive, Rosedale, Auckland 0632, New Zealand
harpercollins.co.nz

Copyright © Cynric Temple-Camp 2024

Cynric Temple-Camp asserts the moral right to be identified as the author of this work. This work is copyright. All rights reserved. No part of this publication may be reproduced, copied, scanned, stored in a retrieval system, recorded, or transmitted, in any form or by any means, without the prior written permission of the publisher. Without limiting the author's and publisher's exclusive rights, any unauthorized use of this publication to train generative artificial intelligence (AI) technologies is expressly prohibited.

A catalogue record for this book is available from the National Library of New Zealand

ISBN 978 1 7755 4263 6 (pbk)
ISBN 978 1 7754 9294 8 (ebook)
ISBN 978 1 4607 3855 9 (audiobook)

Cover design by Darren Holt, HarperCollins Design Studio
Cover images by shutterstock.com
Typeset in Bembo Std by Kirby Jones
Printed and bound in Australia by McPherson's Printing Group

*To all the fine people whose stories these are.
You will be long remembered.*

CONTENTS

Introduction
A principio — from a good beginning   1

Part I	*Dangerous days*	
Chapter 1	For the love of a dog	13
Chapter 2	A burning question	31
Chapter 3	Claws of cancer	47
Chapter 4	Brain attack	65
Part II	*Chance and circumstance*	
Chapter 5	Hard landings	85
Chapter 6	Deliver us from evil	107
Chapter 7	What on earth have you been eating?: part I	126
Chapter 8	What on earth have you been eating?: part II	145
Chapter 9	Covid comes	169
Part III	*Murder most foul*	
Chapter 10	Musings on murder: part I	201
Chapter 11	Musings on murder: part II	223
Chapter 12	My age is against me	249
Chapter 13	'It looks like we've made the wrong diagnosis'	270
Chapter 14	*Semper ad meliora* — always towards better things	292

INTRODUCTION

A *principio* — from a good beginning

I love being a pathologist.

I would not not enjoy the glamour, the glitz or the glory of being a brain or a cardiothoracic surgeon. There is little doubt these super-surgeons are covered in the glow of public esteem and even adulation, whereas it is far more likely that a pathologist will only ever be covered in blood and faeces and foul fluids.

How can any doctor compete with those giants of the profession, who can delicately remove a brain tumour in a twelve-hour operation, or stitch a new valve into a beating heart? An ENT surgeon once ruefully told me that even amongst surgeons such as himself the cardiothoracic boys and girls were considered the royalty of the profession.

'We ENT surgeons are all really lovely, ordinary people,' he told me, 'but the cardios! They kick sand in our faces as they pass, ignore us, and steal our lunch sandwiches from our lockers.'

I am reasonably sure he meant this metaphorically, but you never know what happens behind closed doors in the theatre suite.

Yes, I love being a pathologist.

Every morning it is a joy to come to work to uncover what surprises the day will bring. The one certainty is that something wholly unexpected will turn up, from finding a strange cause of death in an autopsy to solving the mystery of a puzzling patient whose disease will at last be dragged from darkness out into the blinding light of day.

I hear from the experts in these things that we should all aspire to an orderly and predictable workplace, where we clock in at eight and out at five, with an hour off for lunch at twelve. This, apparently, will make us content.

Not for me, thanks. I relish the uncertainty of pathology; the complete unknown of the why, the what and the when of the next surprise call for help. I don't even mind being the bottom rail in the medical fence publicity-wise, for we have our own music, too.

Everyone in the medical profession is fully up to the mark about what happens in, and the point of, the autopsies we do. Our role in diagnosing cancers and other diseases is just as important as those doctors dealing directly with live patients, yet invariably it sits well below the public horizon.

Unless it is your own personal biopsy, and then you will want your answer from us. And quickly, too.

When pathologists feel undervalued by our clinical colleagues and our unseen patients, we are often driven to console each other with comfort food for thought. 'We are the eyes and ears of the surgeons,' we tell each other smugly. 'Without our diagnoses, they would be blind, and wouldn't

A *principio* — from a good beginning

know what to do.' Sometimes, too, we say we are the brains as well as eyes and ears, but I think that is mere braggadocio.

My pathological day is truly filled with the unusual, the strange and the unexpected stories of patients, their diseases and what became of them. In this book I will tell some of those tales, of the travails of some of these patients, and something of the different oddities that fill my days.

Many of these stories are of patients past and present, both long cured or still on their pathological journeys, with destinations unclear. I have used these amazing folk's real names where they have asked me to tell their story openly; others I have fictionalised in name, time or place, as well as the medical staff involved, to protect their identities. But all the events are true and have occurred here in New Zealand, unless specifically stated otherwise.

As Oliver Sacks says in his famous book *The Man Who Mistook His Wife for a Hat*:

To restore the human subject at the centre — the suffering, afflicted, fighting, human being subject — we must deepen a case history to a narrative or tale. Only then do we have a 'who' as well as a 'what', a real person. A patient in relation to a disease.

I have used his style of an empathetic semi-fictional narrative, and, like Sacks, I think this makes these stories so much more readable and valuable than presenting just the mere dry medical bones of the case. I am privileged to be the patients' narrator.

Autopsies are the signature dish for which pathologists are known and for which many have an insatiable appetite, so I will include a number of autopsy cases that are either tragic or odd or make a good point.

We are all by nature fascinated by murders, and I am sure readers will be looking for murder stories in this book. Alas, I have drained the well of local murders pretty dry, although in one way that must be good news for the Manawatū. I would not relish living in the murder capital of New Zealand!

Whenever I give talks to groups like Rotary or Lions, I always get asked about murders but never about diseases, which shows where our fascination lies. A frequent question I am asked is, 'How would I commit the perfect murder?' I am never sure whether the questioner's interest is purely academic, or they have some personal project in mind! The second most common question is one that you will easily guess, and that is: 'What do you think of the "whatchamacallit" murder?'

The 'whatchamcallits' are always famous public cases that I know only from what I have read in the paper or what I have heard as a member of the public. The common contenders are those infamous cases such as the Sounds murders of Ben Smart and Olivia Hope, the Crewe couple, and the Bain family, to name but a few. After being asked about them too many times, I decided to research some of these cases more deeply and look at them with a critical pathologist's eye, so I could give a more informed answer to my questioners. I found them professionally fascinating, with much to ponder upon.

Therefore, as some compensation for the lack of my own murder investigations in this book, I have included my thoughts of a number of these more famous cases. I have done this from the perspective of identifying the critical mistakes the murderers made that made it inevitable they would be caught. I also take a critical look at the quality of some of the evidence.

Critics of the trials of many of the more famous murder cases often are heard to complain, 'The evidence was purely circumstantial', as if this is some sort of 'get out of jail free' card. Yet such circumstantial evidence is extremely compelling, and when analysed thoughtfully can be incredibly powerful. As an example of the power of circumstantial evidence, in this book I have expanded upon my earlier accounts to talk of the explicit and ultimately damning circumstantial clues that Mark Lundy has been unable to overturn in multiple trials.

Supporters and advocates of the convicted perpetrators usually do not like what science reveals when the evidence does not run the way of their preferred story. They often end up earnestly running support groups, constructing unconventional ways to undermine the conclusions. But as popular and highly qualified astrophysicist Neil deGrasse Tyson says, 'The good thing about science is that it's true, whether or not you believe in it.' Astrophysicists like Tyson and Stephen Hawking are to scientists what neurosurgeons are to doctors: they are viewed as top of the academic heap.

Tyson also has an interesting perspective on the value of eyewitness evidence, about which I too am a confirmed sceptic. Later in the book I will talk more of this important eyewitness phenomenon and how it impacted on the Olivia Hope and Ben Smart murder trial.

I hope you find my musings on murder both entertaining and thought-provoking, and that they provide a different view to the pathologist's usual autopsy-based perspective.

The Final Diagnosis

* * *

Our lives were changed dramatically by the coming of Covid-19. The first wave of the pandemic was a time of chaos and change, and in pathology it all occurred so fast that I still cannot quite believe that it happened. We all have our Covid story: for most of us, it is of lockdown and the seemingly endless waiting for the gates of the country to be opened again. Many Kiwis did it tough, and it was a time of frustration.

That was not the case for pathologists and their laboratories, however. In this book (see chapter 9) I have told the tale of what happened to us in our lab. I am sure other labs had similar problems and maybe different experiences, but this is our story.

Before Covid came along, viruses were very, very low on my horizon. My autopsies usually revealed a sudden death or two every year from viral myocarditis. I religiously had my annual flu shot, and I was aware each year when the hospital wards were frantically full of virally afflicted elderly patients over the winter months. That was about the sum of my interaction with the viral world, and quite frankly I had no real interest in these creatures.

When Covid-19 popped its head over the fence in Wuhan in early 2020, I yawned and looked up my registrar notes from 1980 on coronaviruses. All we knew back then consisted of a mere three lines saying there were four known types, and they were a cause of the common cold. Not much to worry about with coronaviruses then, I thought.

With credentials as limited as this, I cannot now credibly pretend to be an expert in viral matters, but we have now

A *principio* — from a good beginning

all become only too aware of how dramatically significant they are to humanity, at the very least in causing disruptive pandemics.

'What's the point of all these viruses anyway?' one of my registrars asked angrily, her training seriously disrupted by the repeated lockdowns. 'Do they even do anything useful?'

It is a good question to ask. I guess we all thought much the same, but when I went to find out more about viruses the answer turned out to be a bit of a surprise. Viruses are now firmly under my fascinated gaze.

Viruses have now got a terrible name from this rogue pandemic, but in fact they are the good guys of our planet, one of the sustainers of life on Earth, and a profound part of our bodies, too. There are more viruses on this planet than there are stars in the universe, but they are so small we usually overlook them. According to one mathematical guru, all the Covid-19 virus ever created would fill less than one Coca-Cola can.

So how are our viral co-lifeforms the good guys? Without them we'd have only about a week to live, for the ocean is riddled with viruses called bacteriophages. They daily eat up and destroy googols of bacteria that would otherwise slaughter all the oxygen-producing plankton in the sea. Without these phages to protect the plankton, the last atoms of oxygen in the atmosphere would soon vanish, although long before this we would all have suffocated to death.

All over the Earth, viruses cuddle up to every other lifeform to create a 'virome' alongside the better-known bacterial biome, making them critical to the health and wellbeing of all other forms of life. One day we may well see human viral transplants following on from the recent fashionable trend of poo transplants and the bug-paste of probiotics we buy from the health shops.

Some viruses have entered our cells and hitched a transgenerational ride by attaching to the DNA of our genes. Surprisingly, this can be very much to our advantage, as a very common virus protects us from a deadly disease.

We have all heard of the deadly Black Death, the plague that wiped out half of the population of Europe — maybe 300 million people — back in the Middle Ages. The echoes of that mega-disaster are still said to ring today in the dark childhood nursery rhyme:

Ring a ring o' roses
A pocketful of posies
A-tishoo, a-tishoo
We all fall down!

In one common interpretation, the 'ring o' roses' is the characteristic bubonic plague rash; the posies are the useless nosegays anxiously carried to ward off the infectious miasma; the sneezing signified the onset of pneumonic plague, with its near 100 per cent mortality; and it all ends tragically with everyone falling down dead.

We have all heard, too, of herpes virus infections, which are both uncomfortable and widespread. One in five of us apparently carries the virus. But why is herpes so common?

There are a few reasons, but the most amazing is that having a herpes infection gives our body cross-protection from the bubonic plague. This odd freak of nature means that humans with herpes also became the chosen survivors during the years of plague, and so that tendency to catch

A *principio* — from a good beginning

herpes has survived in modern populations. Chalk up one for the virus good guys!

Several other viruses are known to boost our immune systems in much the same way, and no doubt we will discover more and more in the future.

Most intriguingly, we owe our very existence as mammals bearing live babies to ancient viruses. One hundred and thirty million years ago, our primitive animal ancestor could only lay her eggs in a nest, though she did produce milk for the hatchlings, a bit like a platypus. The creature was at a primitive evolutionary dead-end. Some biologists have even quipped that the thing this egg-laying, milk-producing ancestor was equipped to do was to make her own custard, but that was about it!

Then one fine day this custard-combo creature became infected by a retrovirus that attached its DNA onto and into the animal's genes. The platypus thing had won the evolutionary lottery, because the virus was able to take over those genes and use them to create a placenta, leading to the ability to carry live young and give birth. Eight per cent of the DNA of the modern human placenta is critical genetic designer software directly stolen from this ancient and friendly virus.

We would be a very different planet but for that virus. Without it, I guess our obstetricians and midwives would today be waddling about nosing our incubating eggs with their beaks, rather than bipeds wearing scrubs in birthing suites.

This new information has changed and softened my viral viewpoint drastically. Covid changed everyone's world view and has been the most significant event in our generation's history. It is to mark this epoch-changing event that I have departed from my usual stories of autopsies and patients to tell you of the backroom frustrations we pathologists went through during the pandemic to reach the relatively calm waters of 2023. We should not tremble with glee, however, because I have a feeling we have not seen the last of this virus yet.

There is no difficulty in beginning; the trouble is to leave off!
— Henry James, quoted in *The Diary of Alice James* by Alice James, 1891

PART I

Dangerous days

CHAPTER 1

For the love of a dog

Pathologists' office, 7.45 a.m.

It was still early but I was ready for the day. My computer was fired up, my microscope light was burning and an anticipatory aroma of freshly made coffee called tantalisingly from close by. That was when the phone rang.

I pressed the receiver to my ear and picked up my pen in expectation. 'Good morning, Dr Temple-Camp speaking.'

'Good morning, Sergeant Brannigan here, Wellington Police. Are you the duty pathologist for autopsies today?' We in Palmerston North were covering the Wellington autopsies that day, as their local pathologist was having a day's leave.

'Yes, that's me. What's happening out there?' I kept it light-hearted, but I knew precisely why the police would be on the phone at this early hour. Someone, or maybe even several people, were somewhere out there unexpectedly very dead, and the coroner needed an autopsy to find out why.

'We had a fatality in the Hutt yesterday morning. Forty-year-old male apparently in a motor vehicle accident.'

'Why only "apparently"?' I heard the nuance in his voice. Something wasn't right here. Over the years I have learnt

The Final Diagnosis

that it pays to listen to not only what information the police give you but how they give it. It's also worth wondering about what they are *not* saying.

'Doesn't look like any vehicle accident we've ever seen. We think it's a suicide.'

Suicide by car. Autocide. That was indeed different.

My mind automatically flicked through everything I knew about autocide, trying to remember what I was supposed to do as a pathologist to prove or disprove that possibility.

Autocide is a stolen word that has been adopted only recently to describe those people who commit suicide by driving at high speed into a truck or a tree, as well as those using a vehicle to murder someone else by running them down in cold blood. Before this modern use, autocide was a seventeenth-century word for a simple suicide. More recently, in the 1960s, the agriculture boffins also pinched the word to describe their method for eradicating insect pests by breeding millions of sterile males and releasing them to falsely impregnate unsuspecting fertile females.

Nowadays suicide by car or motorbike is thought to be quite common, though it can be devilishly hard to prove without something like a final note or a history of other attempts. As far as I could remember, there was usually not a great deal of information to be found in an autopsy to tell the difference between autocide and a straightforward fatal motor vehicle accident, or MVA.

I wondered what I might usefully add. People often ask me why we always do autopsies following traffic and other accidents, where the cause of death is usually so breathtakingly obvious. An autopsy always has to be done just to make sure the findings all fit the scenario. A solitary local, depressed fracture of a skull with no other injuries, for instance, would be odd in a car crash. You would need to discover exactly how that might come about in a situation where multiple injuries are the usual rule. A homicidal blow to the head would be distinctly more probable, so with that sort of isolated injury, we would then have to look further and harder. (This homicidal scenario can indeed occur, by the way — in other places there have been murders that had been cleverly disguised to look like traffic accidents.)

Sergeant Brannigan explained further: 'Peter Jones was driving a Nissan sedan, and at a roundabout went straight through and over the top of it, then raced through the forecourt of a petrol station and swerved off into a private driveway. He went at high speed into the garage, which was empty at the time, and hit the back wall. Made a hell of a mess.'

'Anyone else involved?'

'Nah. One-car accident. The owner of the garage was out in his car, luckily, and the rest of the family were all inside the house. He had left the garage door up, otherwise this bloke probably would have gone straight through that as well.'

'What if he just lost control and careered into the wall? Why do you think it is autocide?'

'I can't see how anyone could do it accidentally. His direction of travel was just weird — not what you'd see if he was out of control and skidding or sliding. We reckon it must be deliberate.'

I could tell the police had already made up their minds. However, I persisted.

'Any note left?'

'No, nothing's been found yet, but it could still pitch up somewhere. Checked his phone, too. No messages or calls in or out.'

So no easy answer there.

'Any depression? Other mental illness?'

'Nothing. We've checked with his doctor. He was fit, and there was nothing to suggest he'd do anything like this.'

This is actually the case in so many suicides, as is the lack of a final letter or note. The families of the victims are often profoundly devastated by these completely unexpected deaths. Of course, all families suffer with the death of a loved one, but there seems to me to be an extra cutting edge when it comes so suddenly and is completely out of character, and they never find any explanation.

'What about family circumstances?'

'What do you mean by that?' The policeman sounded puzzled.

'You know: lost his job, marriage breakup. That sort of thing.'

'Oh, I see.' He thought for a moment. 'He was employed as a manager in the Primary Health Organisation. Quite high level. Managed the local GPs apparently. But he was on leave at the time. His bosses were pretty shocked to hear about it, and so was his wife. Quite out of character, apparently. Don't reckon there's much going on there in that regard — not socially, anyway.'

'On leave? What time of day did this happen?' I was thinking of partying, and maybe recreational drugs.

'We got the call just after 10 a.m.'

'Bit early for a boozy party even in the Hutt, surely?' I was taking the piss with him now.

He chuckled. 'I reckon.'

'Where is the body now? In Wellington?'

'The undertaker has uplifted him and he's on his way up to you now. They left at seven, so should be with you by nine.'

'I'll let you know what I find.'

I thought I had covered all the bases. But there was one fact Sergeant Brannigan did not tell me, which would never even have occurred to me to ask about.

But it was one fact that would change everything.

Mortuary, 9.30 a.m.

'Good morning, doc. He's all ready for you.'

'Morning, Pat. Anything unusual to see?'

Pat and the Wellington undertaker had wheeled the body from the underground mortuary forecourt into which the hearse had driven, the roller doors metallically grinding closed behind it to conceal the scene from prying eyes.

The mortuary assistants are experienced at moving heavy bodies single-handedly, even those patients weighing in at 100 kilograms and more. It's not for nothing that something that is hard to shift is often called a 'deadweight'. It's just possible this word was first thought up by mortuary assistants, who have real-life knowledge of what it really means.

It's not just the body weight that matters — it is the awkward shape of the human body and its rigidity after death, too. We also have to be so careful and gentle not to cause postmortem injury in a stainless-steel-clad mortuary filled with hard corners and edges. The assistants have power lifts to help, but getting a body out of the body bag on the trolley and pulling them across onto the gurney for the evisceration is quite a skill. This effort might seem exhausting, but even our diminutive assistant Simone, at just 160 centimetres tall, seems to do it with admirable ease.

'Nah — pretty standard high-impact job. Head, chest, arms and legs. Wasn't wearing a seat belt.'

I pondered that. It was suspicious, but it was not good-quality, reliable evidence to differentiate suicide from an accident. Suicides can do some bizarre things from habit, such as putting on a seat belt before driving into a tree. Sometimes they've done things that confuse the scene, such as putting a pillow beneath their heads before shooting themselves, so you end up wondering if they were actually murdered while asleep. Why would you go to the trouble of making yourself comfortable when you were about to end it all abruptly anyway?

I went over to the gurney and studied my patient. It was not a pretty sight. His face had imploded upwards into his skull. Shards of skull bone projected through a star-shaped split in his scalp, gleaming whitely in contrast with his blood-sodden dark hair. Brain matter was splattered throughout the injury, and blood was oozing from both ears.

'Fractured base of skull,' I murmured, as much to myself as to Pat. The blood coming from that unexpected place was an unmistakable sign of a massively destructive shattering of the body's very hardest part: the sphenoid bone, running from ear to ear.

His head was also lying at an unnatural angle.

'Looks like the cervical spine fractured and dislocated, too,' I added to the list. I often make my observations out loud, as it helps fix them in my mind. Pat nodded sombrely. He, too, had seen it so many times before. There seemed to be nothing new here.

The victim's chest wall had been crushed by the steering wheel. The deformed breastbone and fractured ribs alone would have been fatal even without the head and spine damage. We do not see as many car accidents where no seat belts were worn as we used to. Dead is dead, I suppose, but the damage inflicted to a body without a belt is truly hideous.

And then there were his limbs.

The force from decelerating in a millisecond from maybe 40 or 50 kilometres per hour to zero had transmitted up through the floor of the car and the brake and accelerator pedals into his legs, smashing them instantly and telescoping them to a fraction of their normal length. That force had also been flung up the steering column and into the steering wheel, where it had unleashed the same compression force on both his arms and shoulders.

There were also countless lacerations and ruptures to skin and muscle and fat all over the body. All had to be photographed and described. I sighed. There was a big job ahead of me.

'Can you smell booze?' I had caught a whiff as I bent over to look at the facial injuries.

Pat nodded in agreement. 'Yeah, I thought there was a bit of a pong. Could be from last night's piss-up, though.'

'It's not you reeking like that then, is it?' I feigned a suspicious glare at him, but he beamed expansively, his walrus moustache quivering. He knew me too well.

'Nah, haven't been near the turps for weeks.'

I smiled back to show I was toying with him. 'Let's do it.' I nodded to Pat to start the evisceration. 'I'm sure the undertaker wants to get back to Wellington before nightfall.'

Mortuary, 12 p.m.

I replaced the dissected heart into the chest. It was ruptured, with the right-side ventricle and atrium nearly completely ripped off, avulsed by the horrific impact.

'We're done.' I turned to rinse the blood and tissue from my gloves. I always have the tap running, as the organs are usually obscured by clotted blood and sometimes in the case of motor vehicle accidents with gravel and stones, so they need cleaning before examination.

'I'll notify the coroner and get the body released. Have you taken blood for toxicology?'

Pat nodded and held up two tubes containing blood and one of urine. 'His bladder was about the only thing that hadn't ruptured, and it was full, so I got some urine, too.'

The urine looked as clear as spring water. Very dilute. He must have been well hydrated to produce that, I thought.

'Should I send them off to ESR?'

I nodded. We always check the blood for alcohol as well as recreational drugs and any prescription medicines. This was where major surprises often come up. Sometimes there are things that the patients never wanted anyone else to know about, but death often lets the cat out of the bag.

'Have you got a spare tube?' I'd had an idea. Both of us had become pretty sure as we went along that we could smell alcohol quite strongly in the corpse. 'I'll take it upstairs to check it out in Chemistry.'

I changed out of my scrubs and ran up the three flights to the lab, arriving breathlessly. It's the only exercise I ever get in this job.

I handed the specimen over to Dave, the Chemistry head scientist. 'Can you do me a favour, please? Could you run an urgent blood-alcohol level and a "drugs of abuse" screen for me on this postmortem blood? We've got a bit of a mysterious death on our hands.'

'Sure thing. We like a mystery. I'll bring you the results in two hours or so.'

Pathologists' office, 3.20 p.m.

'What is the pattern of disease we are looking at?' I looked expectantly at Toni, the young registrar. We were examining a puzzling bowel biopsy that the gastroenterologists had taken earlier in the week.

'Er, is it granulomatous, maybe?'

I smiled. 'Correct. There are granulomas scattered along the lining of the bowel, dug in as tight as ticks on a dog. But why are they there? They are not normally seen in the bowel, are they? What are they doing? What has made them do that? If you can find the answer to these questions you will find what is ailing this patient.'

No matter how busy we are or how many autopsies there are to do, we still have to continually train the young pathologists who will be taking the baton from us.

'Knock, knock!' The door was wide open as always, but Dave always announced his arrival like that. 'Your autopsy blood results on Peter Jones.' He handed over a report sheet.

I scanned it and whistled in surprise. 'His alcohol is 260 milligrams per litre! That's just bloody unbelievable!'

'Checked it twice. It's correct.'

I knew he had, and I knew it was right.

'Thanks, Dave.' I stared pensively out of the window.

'What does it mean? Does this make suicide more likely?' Toni looked at the result with interest.

'Yes, it does look that way,' I admitted. 'I guess on the face of it this could be called a straightforward accident, obviously caused by alcohol. But this is an unbelievably high level for casual drinking, especially at ten in the morning in a middle-class, forty-something man, holding down a responsible job. Teenagers in the middle of a party night, sure. But I've never seen a situation quite like this before. With such a high mid-morning blood alcohol, I suppose the balance of probabilities shifts to an autocide after all.'

I sighed and shook my head. 'Let's get back to our mysterious bowel biopsy, shall we?'

We turned back to the microscope, but we had not even managed to refocus our eyes on the bowel with its enigmatic granulomas when the next interruption arrived.

'Gidday all! TC — signature please!' Pat breezed into the office, beaming at us and disrupting our measured discussion and train of thought. He dumped a pile of forms in front of me. 'Here you are. Toxicology forms to sign, please, for Mr Jones's blood.'

Although I had already arranged for our own in-house tests in our lab, that was only to satisfy my insatiable curiosity for a quick answer. I still had to re-order the same panel of forensic tests from the ESR laboratory in Johnsonville. These ESR results were automatically accepted in court as valid, whereas ours, although identical in every respect, could be challenged on all sorts of grounds by defence lawyers. What is good enough to treat our living patients in a hospital is, absurdly, not apparently good enough for the dead in a criminal case.

I pulled the pile of forms towards me and began filling out the tests I wanted.

'I hear it was a terrible case, Pat. Been a bad day for you guys?' Toni asked sympathetically, turning from our microscope as I was scribbling my signature on the forms.

'Nah, not too bad.' Pat shrugged, smiling at her.

As I wrote, I listened with half an ear to their banter, hearing his tone of gentle understatement. The mortuary assistants always make a point of playing down our bad cases to outsiders, no matter how grotesque they had been. I have always supposed that it was a defensive thing, that the cases were best not spoken of and put right out of mind.

'Nah,' he was saying, looking at Toni. 'It was OK. Weird thing about the dog, though.'

My eavesdropping ear sounded the alert.

'Dog?' I swung my chair around to face Pat. 'Dog? What's this about a dog? I didn't hear anything about a dog from the police.'

'Ah, just what the funeral director told me.'

'What did he say?'

'The bloke had his dog in the boot of the car, apparently. It survived.'

I looked at Pat in surprise. Was this true? What did it mean?

Five minutes later I had Sergeant Brannigan on the phone once more.

'That's right, doc,' he confirmed. 'Golden retriever bitch in the boot. Nice-looking dog, called Bonnie. Luckily quite unharmed, though a bit shaken.'

The Final Diagnosis

I was silent.

'You still there, doc? Doesn't make any difference, does it?' Sergeant Brannigan sounded worried.

'Yes, it might well do. Did you ask why the dog might be in the boot?'

'Oh yes. His wife says he was totally devoted to that dog. Used to take her to the dog park to walk, according to his wife, every single day, and sometimes twice a day. She was glad the mutt had survived.'

'In the boot? He always took her in the boot? Why?'

'Yep. Apparently always in the boot. She's a shedder and he didn't like her fur all over his car.'

I smiled at that. My 20-year-old Subaru was coated with years of shed fur from generations of Labradors, and you could not be a passenger without inadvertently taking a goodly gift of it home with you. About once a decade the car was sent for grooming and a surcharge of $50 was always charged due to the labour required to extract the hairy deposits crammed tightly into every crack and cranny.

This new information might have been a small detail, but it completely changed my mind about the course of events. I could imagine Peter opening the boot and Bonnie joyfully leaping up: 'Dog park, here I come!' I believe it pointed to Peter's state of mind. Surely, he never opened that boot saying, 'Good dog! Jump up, Bonnie! We're off to kill ourselves!'

'I don't think this is suicide. Not in my book,' I said firmly. 'I don't believe that anyone puts their dog in the boot and then drives their car into a wall. Next to him on the passenger seat, maybe, at a push, but probably not even then. It's like taking your kids with you on a death drive. Sure, it happens rarely, but it's just so against human nature,

I'd need a lot of convincing evidence to be persuaded otherwise.'

I thought for a moment. 'Think about it. He doesn't want fur on the seat? Why on Earth would he care if he knew he was going to kill himself and his dog in a couple of minutes? Why bother with the boot?

'The odd thing is his high blood alcohol, isn't it? I suspect you'll find he had a secret drinking problem, which has now been exposed by this accident.

'My gut feeling is this whole sad story is only about alcohol. For me, the dog in the boot trumps everything, and that means this was a nasty accident and not a suicide.'

Toni had been listening intently, following my reasoning.

'Is there any way we can be sure?' she asked once I was off the phone.

That was a difficult question to answer. 'Not really — it turns on what I know of human psychology. Love of a dog is a powerful force,' I replied. 'I may be wrong, but I really think it is highly unlikely anyone would also kill their dog, even if they are suicidal. How could they do it?'

Toni nodded. Her dog, Murdoch, was a spoiled and much-loved terrier, a firm member of their family, so she got my point. 'Dogs are so unconditional in their love for their masters, aren't they?' she said.

I leant back in my chair thinking, the fascinating bowel biopsy forgotten for the moment.

'Yes, that's true. Your dog would knowingly follow you into the Valley of Death rather than be left behind and alone, wouldn't he? I have seen a couple of strange cases involving dogs in my time.'

Toni settled back, looking at me expectantly. I gathered my thoughts for a moment or two and then launched into my story.

'There was an odd case in Whanganui a year or two back. Let me get this straight ...'

Enid was a 65-year-old reformed addict who was regularly active in the methadone programme. This meant she was legally given 50 ml of methadone three times a week as a substitute for morphine. Methadone is a safer drug than morphine, and the idea is to give the patient just enough to stop them having a bad withdrawal and going after the hard stuff.

That October day, her daughter Anita came to visit her, which she did once a week or so. Enid was inconsolable, weeping into a handful of sodden tissues.

'What's wrong, Ma?'

Enid looked up, eyes red-rimmed with sorrow. 'It's little Mitzi. She's dead.' And she wept anew.

Mitzi was a rescue dog. No particular breed, but Enid had chosen her from a yard full of those abandoned dogs whose only hope of avoiding death is to find an adoptive family. In return for her life and her care, Mitzi gave Enid back all the love she had. Mitzi was the brightest spot in Enid's life, and the two were inseparable.

'That's the problem with dogs, isn't it?' I said reflectively. 'We love them, feed them, play with them and walk them, and often even let them onto our beds. We love them even when they annoy us by not listening.

'I know all about that,' I added. 'My Labs have dysfunctional, ornamental ears stuck on the sides of their heads. They just don't hear me whenever it suits them. Whenever they are eating cat poo or off after another dog down along the river, they hear nothing I say, no matter how loudly I shout — but quietly open the fridge door while they are sleeping at the other end of the house, and they will hear it and be there like a shot.

'The problem is dogs just don't live very long, and then they break our hearts when they die. The feeling can often be as intense as losing a member of your family.'

Toni nodded in agreement, and I continued the story.

Mitzi's time had come. She had sickened quite quickly and in a few days she had gone. Enid couldn't bear to part with her, and lay the body on the carpet in the living room, in the very spot where the dog had lain through the past decade.

Anita had consoled her mum as best she could, but she had to go home to feed her newborn baby. 'Have a cup of tea and I'll come back tonight to see you again after I've fed Jack and put him to sleep,' she had told her mother.

Anita had told me Enid had seemed OK — just upset. There wasn't anything to make Anita think she was going to 'do something'. I turned to Toni. '"Do something", of course, is what people say when they don't want to say "commit suicide".'

Anita told me her mother had recently had some good news from her doctor. She had had a breast cancer removed the previous year and was worried the disease had spread to her lungs because she was coughing up blood. But her doctor had said it was just from her gums bleeding, and she was relieved. Anita felt her mother wouldn't have been so happy if she had been intending to take her own life.

Anita returned earlier than she had promised, at 3 p.m. I think she must have suspected something was up. She looked into the living room and saw Enid lying face down on the floor next to Mitzi, her arm over the dog.

'I thought she had been giving the dog a hug and had fallen asleep,' Anita told me. 'She often lies like that after she has taken her methadone, which makes her sleepy. I left her to sleep it off and thought I'd come back later.

'I came back with my partner at about 7 p.m. She was still in the same position. I felt her arm and it was warm, so I thought she was still asleep, and we left again.'

Enid was apparently always hard to wake up after taking methadone, but obviously Anita was still not sure all was well and returned just before midnight. Enid was now stiff and cold. She felt for a pulse but there was none, so she called an ambulance.

I paused in my telling of the story, staring sadly out of the window.

'So was it suicide?' Toni questioned.

I nodded. 'Enid had severe facial and frontal lividity from so long lying face down, so I had to be careful to make sure there were no injuries lurking beneath.'

When the heart stops beating, the blood stops going around the body and sinks to the lowest part. It becomes fixed in the tissues and to the uninitiated looks like severe bruising. And since it can hide real bruising from an assault quite effectively, I made sure that I examined her very closely.

'There was nothing much to find, really. A healed mastectomy scar on her chest and no spread of her cancer anywhere. But it was an overdose that killed her. We got the answer from her toxicology — there was a real cocktail of drugs in Enid's blood.

For the love of a dog

'There was quite a high level of prescription methadone, of course, but she was an experienced user and if that had been all there was, she probably would have handled it OK.'

People on the methadone programme develop a tolerance and can live with phenomenally high levels of it in their blood. Problems can come with naive users who get the drug from legitimate users and inject themselves. Their bodies are not used to it, and they can die suddenly from very much lower levels.

'But,' I went on, 'Enid also had zopiclone, amitriptyline and diazepam on board, in significant amounts. The only thing that was missing was any alcohol. Acting together, there was more than enough medication in her blood to kill her easily.'

'Were they her prescribed drugs?'

I nodded. 'Yes, they were old prescriptions all from a few years earlier. Nothing more recent, other than the methadone. She must have gone to the cupboard and pulled out her old leftover pills and taken the lot.'

'But lots of people have dogs, which must eventually die. Do suicides like this happen very often?'

'No, not really. I can remember only one other case. It was an old gent who lived independently alone with his dog as his only buddy. Bit like Enid and Mitzi, really. But he became increasingly unable to cope with things and his daughter moved him into a rest home.

'Unfortunately, he couldn't take the dog there and the dog was either given away, or more likely euthanised, as it was already old, I forget exactly which.

'Anyway, after a week or so he topped himself with his pills. Left a note saying he missed his dog and just didn't want to carry on anymore.'

The Final Diagnosis

We both stared out of the window. It was a clear day, and we could see the snow-covered peak of Ruapehu 130 kilometres away. The beauty of the vista contrasted with our sad thoughts.

'Yup, the old fellow in the home killed himself for the love of his dog and so did Enid for hers. And his love of that dog in his boot is why I think Peter Jones's death was a horrible accident and not suicide.' I took a deep breath.

'Right, enough of dogs and death now. Let's get back to the living and our mysterious bowel biopsy, shall we?'

Brothers and Sisters, I bid you beware
Of giving your heart to a dog to tear.
— Rudyard Kipling, 'The Power of the Dog', 1909

CHAPTER 2

A burning question

Laboratory reception, 7.30 a.m.

'Can I help you?' Maureen looked up through the serving-hatch window from her seat at the counter. A middle-aged doctor was standing in the corridor, politely smiling at her.

'Yes please. Sorry to trouble you but yes, I would really appreciate that.'

Maureen looked at him curiously. He was much older than the baby-faced junior doctors who usually arrived at this early hour, burdened with late request forms or looking for missing test results from the middle of the night. The juniors were often overwhelmed by dire emergencies and a host of tasks during the night that ate away the hours. There would be a drip to set up, a vomiting child to examine, interrupted by a call to check up on an elderly gent who tripped over his catheter bag while trying to reach the lavatory; so much to do that they didn't always get around to checking the results of tests they had taken earlier in the night. They had to be able to produce those results for their consultant on the ward round at 8 a.m., so an early morning, breathless rush to the lab was a daily phenomenon.

The Final Diagnosis

This doctor was well groomed, Maureen saw, with freshly wetted, combed-over, light brown hair. He was clean-shaven and smiling in a confident manner. These features contrasted with the usual dishevelled house surgeons with their red-rimmed eyes and crumpled clothes after twenty-four hours on the run in the wards and the Emergency Department.

Oddly, he was wearing short trousers with walk socks, and his bare knees protruded from beneath his white lab coat. His ID badge was turned face down, the only thing out of place. A stethoscope was casually draped around his neck, worn more as a doctor's badge of office than for ease of access.

'Thank you so much for your kind assistance.'

He was unusually polite, too. There was none of the hurried snap of stress-driven instructions peremptorily delivered at the hatch, the usual pre-breakfast fare that Maureen encountered.

'I am Dr Elmsley, and I am a consultant psychiatrist from Ward 22.'

Maureen looked at him with renewed interest. A psychiatrist visiting the lab was distinctly unusual at any time of day, as was any consultant this early in the morning. It was a bit of a gala event to have no less than a consultant psychiatrist come calling.

Maureen did not recognise him. She was sure she had not seen him before, but as psychiatrists are rare birds out of their wards, that was not too surprising.

'What can I do to help, doctor?'

'I need an urgent test on one of my patients, please.'

'Do you have his name or NHI number, doctor?'

A burning question

'Certainly: Theo Ten Brink. The surname is in two words. NHI number MSTI273. Date of birth 18 March 1970.' Dr Elmsley reeled this off effortlessly.

'That's impressive, doctor. All from memory, too.'

Maureen was indeed impressed. She was used to harassed juniors crossly scrambling through bulging lab-coat pockets for bits of paper, which they then dropped, or flicking through battered diaries decorated with sticky Bradma labels they had peeled from patients' files on the wards.

He smiled. 'Sure. I've got a photographic memory. And I do make a point of getting to know my patients very personally.'

'Got him.' Maureen had typed in Theo's NHI number and brought up all his results. She looked intently at the screen. 'I see we've got bloods on him from three occasions last night. Gosh, you have been busy, haven't you? Anyway, we do have plenty of blood sample still available, so we don't need another tube taken.'

She looked up. Elmsley was watching her strangely. Maureen felt a momentary unease, though she could not imagine why.

'What test should I add?' Her fingers poised expectantly over her keyboard.

'An urgent testosterone, please.'

Maureen frowned and looked up, puzzled. 'Testosterone? I'm not sure I've ever been asked for an urgent testosterone before.'

Now she was sure something was wrong.

'This is an urgent request.' Dr Elmsley was staring at her very oddly. He was still polite, but his tone was much less relaxed. Distinctly more formal. Maureen sensed he was about to pull rank. She shrugged mentally. He was the doctor, after all. Her fingers keyed in the test code request.

Her screen flashed, unexpectedly popping up 'Declined'.

'Now, why's that?' She stared at the screen, perplexed.

'What is the matter? This is urgent. I want this test right now.' Dr Elmsley was insistent. His tone of voice had now definitely changed. Maureen was sure his tone had become hostile, as she scrolled through her screens to find why the testosterone request had been blocked.

'Ah, here it is! This is odd, though.' She looked at him uncertainly as he stood leaning forward threateningly, now seeming to dominate the hatch between them. 'But I think it's good news for you.'

'What?'

'Mr Ten Brink has already had his testosterone measured during the night. In fact, he's had it done three times on different samples through the night.' She consulted the screen. 'The first was at 9.15 p.m. as an urgent consultant request. Then again at 1.22 a.m., also at a consultant's urgent request. And repeated again on the last sample at 3.47 a.m., as per a consultant telephone request. Do you want the results? I can print them all out for you now.'

Maureen turned in anticipation and pushed the power button to activate her printer. It clicked and buzzed into life.

'No, I don't want those results — I've already got those. I want an urgent new test. And do it immediately. It's an emergency.'

'I'll call Dave, the Chemistry chief scientist — only he can override the system when it declines a test. Please excuse me, doctor, I'll only be a minute.' Maureen could easily have called Dave on the phone, but she got up and left reception

A burning question

to fetch him personally. Something did not seem at all right and she wanted him to come and deal with it.

'Dave, there's something creepy about this doctor and I'm not sure what to do.' Maureen told Dave what had happened. He looked at the record of test results.

'Bloody hell!' Dave looked shocked. 'Three bloody testosterone levels, all done as urgent specimens! There is no such bloody thing as an urgent testosterone, anyway.' He stood up and walked to his office door.

'Wayne!' he called out into the laboratory. 'Can you come here for a minute, please?' The young scientist left the instrument he was calibrating at the bench and walked over. Wayne looked tired, and stubble covered his jaw; it was not only doctors and nurses who spent long hours through the night caring for patients. The laboratory scientists and technicians also put in the grind, and Wayne was at the blunt end of twelve hours' frantic labour at the testing bench.

'Morning, boss. What's up?' Wayne was already anticipating his breakfast and bed.

'You were on all night?'

Wayne nodded.

'What's the story with these three "urgent" testosterones?' Dave tweaked the air with two fingers of each hand to apostrophise the fallacy. 'And they're all on the same patient, for God's sake!'

Wayne smiled ruefully as he shook his head. 'Never seen anything like it. The first request seemed OK. The consultant phoned about eight last night and said he knew it was irregular, but could I do it anyway, as they had an urgent situation on hand. I thought it was bloody odd for the psych ward, as they never ask for anything urgent from us. I agreed only because they ask so rarely.'

'And the second?'

'The consultant came personally here to the lab with his blood sample. He said he was Dr Elmsley. He needed a repeat testosterone, and he said it was because they weren't sure the first was right. I sort of tried to argue with him, but he was insistent, so I gave in, overrode the computer block and did it again. Same answer, same normal level. I phoned it through to the extension he gave me. He sounded happy enough with that and thanked me. I thought that was that.'

'And then?'

'I was taking my meal break. He phoned ... oh, about four o'clock and got hold of Tracey this time. He gave her some cock-and-bull crap and persuaded her to repeat the test on the last sample. Said it needed to be checked. She agreed. Same result again.'

'Right. Thanks for that, Wayne. Come on, Maureen — let's go and have a chat with Dr Elmsley, shall we?'

Pathologists' office, 8.05 a.m.

'Morning, TC. We've got a curly one.'

I swung my chair around. 'Morning, Dave. How's Chemistry this morning?'

'The department's fine. It's your bloody consultant colleagues that are the problem.'

'Who is it this time?' My mind turned immediately to the specialists in the Emergency Department and Intensive Care Unit. They had dozens of hugely puzzling and dangerously complex patients to care for, and they often needed unusual,

A burning question

urgent laboratory tests done at odd times out of normal hours. Some of these tests were either difficult or impossible to perform, or took so much time in the middle of the night that unless specialist scientists could be found to come in to do them, they had to be deferred until the next morning. Midnight tensions between the clinicians and scientists were not uncommon, and it was always a part of my role to bring a sensible clinical mediation to any of the heated arguments.

'Do you know Dr Graham Elmsley? The psychiatrist?'

I nodded. 'Yes, I do — vaguely.' A psychiatrist as a nocturnal problem was the last guess I would have made. 'At least, I haven't ever met him in person, but he was on the phone a couple of times to me last week.'

'Was it by any chance about this patient's testosterone levels?'

He shoved Theo Ten Brink's results at me.

I looked at Dave in amazement. 'How the hell do you know that?'

'Just a hunch!' He was smiling.

Dave then filled me in on the night's testosterone charade.

I was intrigued. 'What did he say to you?'

'He launched into a complicated story about testosterone metabolism when I asked for some justification for his repeated requests. Some of it sounded plausible, just possibly, but most of it seemed like crap to me. He then said, "I need to know how artificial testosterone can affect the blood level. It is urgent." I asked him what he meant by artificial, and he said, "From medical implants. How can you reverse the effects?"

'He wasn't going to budge or piss off. After all, he is the doctor and a specialist, so I agreed to do it this once more.

But I told him he would have to call you to get the result. It's the same level, by the way. Plumb bloody normal.'

'Leave it with me. I'll give him a call.'

Psychiatry offices, 8.15 a.m.

'Morning, Alexander. What on earth is Graham Elmsley up to?' I had diverted from my journey down to the mortuary to begin an autopsy to drop into the psychiatric department to sort out the testosterone problem. I usually found problems were most amicably and quickly solved face to face. I had barged into the office of Alexander Anderson, a senior psychiatrist.

'Graham?' Alexander looked puzzled and shook his head. 'Nothing, as far as I know. He's been away at a conference in Sydney for a couple of weeks. Why?'

Now it was my turn to look puzzled. 'But I was talking to him only on Monday.'

Alexander shook his head again. 'Not unless you were talking to him in Sydney you weren't. Why?' he repeated.

I began to explain the events of the night. Alexander listened intently. At the mention of testosterone, a light dawned in his eyes, and he began to nod.

'I think I know what this is about. Is the doctor mid- to late thirties, light brown hair, a bit stocky and very polite?'

'I haven't actually seen him, but that sounds about right.'

Alexander laughed. 'Graham Elmsley is tall with dark hair. Your "doctor" must be one of our patients, Theo Ten Brink.'

'Patient? Well, that's the testosterone patient's name all right, but if he's a patient he's at large in the hospital by night, and he's wearing Graham Elmsley's white coat. Got his stethoscope on, too.'

A burning question

'I doubt that.' Alexander laughed. 'Graham doesn't wear a white lab coat or a stethoscope or even use one, I am sure. None of us do — I have seen our registrars wearing them, though buggered if I know why they do. They're no bloody use in psychiatry. So what's Theo been playing at?'

I explained the farcical tests of the previous night.

'What on Earth is this all about?' I asked. 'Can you tell me what's going on? He is your patient, is he?'

'I'm not entirely sure what is going on,' admitted Alexander, 'but he does have an interesting backstory.'

Apparently, Theo Ten Brink had first presented to his GP, Phillip Vaughan, in Wellington, a few months earlier, asking to have the testosterone level in his blood tested.

'Why is that?' Dr Vaughan was a very experienced general practitioner.

'My levels are very, very high and they're going to kill me. I know high levels give you liver cancer. I have read all about it, and I know.'

'Why do you think they are so high? Is there something in your medical history that makes you think that?' Vaughan knew there were rare testicular cancers that could produce testosterone and he wondered briefly if Theo had a cancer of which he was unaware.

'I have an implant. A testosterone implant.'

'Oh, that's different. When was this done, and why?'

Vaughan wondered why he did not already know this, from Theo's earlier visits. Maybe it was because all of the earlier consultations were for routine, banal, day-to-day afflictions, and he had never thought to probe any deeper?

'It was done in secret while I was asleep. I don't know why.'

'You mean under anaesthetic? Which hospital was this at?'

'No, it happened at home while I was asleep. They came in and inserted Testopel pellets into my leg.'

'Your doctor did it at your home?' It seemed odd, but Vaughan thought it might be possible to do under local anaesthetic, though he had never heard of it. But why on Earth would any doctor want to do that in a person's home?

'No, not by my doctor! These people did it one night while I was asleep! They crept in and injected them into me.' Theo showed emotion for the first time.

'"They"? Who exactly is "they"?' Vaughan was perplexed.

'It was them. They sneaked through the side door and injected me with the pellets. It was them.'

Phillip Vaughan looked at Theo with a dawning recognition that this was a much bigger issue than he had thought or was qualified to deal with. It was surely an issue of the mind and not the body.

'So it began,' Alexander continued his story, 'but it got worse quite quickly.'

Phillip Vaughan did do a testosterone level just to show Theo that all was well, but of course that made no difference to his aberrant beliefs at all. Theo was back in the surgery pretty much daily, badgering the nurses, demanding repeated testosterone tests, insisting to Phillip that the implants were in his thigh and threatening to cut them out himself unless action was taken.

Vaughan knew he was out of his depth. In desperation he referred Theo to the psychiatrists at Wellington Hospital. As expected, the same scenario played out there. He became a real nuisance, hanging around the wards and abusing the nurses.

'He seemed to have had a further delusion, or maybe it

A burning question

was actually a hallucination, real to him at least. He told one of the nurses that she was "a vampire bitch who wanted to stick her fangs into his neck". Or maybe that was just a colourful insult? He called another one "a psychiatric bitch" — not quite so impressive a description as a vampire but who can tell, perhaps it was rational and accurate?'

'Why is he in hospital here in Palmerston, and not back home in Wellington?'

'They had to trespass him from going into the hospital there, as he was so disruptive and was becoming quite aggressive with his threats. He then shifted up here, and we're now going through virtually the same saga.'

'But what's wrong with him? Surely this is a mental illness?' In common with most pathologists, I know little of modern psychiatry.

'It's hard to pin down into a specific diagnostic category. It's clearly a delusional belief centred on a real fear of harm coming to himself, and it sure has him preoccupied. There is some degree of paranoia, too, with the unidentifiable "them" sneaking into his room to do him mischief.'

'Can't you treat him? Sounds a bit like patients we've had with delusional parasitosis.' This is an awful condition where patients are convinced there are real parasites, and sometimes even seahorses, crawling out of their skin. Afflicted patients are always turning up to the lab with bottles and tissues of squamous skin scratchings, bits of stick and other detritus clawed from themselves in a futile attempt to prove their illusionary creature's existence. 'They get better after a while, but this sounds a bit different. It must be a bloody awful thing to be going on and on in his mind. Poor bloke — can't you give him some pills or something?'

'We've done what we can to stabilise things, but as you see we're not making much progress so far. Of course ...' I could see a glint of humour in Alexander's smile ... 'you pathologists can play a part in his therapy, too, if you like. Look at it this way: you could just keep doing the tests and reassuring him, and eventually the delusion might well burn out.'

I shuddered. Endless nights of repeated testosterone tests stretching to some distant time horizon sounded horrific, even if it were possible.

'No thanks! I've already wasted an hour or so talking to him about testosterone metabolism and answering his daft questions on the phone last week. I think Theo has had more than enough therapy from me!'

'Didn't you suspect he was a fraud?'

'No, not even for a second. I mean, I thought he was Graham Elmsley, and we don't really think you psychiatrists are really that clued up on chemistry anyway. Probably on a par with what I know about psychiatry. His questions didn't seem all that strange.'

'Thanks a lot for that!' Alexander laughed. 'But I do know what you mean.'

'In fact, I did a really embarrassing thing.'

'Oh, what was that?'

'Well, Theo made some sense, but I wasn't completely sure of my ground, so I put him through to Professor Peter George. You might not have come across him in your line? He's the professor of chemistry at Canterbury Health Laboratory in Christchurch. They're the lab where we send all our sophisticated tests to be carried out. He's one of the top biochemistry guns in the country.'

'Oh God, no!' Alexander was laughing more at my

A burning question

embarrassed discomfort than anything else. 'What did he say?'

'Well, I called him soon afterwards and asked how it went. I reckon he was fooled too. He told me that he and Theo had talked for about twenty minutes.

'"What did you make of his questions?" I asked Peter.

'"Oh, he made some interesting observations, I thought. He clearly knew a little bit about testosterone. Some were very odd, though. But no odder than those I sometimes get from some of our physician colleagues. I thought he was just a happy fool, really. He probably thought I was one, too. We cheerfully parted company on convivial terms."

'Now I know this, I am surprised that it went so well. Theo must sound very plausible. God knows what Peter will think when I tell him.'

Alexander was still laughing. 'Your worries are close to an end, so don't worry about it.'

'How's that?'

'Today just happens to be the day we take him to court to get a trespass order against him, to stop him coming here, other than for his regular scheduled consultations and therapies. That's this afternoon.'

'Poor bastard.' I felt somehow sad for Theo. 'It doesn't really solve his problems though, does it?'

Pathologists' office, 3.30 p.m.

'TC, have you heard the news?'

It was Alexander. He looked bothered and his face was flushed.

'No, what's that?'

'It's Theo Ten Brink. He's really done it in spades this time.'

'Not more testosterone tests, surely? We've permanently blocked those on the computer.'

'No, it was in court this afternoon. You remember he was going to be trespassed from the hospital?' I nodded. 'Well, we sent him along with one of our male nurses and a security guard, and they've just come back and told me what happened.'

They had been sitting in the foyer outside their designated courtroom, waiting to be called for the session, when Theo asked to go to the toilet. The nurse looked up and down the foyer, spotted the sign for the gents, and nodded.

'OK, it's just over there.' He pointed at the sign. 'We'll wait here for you. How long will you be, in case they call us?'

'Only a minute or two. It's just for a piss.'

The nurse and guard watched Theo head down to the lavatory. There was no way out except past them, so they were not too concerned. They might have been if they could have seen his face. He was grimacing with a deep emotion, and he had a hunted look to his eyes as they cast here, there and everywhere.

'Fuck! Will you look at that joker's face!'

Two young men were seated near the toilets opposite the courtroom in which they were both about to appear on a charge of breaching the peace. Reece Waugh and Liam Hayes were best of mates but had got into a spot of bother in a bar on Saturday night. They had finished three handles of beer and were well into their fourth when they fell into one of those senseless arguments that friends can get into, from time

A burning question

to time. Words were traded and these were exchanged after a while for fists. Quite a bit of damage to the bar was done before the bouncers managed to separate them and the police were called, and here they were now to answer for it all.

'Looks pretty sick, doesn't he? What do you reckon he's done?'

'Dunno, but it must be bad.'

They sat staring at the door Theo had gone through.

Then the toilet door suddenly crashed open, and Theo staggered out, his head in flames. His jersey was well alight, and the flames licked voraciously at his neck and face. Everyone looked up, startled by the explosive opening of the door, and stared in disbelief at the walking pyre.

'Christ, no!' I was horrified by the story. 'What had happened to him?'

'Apparently he had a cigarette lighter, and he poured lighter fuel over his head and jersey and set fire to himself. Fortunately, he immediately came out into the foyer, otherwise it would have been too late.'

Most people were stunned and just stared, but not these two young men. They had been watching the door for Theo to come out so they could have another look at him. They didn't hesitate for a second, leaping up and pulling him to the floor, then smothering the flames with their jackets. It didn't take them long, but even so Theo was pretty badly burnt.

'That's bloody terrible! Where is he now?'

'Down in the Emergency Department. He's OK and is stable but they're transferring him to the Burns Unit at Hutt Hospital. His burns are too complex for us to handle locally, apparently.'

The Final Diagnosis

'Why did he do it? Did he say?'

'Yes, I went down to ED and spoke to him before coming here. He says he was terrified of getting a jail sentence and it was all he could think of to avoid it. Of course, that was never even on the cards, but I suppose he wasn't to know that.'

'Bugger,' I said. 'What an unmitigated bloody disaster!' I do confess, though, that I was mischievously wondering if the Hutt Hospital lab would soon be doing plenty of after-hours testosterone tests.

'No, you're wrong there.' Alexander replied. 'There is one good thing that has come out of this crappy day.'

'Oh, what was that?'

'Those two young men up for disturbing the peace? They were facing a serious punishment, but the judge called them in and commended them both for their quick action and their public-spiritedness. He then discharged them without conviction as a reward, so for them at least it's been a gala day.'

'When we have done our very best, Papa, and that is not enough, then I think the right time must have come for asking help of others.'
— Charles Dickens, *The Magic Fishbone*, 1867

CHAPTER 3

Claws of cancer

Operating theatre, 8.20 a.m.

'You can begin.' The anaesthetist nodded her assent to the consultant surgeon Richard Coutts. He was scrubbed, gowned, gloved and masked. Opposite him stood Tim, his registrar, who, similarly dressed, was there to assist with the surgery. The theatre nurse stood close by Richard's side, her hands hovering expertly over her carefully arranged instruments. Her eyes flickered between the patient and Richard, ready to anticipate his need for any instrument.

Between them lay the sleeping body of the patient, Elizabeth Shortall. She was draped in green towels, her head screened off and under the watchful care of the anaesthetist, monitoring her vital signs. Only her belly was exposed, and this was already marked by an old midline scar. An ileostomy stoma protruded through her right side, bypassing her large bowel.

This was not her first rodeo. Elizabeth had been here before and under more serious circumstances.

'This operation will be a cancer hunt with a vengeance! Like the Hunting of the Snark!' said Richard with obvious relish, as his scalpel expertly slit through the scar down to the delicate peritoneal membrane beneath. He looked down at his incision with satisfaction. 'That's the first hurdle over. I was worried that there might be adhesions and the bowel would be stuck to the back of her scar, which would have been messy. But look!' He gently lifted the glistening peritoneal membrane between his forceps. 'As clean as the day she was born. You'd never believe that last year I grubbed out half her guts and left a huge raw patch and God only knows how much cancer behind in here.'

'So, what exactly is this search for? I thought we were just closing the stoma and taking out the uterus?' Tim asked.

'Elizabeth has tiptoed along a very narrow and crumbly path past a deep precipice to be here today. Do you know her story?'

Tim did, but he could see Richard wanted to yarn as he worked, so he shook his head. 'Not really. Some of it, of course, but most happened before I started this job.'

Richard settled to his tale. 'Elizabeth pitched up in ED about a year and a half ago and said she had been well but woke up one Sunday morning feeling really bad. This had come up literally overnight. The ED docs were suspicious of a bowel obstruction, so they summoned the general surgeons on call. They were onto her in a trice and arranged an urgent CT scan.'

It was bad news. The radiologist studying and scrolling rapidly through Elizabeth's scan turned to Chris, the on-call surgeon, who was watching intently.

'I thought it would be. What is it — malignant?' he asked.

The radiologist nodded sombrely. 'Looks like cancer throughout the peritoneal cavity. It's caking all the membranes and encircling the bowel. I'd put my money on peritoneal carcinomatosis, for sure. Tuberculosis or any other infection are so unlikely as to be also-rans, I'm afraid.'

'Could it be lymphoma?' Chris asked hopefully, for at least that was potentially curable, with the right chemotherapy. Surgeons often grasp at lymphoma when they hit an irresectable malignancy, one that can't be surgically removed. No one likes telling their patients dire news without any glimmer of hope. The possibility of lymphoma is usually raised more out of wishful thinking and desperation than in any real expectation that it is a likely diagnosis. But you never know what fate has in store for you. Sometimes it does indeed turn out to be tuberculosis or lymphoma, or something else unexpected that is completely treatable or even curable.

'Unlikely, but I wouldn't say never.' She shook her head. 'A carcinoma is most probable, and it looks to me as if the splenic flexure of the colon is encircled by the tumour. The odds are this is a colon cancer arising from there that has spread throughout the abdomen.'

'That fits.' Chris was downcast. 'She is presenting like a bowel obstruction.'

It was the worst of news. If the cancer was from the bowel, then it was both inoperable and quite untreatable. Chris persisted in his search for some comfort to offer his patient.

'What about the ovaries or uterus as the origin?' Those particular cancers are potentially treatable in many women, using a strong cocktail of carefully chosen chemotherapeutic drugs.

The radiologist scrutinised the screen closely but shook her head again. 'Both ovaries are normal, and the uterus is small and unremarkable. It hasn't come from there. Her colon is definitely the culprit here.'

The Final Diagnosis

'I'll take her to theatre and do a colonoscopy under sedation to grab a bit of the tumour for the pathologists to confirm the diagnosis,' Chris said. 'I'm not sure she can stand much more anaesthetic than a mild sedative anyway. She's a lot sicker than we thought at first.'

Chris got her straight into theatre and passed a flexible colonoscope from one end of the bowel to the other, peering intently at every centimetre of the gut lining. It was clean as a whistle — no cancer anywhere! The bowel obstruction must have been caused by an intra-abdominal malignancy, compressing the bowel closed from outside. So where in hell had the bloody thing come from?

Elizabeth was sinking fast, and a final diagnosis was desperately needed if there was to be any hope of finding any last-minute chemo-cocktail to bring her back again.

'We'll just have to laparoscope her and biopsy the tumour inside the abdomen,' Chris decided. 'That's now the only option for a biopsy.'

It was back to theatre that same day, with a general anaesthetic needed this time. The anaesthetists were disapprovingly sucking air through their teeth and shaking their heads. Elizabeth's condition had now deteriorated so much that she was a very poor anaesthetic risk, and having someone die on the table is every anaesthetist's and surgeon's personal nightmare.

Chris passed the scope through a port punctured through into Elizabeth's belly just beside her umbilicus. Cakes of cancer met his eyes as he peered intently into the eyepiece. Some areas were white with infiltrating cancer and others were a horrible blotchy yellow, as the rapidly growing tumour outgrew its blood supply and rotted into a necrotic mush. It was the work of a minute to snip off a good sample of the tumour, and off it went to the lab.

The pathologist's answer was not quite what had been expected. I reported my findings back to Chris. 'It's a carcinosarcoma — a poorly differentiated one, with both malignant glands and a very high-grade sarcomatous component.'

'Where's it from?'

'Looks like it's been biopsied from the peritoneum to me.'

'I know that, you dork!' Chris exclaimed, laughing. 'That's where I biopsied it from.'

'Really? Your request form was quite blank. There's nothing at all written there about what it was or where the biopsy came from.'

Surgeons don't always get round to filling out the wheres and whys of what they have done during a surgery on the request form, even though it is important to assist the pathologists to make some sense of the tissues they are examining. We are understanding of these omissions: after exhausting hours on their feet operating and then worrying about post-op care for their patients, it is not surprising that lab forms are a low priority. The blank form is an old joke often batted to and fro between pathologists and surgeons. The pathologists say they need accurate information to make the right diagnosis, to which the surgeons perversely retort that by failing to give any information we could both be sure that our diagnoses were completely unbiased.

'Sorry about the empty form. Where's the cancer come from? That's what we need to know.' Chris was smiling apologetically.

I smiled back. I knew that was what he was after all the time. 'I'm ninety-five per cent sure it's gynaecological, according to the markers. Try the ovaries or endometrium of the uterus. That's where the bastard will be hiding away.'

'CT scan says they're both normal.'

'Still must be gynaecological, though. If there really is no cancer in the uterus, tubes or ovaries, it might have started in a distant peritoneal deposit of endometriosis well away from the uterus and ovaries. It does happen, but it's not common.'

It is not rare for women to grow spots of endometrial lining on the peritoneum of the pelvis and even further afield, on organs such as the bowel or appendix. Endometriosis is a painful condition, as these misplaced pieces of tissue often go through the same periodic monthly cycle of growing and bleeding as the woman's normal lining within the uterus. This can cause a monthly cycle of pain and discomfort.

It is thought that in many cases these implanted pieces of tissue begin with menstrual blood containing fragments of living uterine-lining cells back-flowing up the fallopian tubes instead of out through the vagina. The bloody reflux contains fragments of living endometrium, which then bed down and grow on the peritoneal lining.

This misdirected menstrual reverse-thrust has been recognised as a particular risk for female astronauts in the weightlessness of space, away from the Earth's gravitational field. These astronauts are injected with progesterone to stop uterine bleeding while they are weightless and aloft, and thus avoid developing endometriosis. One rare but serious consequence of endometriosis is that endometrial cancers can and do, from time to time, grow from these misplaced patches of tissue.

'And remember also, the CT scan is not always right,' I added as a reminder.

Like all tests, CT scans have their limitations, and they can give false negative as well as false positive diagnoses. So does pathology, of course, but the tissue under the microscope is usually the best arbiter of the final diagnosis.

Richard worked on as he told Tim the tale, skilfully removing the adhesions and scars of tough tissue from her old surgery and packing the bowel neatly back into the abdominal cavity. He looked at his work with satisfaction.

'That looks tidy enough. Time for the general surgeons to bow out for a bit and let our gynaecological maestro snaffle the uterus. Over to you, Nasser. We have left you an open and clean field, and your patient awaits you!'

Nasser Shehata was a highly skilled gynaecologist, and he was scrubbed and ready to take over and remove Elizabeth's uterus and cervix.

'It all looks very normal to me, Nasser,' Richard said. 'No cancer coming out this way, at any rate. What do you think?'

'I agree. This looks so normal that I'll just do a simple hysterectomy and hand her back to you.'

'That'll be great. The pathologists are eagerly awaiting your efforts so they can confirm their previous diagnosis.'

Richard and Tim stood back, gloved hands clasped in front of them, watching Nasser at work as he gently mobilised the uterus and tied off its blood supply, vessel by vessel. Richard turned to explain to Tim.

'I'm getting a bit ahead of the story here, but the pathologists have always insisted that this cancer must be from the gynae tract. Last month Elizabeth had some pelvic bleeding, so a biopsy of the normal uterus was taken. The pathologists think they spotted the malignant beast in its lair, and that the cancer comes from inside there. It's hard to see how that's possible, as it all looks absolutely OK to me, but we thought we would get in Nasser as a guest performer to do a hysterectomy and pluck it out while we are tidying up the surgical mess we made here last time.'

Richard then continued with Elizabeth's story as they waited to be called by Nasser to return to the operative fray to finish up.

* * *

The decision of what to do after the CT scan was no real surprise to anyone. Elizabeth was deteriorating hourly before everyone's eyes.

The surgeons in charge quite reasonably decided the only course of action was for her to receive palliative care. There was no way she was or ever would be fit for more surgery or chemotherapy or any other treatment. She was referred to hospice for end-of-life care. Under the circumstances, it seemed sensible — the doctors had done all they could.

'That's when I first came across Elizabeth,' Richard told Tim. 'It was on our combined ward round. The hospice decision sounded depressingly right to me, but I noticed her age on her folder notes. She was younger than I am! I thought, This is appalling! We must do something. I can't just leave her to die without some sort of a chance at life!'

It was the typical Coutts in full flight. None of this made any medical or surgical sense but he was going to do it anyway.

'I decided I would talk to the oncologists and her family

and see if we could find a way to drag her back from the final drop.'

Hard discussions followed. First there were the meetings with Elizabeth and her family. The first was very revealing.

'I don't know where this cancer came from,' Elizabeth said to Richard as she lay wanly against the pillows in her side room off the ward. 'It wasn't that long ago I was on the field playing defence in my senior women's soccer team. I don't know what happened, but there was a catastrophic fall-off in my performance. I just couldn't move and was just useless. It was like wading through treacle. Where did this come from?'

'I don't know,' said Richard, 'but I reckon if you could do that not long ago and you're such a good soccer player, I'll see if I can get the troops moving to do something for you. And I know just who to ask.'

* * *

'Richard!' Richard Coutts called out as he spotted his namesake Richard Isaacs, one of the top oncologists, walking down the corridor in front of him. 'Hold on, I've got something to ask you!' Richard Isaacs is a quiet and thoughtful man, but importantly, both Richards are cut of the same buccaneering cloth.

'Yes, Richard. What do you want this time?' Isaacs was guarded. All the medical staff knew to engage a certain wariness in the face of Coutts's unbridled and optimistic enthusiasm.

Coutts explained Elizabeth's dreadful dilemma and began enlarging on it, waving his arms as his face became more and more animated. Isaacs listened and nodded. Isaacs had been awarded the QSM for his work on breast cancer, so his opinions on cancer treatment were widely respected and valued.

Isaacs sighed internally, however, suspecting it may already be too late and that this task would be next to impossible. Coutts's hopes for his patients did on occasions fly in the face of anything that could be reasonably expected, and a forced descent to Earth was sometimes necessary.

'Yes, this is all very dreadful,' Isaacs thoughtfully interrupted. He had to deal with the emotions around cancer all day and while they were important, he had business at hand that needed to move on — heaps of cancer patients were awaiting his attention. He also knew that Coutts could develop this theme for some time yet. 'My answer, Richard, is a yes. *But* — and this is a big but, Richard, so listen to me carefully — first, I'll have to check with the pathologists that they are sure this cancer has come from the uterus or ovaries. Only those cancers will have any hope of responding to my treatment, otherwise why actually do it? It would be pointless if it's from the pancreas or bowel or somewhere.

'Your job is to go inside her and remove the bulk of the cancer — say at least ninety-nine per cent of it — surgically. Only after Elizabeth has recovered from her surgery and her gut is up and working well will I treat her. It's a big job for you, mate. Agree? Will you do that? *Can* you do that?'

'I'll do it!'

The improbable, perhaps even the impossible, was rashly promised. So the wheels of cure began to slowly turn.

* * *

Claws of cancer

Richard watched closely as Nasser put the final touches to his elegant hysterectomy.

'Over to you now. My modest bit is done. The uterus looks and feels entirely normal to me. I am not convinced of the pathologists' diagnosis of uterine cancer — there is nothing here.' Nasser bowed out, passing the surgical baton firmly back to Richard.

Richard frowned over Elizabeth's abdomen, feeling deep in the pelvis as well as peering intently into the cavity.

'I decided that what I was going to do here today,' he explained to Tim, 'could only be based on what I found on the inside. Elizabeth and her family agreed that I could do whatever I saw fit.

'I can feel the pelvic lymph nodes here on the right side. They feel fleshy and soft with squishy fat around them.' He shook his head. 'I reckon they're benign, but I am going to dissect the right pelvic wall and send them off to the paths to make sure.'

He shifted his reach and probed deeply again.

'I'll leave the left side alone. It's pretty scarred up from what I did last time, but I can't feel any cancer in there either. I don't want to snaffle it and find out that I've opened her veins, which must be buried in there somewhere. No, better to give that side a wide berth.'

He set to work deftly plucking the lymph nodes and dropping them into the pan obligingly held out by the theatre nurse.

'Now where was I in her story?' Richard glanced up at Tim, who was diligently retracting the bowel out of Richard's operating field. 'Ah, yes. So, with Richard Isaacs lined up to poison the cancer, I met again with Elizabeth and her family. I put it pretty bluntly, I can tell you, but time was running out.'

* * *

'There's absolutely no treatment that's going to give you any chance at all the way you are, and you're going off the boil pretty fast. Your belly is tense with fluid, your vena cava is squashed flat by the pressure, and your legs are swollen up to your thighs. Now, with your bowel obstructed, you'll never be fit enough to even sniff at chemotherapy. I estimate you might last the rest of this week but no more.'

Elizabeth and her family listened intently to Richard's summary. The room was tense and silent, with not a single movement. Even breathing seemed suspended.

'There's only one hope and it's a tough one,' he continued. 'I can operate and clear out as much of the cancer as I can get at. It's called "debulking", and it's really a toilet procedure to cut out the worst of the crap, not aimed at a cure at all. I'll also bring your small bowel out to the surface, with a stoma to bypass your obstructed colon.

'It'll be very dangerous, and the big odds are you won't make it through. Just draining all the cancerous fluid in your abdomen is a serious risk by itself and can lead to you suddenly dying from shock. You'll definitely need a long stint afterwards in ICU to get over this, even if you make it through the operation.

'There's a distinct chance that I'll make your life even more miserable and shorter, but — and this is the big but — if you recover from the surgery and your gut starts working again, then Richard Isaacs says he'll give you some chemotherapy.

Claws of cancer

I reckon he'll wheel out the real big guns to nail this cancer, so that'll be a hard road to follow. And there are no guarantees that it'll work anyway. But without all this there is only supportive care in the hospice. What do you think?'

Elizabeth was composed, though her family clearly were shocked at the bald facts they had just heard.

'I want to live. I'll take any chance to get a bit more time, even with all those risks. I mean, it doesn't sound as if I've got much to lose, does it?'

And so, they operated. Richard was assisted by fellow consultant surgeon Bruce Rhind, and they took turns to operate, as it was just too much for one person to handle. There was an immense amount of tense ascites — fluid in the abdomen — four litres of which was drained. Her legs and abdominal wall were massively oedematous, with fluid leaking out of the tissues through which Richard had made his incision into the abdomen.

The cancer was a huge cake, plastered around most of her large bowel as well as binding up several loops of the small bowel. The surgeons took the whole lot in one large block. She lost a lot of blood, but the anaesthetists did a great job of keeping up, and Elizabeth handled it all well.

'I reckon being a fit soccer player was her contribution to pulling through,' Richard said.

'Despite the pathologists insisting this was from the uterus or ovaries, they looked perfectly normal. I whipped off the ovaries and tubes, really to placate the paths and prove they weren't the villain, but Bruce and I decided to leave the uterus. It looked plumb normal and clearly wasn't the site of the tumour. She had already lost a lot of blood and we would have been pushing it a bit too far to do any more.

'We looped her ileum out into a stoma on the abdominal wall and closed her up. Even having her not perish on the table was a victory that I had not counted on.'

'That was eighteen months ago, wasn't it?' Tim was still following the story closely.

'Yes, that's right. Elizabeth recovered really well. The pathologists confirmed it was a high-grade carcinosarcoma, and they still insisted it was from the gynaecological stable. They found it stuck on the surfaces of the ovaries, but it had only spread there and not arisen from them. They reckon it must be secreted away inside the uterus.

'After a few weeks Elizabeth was back up to speed and ready for anything that Richard Isaacs could do, so it was off to the oncologists at the Cancer Treatment Service with her. But I had a strong disagreement with the good Dr Isaacs over her treatment. He gave her single-agent carboplatin, which I reckoned was a weak option, kept only to palliate little old grannies. I wanted him to nail this cancer with every toxic big gun he had, just to give her a fighting chance at a cure. But he was quietly insistent that this would be enough to do the trick. Nothing I could say would persuade him.

'And I have to say that it now looks as if he might just be right.' Richard waved his hand over Elizabeth's open abdomen. 'Despite a very determined search, there is not one skerrick of cancer to be found. I thought I was going to find chunks of it everywhere, and I was looking forward to telling Richard that I had told him so. Now it looks like I am going to have to eat a slice of humble pie — he's right, and it's gone. My gut feeling after eighteen months is that Elizabeth is completely cured.

'There doesn't seem to be any reason why we shouldn't reverse her stoma here and now, reattach her small bowel to her sigmoid colon and get her back to a normal life again. Can you finish that up, Tim, and close up? I've got a laparoscopy to do in Theatre Seven.'

Richard paused as he left the theatre and turned back for a last look.

'Who knows, maybe she will soon play soccer again?'

Pathologists' office, 2.25 p.m.

Richard Coutts arrived in the lab an hour later, the creases of his surgical mask still imprinted on his face.

'I can't stand the suspense! What have you found?'

I turned from the biopsy I was studying, sighing inwardly. I knew of old that Richard was unstoppable once in full flight.

'Which patient are we talking about this time?' Richard often came in to get the latest on his patients and he usually didn't provide any details for us on which patient and which biopsy he wanted to talk about. We were diagnosing 35,000 patients' specimens each year and there was no way we could remember all the details and have all the information at our fingertips.

'You know — Elizabeth Shortall! Her cancer's gone! I've been right through her belly, and it's just melted away! You boys have always said it had to come from the uterus but that's clean for sure. Can't we just open it and have a quick look?'

Eventually we tracked down where the freshy removed uterus had got to in the lab system. There was nothing for it but for us all to trek over to the cut-up room and have a look. I, too, was intrigued to know the answer. All the markers had told us this cancer came from the endometrium, and they weren't often wrong.

I lifted Elizabeth's organs out of their container onto the cut-up bench. 'I'll open her uterus and we'll see once and for all if we were right.'

The uterus certainly looked normal, with a smooth, unblemished surface and a healthy-looking cervix.

'It only weighs fifty-six grams — not impressive for a cancer, I'll agree with you there. I'll open it anteriorly through the cervical canal.'

As I peeled the muscular coat back, the uterine cavity came into view. And we saw it.

'A-ha!' I exclaimed. 'That'll be it!'

There, attached to the inner lining, was a tumour: a soft, cream-coloured polyp mottled with areas of haemorrhage.

Richard looked doubtful. 'It's a bit small, isn't it? I mean, the gut was caked with a huge cancer. How could something so big come from something that's so small?'

'Sometimes children grow to be bigger than their parents. It also happens from time to time with cancers, too, though not very often. I'm going to take a sample piece and we'll do a frozen section right now, to prove it is malignant. Can you please help us here?' I called out to Jackie, the scientist running the lab.

I cut a sliver of the tissue off the polyp with my scalpel and dropped it onto a metal chuck Jackie held out to me. She squeezed gel over it then opened a cylinder tap. There was a sibilant hiss as clouds of smoky evaporating nitrogen gushed past and the wafting air grew noticeably colder. The gel whitened, hardened, and finally froze solid under the icy stream of gas.

In less than five minutes Jackie had sliced a microscopically thin section off the icy block and had it mounted on a glass slide and stained. Richard and I went and sat at the double-headed microscope.

'Moment of truth, eh, Richard?' I was enjoying myself as I focused the microscope. The pink and blue image swam into view. We stared.

'There you are! The enemy in arms at last. It's a carcinosarcoma of the uterus, hideously revealed for the first time. This is the beast where it all began.'

'Well, I'm amazed! I was absolutely wrong about that then. Bloody glad we took it out before it could do any more mischief.'

I nodded. 'Just as well you got it out. This cancer looks alive and kicking to me. Richard Isaacs may have wiped the metastases, but his pills didn't touch this cancer. In time it probably would have spread throughout her belly again.'

Richard was beaming with joy, as he should have been, with this phenomenal result. He turned to me thoughtfully.

'Do you know what Elizabeth said to me? When I first told her the cancer had miraculously vanished, she said she just couldn't believe that her life depended entirely on one chance encounter with a surgeon on a ward round, and a second chance corridor encounter with an oncologist.'

I nodded in agreement. Life, like Lotto, is a game of chance. 'Do you remember what Perce Bydder once told one of his cancer patients about it all?'

Richard shook his head, smiling. Perce was a West Coast man and a brilliant but very unconventional, old-style

The Final Diagnosis

radiotherapist. He was refreshingly blunt and for that, much beloved of his many patients. Perce's stories over the years were legend throughout the hospital.

'His patient had just been given their cancer diagnosis and they were naturally stunned at the news. "Why did I get my cancer, doctor?" they asked him. "Well," Perce slowly drawls, leaning his large bulk back into his chair and putting his hands behind his head. "We don't really know, do we? Some folks talk about genetics and some folks talk about the environment. Myself, I think it's just fucking bad luck."'

We both laughed.

'Sometimes it's very good luck, too. All the holes in the Swiss cheese have lined up in a good way for Elizabeth. That's often the way of it with life and death, isn't it?'

Diseases desperate grown,
By desperate appliance are relieved,
Or not at all.
— William Shakespeare, *Hamlet*, Act IV Scene II, 1601

CHAPTER 4

Brain attack

Ward round, 8 a.m.

'This is Carol Laurence, the young lady who came to us from the psychiatrists.' Janice Fulton, a medical registrar, was presenting the patients on the ward round to Alison Reubens, the consultant neurologist. The young girl in the corner bed sat upright and stared ahead, avoiding eye contact. She was nineteen. Her fingers plucked anxiously at the bedclothes, fingering the sheet and twisting it this way and that. Her amber-coloured eyes were anxious, though what was causing her nervousness was not clear.

'Hello, Carol. How are you feeling today?' Alison leaned forward and patted her on her forearm. Carol shrunk back with a grimace, making no reply. 'Did you manage to sleep last night?'

The ward staff nurse stood behind her trolley of files. She shook her head as she looked at the night report. 'Carol tossed and turned all night. I'd be surprised if she'd had more than an hour's sleep. Two at the outside.'

'The same pattern as before, then. Are you eating anything, Carol?' Alison persisted in trying to make contact with the troubled young girl. Carol did look at her, but it was only the briefest glance as she spoke.

'Are you eating, Carol?' she mumbled unexpectedly, repeating Alison's words.

'Are you managing to eat anything, Carol?' Alison gently asked again.

'Are you managing—' Carol repeated but this time, less surely.

'Echolalia!' exclaimed Alison. Everyone looked at her with interest.

'Echolalia?' questioned Janice, half-frowning, half-smiling.

'Echolalia,' Carol whispered back. They all heard her, and stared at the young girl, perplexed.

'An automatic repetition of words. It's probably just due to her background brain injury — it isn't a specific diagnosis in itself,' Alison explained.

Carol didn't repeat this, though. She stared mutely ahead. Alison turned back to the staff nurse. 'She's not eating at all well — not even fluids.'

'She was becoming dehydrated at about nine last night,' Janice volunteered. 'I was paged, so I put up a drip and we've got that sorted now. But she's still showing no interest in eating. We may have to look at parenteral feeding.'

Alison frowned. Getting all your daily nutritional needs through a drip was possible but it was not without its own risks, and Carol already had enough problems to deal with.

* * *

Carol had been brought into hospital a week earlier by her worried parents. They told her story to the harassed

Emergency Department doctor, who impatiently drummed his fingers to hurry them on. He had a waiting room bursting with unseen patients, several with bloodstained towels wrapped around clenched hands or held firmly onto lacerated foreheads and scalps. He just wanted to say, 'Come on, come on! Get on with it!' but kept that thought to himself, while smiling encouragingly at the family.

'She's not herself at all. We just don't know what is wrong. She's not eating and wanders all around the house, all jittery. She says she's not been sleeping well. It all started when she had a row with her boyfriend, and they broke up. She's taken it really hard.'

The doctor wrote in Carol's notes as they spoke. 'Sounds not too unusual in those sort of circumstances,' he said. 'So why have you brought Carol in today? I mean, what has particularly changed here and now, tonight?'

'She doesn't answer us sometimes. It's like she's on another planet and not hearing us talking to her.'

The ED doctor scrawled '? Psychiatric' in the notes. After a quick examination revealed nothing obviously amiss, he phoned the on-call psychiatrist and Carol was admitted to the Psychiatric Unit.

It quickly became apparent that her illness may have been mysterious, but it was real enough, and not of her mind at all. Her symptoms maddeningly came and went. A fever arose but also disappeared just as abruptly. Psychiatric symptoms may be puzzling and mimic just about anything, but they do not usually cause a genuine fever. That was the key that something organic, something substantial was simmering inside her.

Then the proof of that came to light. Stephanie was a novice psychiatric registrar, and her job was to examine all the new patients and carry out investigations to make sure that the patients had no hidden physical diseases. She decided Carol needed a lumbar puncture to see what was happening in the fluid around her brain and spinal cord.

Stephanie was scrubbed up, gowned and masked. She took up a Menghini needle and gently inserted it into Carol's back, probing between the vertebrae of the lumbar spine. It clicked, palpably popping into the space containing the cerebrospinal fluid bathing the brain and spinal cord.

The fluid ran out into the collecting tube. The pressure was up a little but to Stephanie's eye it was as clear as fresh spring water.

'That has to be normal,' Stephanie murmured to herself, as the fluid dribbled into the test tube from the needle sticking out so shockingly from the middle of Carol's lower spine. The precious fluid from the lumbar puncture was rushed to the laboratory and examined microscopically.

But the lab found things were not as good as they looked. The sample was not normal at all.

'There are a significant number of white cells present, mainly lymphocytes. Twenty-seven million of them per litre, actually! This is an encephalitis or a meningitis.' The scientist sounded excited as they phoned the result through to Stephanie.

But what was the cause? There were no bacteria or viruses to be found in the spinal fluid, and there certainly was no cancer, although she would have been very young for that sort of dire diagnosis.

Strange things then began to happen to Carol. Her heart rate raced randomly then inexplicably slowed to a crawl. Her blood pressure, too, went up and down without discernible cause.

It was a puzzle. But at least the doctors knew the answer lay not in the realm of psychiatry — Carol was in the wrong ward for certain. Stephanie had rung through to the medical specialist on call and, after several transfers to different extensions and many delays, spoke to the consultant. He sounded harassed, with eighteen new admissions waiting for his examination and assessment.

'Sounds neurological to me. Not mine, anyway. Try Dr Ruebens.' Expertly, he 'turfed' the problem on to someone else. Turfing patients to another speciality is a sad but probably inevitable characteristic of super-specialised modern medicine.

Stephanie sighed heavily and started the referral process again. Selling the 'turf' to a specialist consultant was often the role of the junior registrar. It did, however, teach them to concentrate accurately on all the relevant facts and improve their diagnostic skills, as well as teach co-operative persuasion. All these skills they would find essential to follow a useful and enjoyable career in medicine.

Stephanie was successful on this attempt. Alison Ruebens' interest was piqued, and she agreed to come to see Carol. Alison was an experienced neurologist and a clever diagnostician. If anyone could throw some light on the illness, it was her.

But much more hard thought had yet to come before that would happen.

* * *

'Has Carol had any more seizures?' Alison asked Janice at the bedside.

'Not since Monday. Her fever is more settled, too. Maybe the acyclovir is working?'

Alison shook her head. They had started Carol on the wonder anti-viral drug on the off chance that her illness was due to a herpes virus. This virus is everywhere in the world around us, and it can and does get into the brain, causing serious encephalitis.

'No, I really don't think the drug has made any real difference. This presentation isn't like herpes at all. This is something else altogether. Remind me what the EEG showed?'

Janice paged through the medical folder until she found the result form she wanted. The electroencephalogram, or EEG, report was to the point.

'There are diffusely scattered delta waves in all leads. The pattern suggests an organic delirium.'

'Mmm. A toxic delirium. I wonder—' Alison was musing to herself.

The doctors and students on the ward round looked at her expectantly. The consultant was the font of knowledge and Alison now carried the responsibility of what to do next. She reached a decision.

'I wonder whether this might be autoimmune encephalitis. We need to investigate that possibility.'

'You mean like systemic lupus?' asked Janice. Systemic lupus erythematosus, or SLE, is a fierce disease in which the sufferer's own immune system loses the plot and attacks and tries to destroy organs all over the body, from kidneys to joints and skin as well as just about anything in between. Not for nothing was it given the Latin label of 'lupus' or wolf, a fierce animal that will attack relentlessly.

'Lupus is a possible diagnosis,' Alison agreed, 'but I was actually thinking of a much rarer type of autoimmune disease — an anti-NDMA-receptor encephalitis.'

Janice and the team looked blankly at Alison. 'What causes that?' she asked.

'It's caused by an antibody the immune system accidentally makes that attacks the brain's nerve process dendrites, destroying the channels along which nerve impulses are carried from cell to cell. Without them all the nervous system's electrics fuse and the lights start dimming and eventually go out altogether.'

'What causes it?' Janice had her final Fellowship exams coming up in July and was like a terrier after a rat in her pursuit of any grain of knowledge that might prove useful.

'More than half of them have a teratoma or dermoid cyst of the ovary. As you know, those cysts are lined by skin and matted clumps of hair, as well as having teeth, gut and bronchus all jumbled together. Often they also have brain tissue in the mix.'

'What are they for? I mean, why have they got all those weird things in them?' The student intern Bryan Sichel was a final-year medical student on attachment to Alison's medical team to observe, learn the ropes and even undertake a few of the less invasive procedures on willing patients.

Alison smiled. 'They're not exactly *for* anything, Bryan. They are a tumour, an aberration, a mistake. Probably a genetic snafu.

'But it is the brain tissue in them that is the cause of the problem. The brain tissue in the skull and spinal cord are normally hidden from the body's immune system because there is a blood–brain barrier that seals it off, a bit like a border control. Antibodies cannot be made against the brain, or if they are, they cannot get through the barrier to attack.

'But the brain tissue in the ovarian cyst is in the wrong place, and there is no barrier, so the brain tissue is able to get out and antibodies can get accidentally made against it. Then if there's any breach of the actual blood–brain barrier, these wild antibodies are there ready and waiting to cross over and destroy the real brain's neurone receptors.'

'It sounds pretty serious. Can we treat it?'

Alison nodded. 'Yes. The response to steroids is good, and we can do a plasma exchange by plasmapheresis and wash the existing toxic antibodies out. Also, we must remove the source by getting any ovarian dermoid out as soon as possible. But we need to confirm the diagnosis first.

'There's a test for the antibody, and I think we'll need it today if possible. I'll go and call the pathologists to arrange it urgently. If Carol has this type of encephalitis, then time is becoming critical. She is still deteriorating and the later we start treatment, the lower the chance for a complete cure.'

'Should I arrange an ultrasound scan to check her ovaries for a dermoid cyst?' Janice was onto the problem. She would be a good physician.

Pathologists' office, 10.50 a.m.

'Yes, of course we can do that urgently,' I agreed.

Carol's state was so worrying that Alison had come personally to the lab to ask for the anti-NDMA-receptor antibodies test to be performed as soon as possible.

'We do have enough cerebrospinal fluid left from Carol's original lumbar puncture, so that's one less thing to worry about,' I reassured Alison. 'We'll have a result for you by tomorrow afternoon, say, four o'clock. Would that be OK?'

Brain attack

'That would be fantastic. If it's positive I would like to treat her with a plasma exchange to wash the antibodies out of her system. But the haematologists won't accept her for a plasma exchange unless we have a proven diagnosis.'

I nodded. 'I'm not surprised. The exchange takes their whole department out, day and night, and costs an arm and a leg, too. Not that that should matter, but I guess dollars are always at the back of everyone's mind.'

There was never enough money for every new drug or every treatment, and like it or not, the doctors often had to make hard choices.

Alison explained the weird nature of Carol's suspected disease while my registrars and I listened with great interest. This was a completely new disease to all of us and we were fascinated.

'I really want to have a careful look at her dermoid cyst if we can get hold of it,' I said. 'I want to see if there is anything unusual in any of the dermoid's brain tissue. Maybe there will be lymphocytes attacking the glial tissue there?' I paused. 'Imagine it! Encephalitis of a dermoid cyst! No one has ever seen that. It would be the world's first case, for sure.'

We saw many dermoid cysts every year, for they are common tumours. We were used to seeing all manner of tissue types inside them, thrown eclectically together. There was often brain tissue, but it looked no different from the normal brain tissue we saw in our daily autopsy cases.

'So why does the ovary make this tumour, with hair and teeth and brain and all the rest?' Karen was a first-year registrar and was at that stage of asking difficult questions for which we old-timers couldn't easily find answers — at least not scientifically proven answers.

The Final Diagnosis

'My old professor of gynaecological pathology used to say he thought that the tumours were only trying to carry out the grand plan that Nature intended for the human ovary, and these tumours are an attempt to imitate the various parts of a normal pregnancy.

'He told us one type of ovary tumour, the dysgerminoma, looks like and is trying to be the original unfertilised ovum. Others become choriocarcinomas, which are bizarre, malignant copies of a normal placenta. Then there are the yolk-sac carcinomas, which are copying a chunk of tissue normally stuck onto a normal placenta. Finally, we get these dermoid cysts with their skin and teeth and hair and brain — they are just the tumour's stuffed-up attempt to create a foetus, according to the old prof.

'But we don't really know at all. The old prof's idea is probably a bit fanciful, but I reckon it is a good way to think about it.'

'Do the dermoid tissues cause other diseases in the body? Like this encephalitis, I mean?'

I sighed. The day's routine work still beckoned. But the young registrars must be answered — that is how they learn.

'I haven't seen one myself, but there is a very famous case. More than sixty years ago, a famous London-based pathologist William Symmers reported a strange case.'

The registrars smiled at each other and settled back in their chairs. They had got me going on one of my stories and now they could be entertained. This was a great diversion from their mental flogging as they struggled to solve the patients' diagnostic puzzles coyly hidden in our daily slides. I began my story.

Brain attack

Symmers was a great pathologist and wrote the best textbooks of his day. He was a great observer and collected a pile of case studies of his patients and their odd diseases. They were all put into a brilliant book called *Curiosa*, which persuaded me as a young medical student that pathology was for me.

He told of the case of a 40-year-old woman who found a lump in the side of her neck. A surgeon took it out, and it turned out to be a carcinoma of the thyroid that had spread to a lymph node in her neck. The surgeon decided to take out half of the thyroid gland from the same side as the node, figuring the original carcinoma logically had to be on that side. And, to be fair, the lymph glands a cancer like this spreads to are usually on the same side as the cancer.

The surgeon ran into a problem, though. He got the right side of the thyroid lobe out and sliced it open, but there was no tumour there, just a normal-looking gland. He went back to the anaesthetised woman and rather belatedly had a good feel of her neck and the remaining thyroid gland.

The cancer was still in the neck all right, but awkwardly it was in the left lobe, sitting right on his dissection line. It must have taken the wrong lymphatic channel and spread to the right side. He now had to remove the rest of the gland and its cancer. Initially he hadn't wanted to, because he knew that would sentence her to a lifetime of taking thyroid hormone supplements.

But he had run out of options. In hindsight, perhaps he should have felt her glands before leaping in with his initial surgery.

After the surgery, the woman was started on replacement thyroid hormone pills immediately, and fortunately she recovered really well. She took her pills daily and conscientiously, although privately she thought they were a waste of time, as she had never felt so well.

'A couple of years later, she had a relationship breakdown and decided to move on with her life by going to Australia, where she had a sister,' I continued. I glanced up at the clock: twenty past eleven. The day was half run and there was still plenty of diagnostic work to get through. I had better get a move on. But the registrars were watching and listening intently to the story. If only they could always listen that carefully when being taught the boring bits of pathology!

'Her sister was part of a religious sect — I think it was the Christian Scientists. Whatever, it was a group who didn't believe in medical intervention. She fell under their influence and joined the sect. She biffed her pills and then what do you think happened to her?'

I looked questioningly at the registrars. I would make them earn their story.

'She became hypothyroid?' Karen ventured.

'Logically the correct answer, or so you would think. But no, this was truly a miracle. She remained perfectly hale and hearty. You might think the Christian Scientists were onto something after all — or so it must have seemed to our lady after all the dire warnings she had been given over the years by her doctors never to miss her thyroid replacement medicine.'

'How is that possible?' Karen asked. 'Was she secretly taking thyroxine pills all along?'

'Apparently not. She wasn't taking any medication at all.'

But then, I told them, she fell out with the sect after a couple of years, left their church and decided to return to England. Though she no longer believed in their teachings, quite understandably she saw no point in seeing a doctor and restarting on the thyroxine.

Several years passed and she continued in robust health, until she began to have increasingly heavy and erratic periods. Medical treatment did not improve the bleeding, so she opted to have her uterus, fallopian tubes and ovaries removed, and be done with them and the bleeding.

Symmers was the examining pathologist, and he found there was a six-centimetre dermoid cyst in one ovary. These are, of course, common, and are benign and are usually of little importance, as we all know. He did find, however, that there was a solid part in the tumour, and this was composed entirely of thyroid-gland tissue. Of course, you usually find hair and skin and teeth, bronchi and brain in these tumours, and thyroid is just another tissue type. Like the other tissues, the thyroid there is usually of no significance. It's a condition called struma ovarii, though why we've kept an obscure Latin name from a couple of centuries ago for this particular type of dermoid beats me.

'Anyway, back to our lady. Within a few months she had become pitifully ill. Her hair was dry and came out in tufts. Her face had become rounded like the moon and her voice was hoarse. She felt dull and listless. What was wrong with her?' I put the registrars back on the spot.

'Now she *does* have hypothyroidism.' Karen was quick off the mark.

'That's right. She now had typical myxoedema, but it's hard to recognise if you see the sufferer often, as it comes on so slowly. Her GP missed it; he thought her symptoms were all menopausal from having her ovaries removed, so he gave her replacement oestrogens.

'Of course, he was half right in that her symptoms *were* brought about by removing her ovaries. But he chose the wrong replacement hormone to treat her. She had, of course, lost her only remaining thyroid hormones when the dermoid and its thyroid tissue came out. Although the thyroid was in the wrong place altogether, it had been working away perfectly as a replacement for the gland the surgeon had taken out. She was now onto the slippery slope towards advanced myxoedema and certain death.'

'I've heard stories of patients with hypothyroidism who were misdiagnosed and put in asylums back in the old days. It can be easily misdiagnosed, can't it?' Karen asked.

'Yes, that's right. All those endocrine diseases can be hard to pick up. Fortunately, the woman fully recovered after getting back onto hormone replacement.

'And now, back to work. We've got a pile to do. Now, where's that case we were looking at?'

Radiology department, 2.20 p.m.

Carol was wheeled into the department by Gary, a grey-haired, stooped orderly. Gary had wheeled patients and sometimes their deceased bodies to and from every nook and cranny in every department in the hospital for the past 35 years. He knew that the small room where the visiting podiatrist came monthly to trim the nails and corns of the diabetic patients was improbably situated next to the cafeteria storeroom. He could even remember when that same room had, in a previous stage in the hospital's life, been the repository for the mops, polishing potions and brooms of the hospital cleaners.

'Hello, love,' he called out to the receptionist. 'You married that fellow of yours yet?'

She smiled back at him and shook her head. 'Not till November.'

'Hard luck. Just have to wait, won't you? Got a patient here for ultrasound.'

'Wheel her through.' She gestured with a movement of her head. 'Sheila's there with the medical registrar and they're waiting for Carol in the examination suite.'

* * *

'There it is!' Janice sat intently watching the screen, as Sheila, the head sonographer, expertly manipulated the instrument over Carol's lower abdomen, getting the best possible contact through the gel she had smeared on. The screen was fuzzy with green and white shimmering lines. It looked a bit like the weather map on the news.

'A tumour in the right ovary,' Sheila said. 'It's solid, with cystic areas. About four centimetres across. It could be a teratoma, I suppose. Pity I can't see a tooth — that would clinch the diagnosis for sure. Teeth are only visible in about ten per cent of cases, though.'

'Great! Thank you. I had better go and find a gynaecologist to whip it out as soon as we can.'

'Will that cure her?' Sheila was looking curiously at the oblivious patient on the examination couch. This was not the usual sort of patient she saw down here.

'Yup, should do. We'll whip it out and some steroids should turn the auto-immune reaction off, and she'll be back to normal.'

The Final Diagnosis

The brain is an amazing organ, we all know that. It can do advanced maths and philosophy, and direct everything from painting an exquisite work of art to building a skyscraper — most of the time.

But, like my laptop, my brain, and yours, can behave annoyingly, jamming up unexpectedly, forgetting things, losing thoughts and sometimes even making up completely new ones that are just not true.

It is intricately wired — much more so than even a supercomputer. There are 100 billion neurons, which are the smart brain cells doing all the calculations, and they are wired up with a 100 trillion connections. That's way more than there are stars in the Milky Way. It's much faster and cleverer than a computer by 100,000 times … though sometimes I wonder when I listen to talkback radio!

The problem is, it is all a very fragile network, which falls over for the slightest of reasons, and sometimes for none at all. I can personally confirm that mine loses its edge after a few glasses of wine, though it's usually hard for any of us to recognise what we are like when we are listening to ourselves from the inside. Try listening to a dinner party conversation when you are the sober driver. Not only is it all much louder than usual, suggesting the ears are an early victim, but it is also intellectually often pretty poor quality, too.

What's true for booze and the brain is also true in many diseases. When people feel distant, as if they're not at home, can't find the right word, have ringing in their ears or dizziness, it may well be 'nothing', as my mother always used to reassure me … but just sometimes there may be some deeper illness tucked away. The doctors will then stand around scratching their heads and looking at each other and at the poor patient, the one with the strange symptoms, the normal lab tests and the pristine MRI or CT scans, and they will wonder.

The sensible thing would be to say, 'What have I missed?', but too often we cannot believe we don't know what's going on, so instead we say, 'It's all in his or her head', and they get labelled psychosomatic or neurotic, and sometimes, even worse, psychotic. And the results can be devastating.

When I was a young medical student in Harare Hospital in Rhodesia back in the '70s I remember a physician, Dr Wicks, telling us that he had studied a whole pile of cases of local patients who had been confidently diagnosed as 'psychosomatic'. Nearly half of them were dead within six months, succumbing to a variety of illnesses completely missed by all the specialist doctors.

That happens even with the best and most modern investigations in the top teaching hospitals in the world. Diseases can be maddingly evasive, hiding themselves in peculiar presentations and diagnostic dilemmas.

Carol was one of the lucky ones. Her rare illness was astutely recognised early by a clever physician before any lasting harm was done. Her test results were returned positive and as a bonus it was treatable, and even curable with surgery.

Carol's brain would now happily resume normal service.

Canst thou not minister to a mind diseased,
Pluck from the memory a rooted sorrow,
Raze out the written troubles of the brain,
And with some sweet oblivious antidote
Cleanse the fraught bosom of that perilous stuff
Which weighs on the heart?
— William Shakespeare, *Macbeth*, Act V Scene III, 1623

PART II

Chance and circumstance

CHAPTER 5

Hard landings

Pathologists' office, 10.25 a.m.

'The police are on the phone. It's urgent.'

I sighed. Why did this always happen on a Friday? I hoped it was something that could be quickly dealt with. A murder would be the worst thing right now. Or so I thought then. I never dreamt there might be something much worse brewing out there.

I had planned on going to the movies to see *Braveheart* that night, and if the weather cleared I was keen to get in a couple of hours of flying on Saturday. I was doing an aerobatics course with my affable, cigar-smoking instructor Darryn Tuttle, and we needed lots of clear sky and altitude to do that. It wasn't looking hopeful if today was anything to go by; there had been full cloud coverage when I came to work that morning, and now it looked low to me, maybe 2000 feet. The wind was icy from the southwest and there were spots of rain. Out of habit, I looked at the Tararua Ranges. Clagged in under wet cloud as usual. None of this boded well for flying.

'Good morning, doctor,' said the policeman on the line. 'We've lost an aeroplane.'

That woke me up all right. 'An aeroplane? How? Where?'

'An Ansett Dash 8 failed to arrive at Palmerston North. It was due in at 9.15 a.m. Twenty-one passengers and crew on board. Can your mortuary cope?'

My mind reeled at the enormity of the tragedy. Cope? *Could* we cope? We would have to, but we would need help, for sure. Lots of help.

Strangely, in those days there was no national disaster plan for pathology in place, and even today it's a bit thin. Both the Christchurch earthquake and the mosque massacre autopsies were professionally and rapidly done by the determined performance of only a handful of forensic pathologists.

My mind flashed back to the Ahu Ahu Valley air crash in 1988. That had nine victims for us to identify and reunite the fragments of their bodies, and it had taken all our mortuary space and all our pathologists a full three days to complete. How the hell were we now going to handle 21?

'Where has it gone down?'

'We believe just short of the runway, in Kelvin Grove. The rescue and fire teams are on their way there now, but I have no information on its precise location at this point. We'll call you as soon as we know.'

'Thank you. I'll need to go to the site to make sure the body-retrieval procedures are OK for our investigation.'

I hung up and stared at the wall for a good while. This was difficult. I called our pathologists together. There were only three of us: James Pang, Bruce Lockett and myself. That would never be enough. We sat trying to work out what the hell we could do. I had my radio tuned to the Palmerston North Control Tower frequency while we talked, but the airwaves were silent — deathly quiet. They were off the air. The airport was now closed to all traffic, the sombre sign of a disaster.

'We'll need the Wellington pathologists to help. Probably a team from Auckland as well. Better get on the phone and give them a heads-up on what's happened.'

'Where can we put the bodies for identification? The mortuary is far too small,' James said.

'Ohakea is our best bet.' We had talked about using the air base for something like this many times before. 'We can use their hangar floors to work on. It's secure, too, and they will be able to supply any extra labour or support we need.' Our minds were fixed on the massive degree of destruction usual in air accidents, and the Disaster Victim Identification (DVI) difficulties that high-speed impacts always cause.

Kirsten Holst came up to our office. 'Have you heard the news?' Kirsten was a senior medical registrar and was found everywhere around the hospital, seeing patients, doing procedures and arranging CT scans and other investigations. She was insatiably curious and could be relied on to know everything that was happening. She was also a great cook and could easily have followed her famous mother, Alison, into the world of celebrity chefdom.

We nodded. 'What's the latest?'

'We've cleared the Emergency Department and we've been assigned to trauma teams. It's all been arranged by Alan McKenzie.' We all had great respect for Alan as the head of ICU. He was a highly competent ICU specialist and anaesthetist — just the man for such a job.

'I suspect this time the work will be all ours.' I gestured to my colleagues. 'No one survives an impact with the ground at 130 knots.'

The Final Diagnosis

* * *

But the Dash 8 wasn't anywhere in the suburb of Kelvin Grove. The policemen, medics and firemen raced there and ended up looking around and at each other in perplexment. Ansett Flight 703 just wasn't anywhere. What had happened? Where the hell was it?

The story of what happened to those on board has been told many times. It was basically a stuff-up, but the story also had some odd legal twists, and emotions added a further patina to an already overloaded canvas.

I was involved from the beginning but the pathology, although important, was uncontroversial. As a pilot I was interested in the technical and piloting aspects that had led to the crash, and as a pathologist in the impact of the accident and its effects on the passengers and crew, as well as in the legal wrangle that followed.

I try to follow the outcomes of my patients on their last journey, so I can learn from their experience, too. Many people have told their version of Flight 703 or have written their opinions, but this is what I saw and know.

The Dash 8, flying on instruments, turned west onto its final approach to the runaway at 14 nautical miles out, aiming for Runway 25. They would then have been just above the school at Papatawa, on State Highway 2 a few kilometres west of Woodville.

At the start of their journey, the flight crew — Captain Gary Southeran and First Officer Barry Brown — had planned for an easy descent from the west for Runway 07. If they had gone that way, they would have avoided the approach across the Tararua Ranges on a flight path that had been operational only for the past few months. That original option over the westerly Manawatū Plains was not available, however, for another flight had grabbed that slot and was already climbing out from Runway 07. Flight 703 was diverted to circle in from the east and begin her descent over the mountains.

The plane's black box recorded the pilots' conversation. At 12 miles out, Southeran requested the undercarriage lowered. Brown lowered the undercarriage extension lever.

'OK. Selected and on profile, ten miles DME. We're looking for 4000 feet — we're a fraction low.'

'Check. Flap fifteen degrees.' Southeran quickly and confidently confirmed the position and height Brown had just given him, not noticing that both check calls were quite wrong.

Brown had immediately realised his error and saw that his position was out by two miles and began to correct himself. 'We're not ten DME—'

He never finished his sentence. Southeran, staring at the instrument panel, interrupted him, whistling in surprise.

Brown looked down at the panel Southeran was staring at. 'Look at that!' he exclaimed.

The right-hand main undercarriage light was glowing red. It had failed to lower and lock.

'I don't want that!' Southeran exclaimed.

'No, that's not good, is it? So she's not locked? So, Alternate Landing Gear—?'

Brown pulled out the quick reference handbook, which is a checklist of all the emergency procedures.

'You want to whip through that one. See if we can get it out of the way before it's too late. I'll keep an eye on the aeroplane while you're doing that,' Southeran ordered.

Brown began to work his way through the checklist, but Southeran wanted him to skip some basic checks and get to the guts of it. However, the quick fix he had in mind still eluded Brown.

It's strange to tell, but this failure of the wheels to lower was not an unusual event. It had already happened recently a dozen times in Ansett's two Dash 8 aeroplanes, due to problems with the aircraft's uplock gear. Later investigation would reveal the lowering gear showed the 'wear condition was sufficient to have prevented release of the undercarriage leg using the normal undercarriage extension procedure'.

That wear and tear should not have prevented the easy manual alternative release, however. It was that alternative method that Brown was not certain of and was struggling to find in the manual. Southeran was no doubt watching all Barry's fruitless efforts impatiently and probably with increasing irritation and anxiety.

He certainly didn't notice that the altimeter was slowly but steadily unwinding, and they were now well below their minimum safe height.

* * *

In the cabin, a passenger, William McGrory, had also noticed the problem with the undercarriage. McGrory was to become nationally famous for his actions on this day. He called out to Karen Gallagher, the stewardess, and pointed out that the right wheel wasn't properly down.

She went up to the flight deck with this news, to make sure they were already onto it. She came back into the cabin and told McGrory, 'The pilots are looking through the manual to see how to get it down.'

She leant over the seat to look out of the window at the stubbornly closed undercarriage doors sealed beneath the engine nacelle.

It would be the last thing she ever did.

* * *

'You're supposed to pull the handle—' Southeran perhaps was still frustrated watching Brown's fruitless efforts. He would no doubt be thinking that the Palmy runway was getting closer and closer. He did not want to overshoot and have to go around for another approach. And to top it all, Karen had come in and interrupted, telling them what they already knew.

The Dash 8's altitude continued its inexorable decline.

'TERRAIN! *WHOOP! WHOOP!* PULL UP! *WHOOP! WHOOP!* PULL UP!'

This must rank as one of the most terrifyingly strident sounds a pilot could ever hear. The ground-proximity warning system is a complicated computer that does exactly what its name suggests: it says you are about to hit the ground in a very unplanned and unpleasant way.

It is a cacophonic and compelling call that cannot be ignored and is guaranteed to pump a pilot's adrenal glands dry of every last drop of adrenaline, urging them to do something about it right now — and fast.

Research has shown that the average pilot-reaction time in responding to this warning is 5.4 seconds. That's still pretty fast for most of us who aren't pilots, believe me. Gary

Southeran was certainly above average. You don't get to become an airline captain by being just average.

Dash 8 November Echo Yankee first hit the Tararua Ranges a scant 4.8 seconds after that alert sounded. What happened in those few seconds is controversial.

What is certain is that the nose wheel contacted a gently rising grassy knoll in a large fenced paddock on the Hall Block Farm, lying on the eastern slopes of the Tararua Ranges. This first unplanned touchdown was followed by a glancing blow to the belly of the aircraft, leaving paint flecks behind but no destructive debris. Flight 703 headed airborne again from the knoll but only briefly, and now certainly no longer under Southeran's tight control.

Prosecutors claimed later that the first random impact with the knoll, pitching Flight 703 upward, was all that saved anyone from a certain death.

Maybe.

Or maybe Gary Southeran had just managed to react in time, snatching the controls back? Even though November Echo Yankee was throttled back to only 38 per cent power for the descent, by doing so had he just created that fractional lift that created the vast difference between life and death?

The fine margin involved here is rather like Chesley Sullenberger pulling off 'the Miracle on the Hudson' on US Airways Flight 1549 14 years later, by gliding an unpowered Airbus A320 to safety onto the Hudson River, without any loss of life.

You should ask what is the margin here between being OK and being dead? Personally, I reckon it wasn't very much, and in this case I would give Southeran all credit for pulling the Dash 8 up, and it was lucky he did.

Hard landings

That first contact was only the beginning, not the end of the tragedy. The propeller marks chopping a regular pattern over the paddock grass showed the Dash 8 was now flying at an airspeed of 122 knots. Ten knots had been bled off in that initial nose-wheel contact and glancing touch. The extra energy tucked away in those ten knots could make all the difference between complete body rupture with fractured, fragmented bodies and breathing people still full of life. But despite this, that initial impact had its first fatality.

Karen Gallagher was unrestrained, as she was up and performing her duties as a flight attendant. She was almost certainly the first to die.

Her body was eventually brought out and delivered into our care at 4 o'clock that wretched afternoon. That first impact, estimated at 30 times the force of gravity, snapped the junction of the first and second cervical vertebrae of her neck instantly.

The 'Hangman's Fracture', it is called. Death was certainly immediate and painless.

Always keep your seat belts fastened, the airlines endlessly tell us, until we are sick of hearing it. It's irrelevant usually, until the rare event such as a crash like this. Then it certainly does matter. There would be other dead come to us alongside Karen, but, thank God, not the 21 we were expecting.

Having bounced off that Tararua hillside, the uncontrolled November Echo Yankee just managed to clear the left of the knoll with her fully extended left undercarriage. The right wing then barely touched and danced off a nearby hillside.

Each glancing blow and bounce bled off more speed and more destructive energy.

Another bounce, and 25 metres further uphill she hit a grass spur. The outer right wing and outboard flaps were torn away together, along with more of the deadly speed, which was at last getting down into an envelope where humans could survive.

Somewhere in this chaotic flight, fragments of the fuselage or wings were ripped off and flung across the peaceful paddock. Three grazing sheep were sliced to death by the flying shards of metal.

The fuselage and its fragile human cargo continued flying, soaring 60 metres over a gully before bouncing again, snapping off her tail, her left wing and its engine. The vestigial cabin and right-wing stub and engine continued to pancake up the hill, slewing around and coming to rest 235 metres from that first impact on the grassy knoll.

The fractured fuselage lay still at last, spilling its entrails into the cold, wet fog covering the ranges. Within the aeroplane's cabin the scene was a chaotic shambles. It must have seemed surreal to the passengers as they regained their wits and their consciousness. Nothing would make sense. The seat-floor mountings were buckled and deformed but largely they had held. Many seat backs were broken, and the ceiling and overhead lockers were partially collapsed. The right side of the floor was a metre higher than the left.

They had suffered a massive deceleration, both vertically and backwards, from the various impacts, and they had all been thrown forward and downward as a result. All were injured, many seriously, and the pilots were trapped on the flight deck, both with head injuries. They would have to be cut out.

Karen and two of the passengers were dead. Others would surely die of cold on that exposed, fog-shrouded hillside unless rescue arrived soon.

Hard landings

* * *

The mystery to all of us on the ground was still where the hell was Flight 703? It just wasn't anywhere it was supposed to be.

The breakthrough came when William McGrory, the passenger who had first spotted the undercarriage failure, contacted 111 on his cell phone and galvanised the search, directing it to the right place. The helicopters were vectored in by McGrory listening to the sound of their rotor beat through the opaque mist, until there before them was Flight 703, in a large paddock at the top of the Hall Block Road.

I know this road well, for it is down here that the body of Arjun Krishnan was carried in 1991, after six years lost to his family in these mountains. It is a winding gravel road climbing through the bush-covered eastern slopes of the Tararua Ranges, riven by gullies and spurs. The top of the road passes through open grazing land that runs over the top of the ranges and undulates down the western side to the Manawatū River. These days the Manawatū's famous giant windmills also dot that hillside, their blades singing to the unconcerned sheep below.

And now up this road came the rescue teams. The injured were succoured, and gently lifted off to the waiting trauma teams. By three o'clock that afternoon, both the living and the dead were off the mountain.

I looked bleakly around the mortuary and prepared to start the autopsies. We were caring for three bodies: not as many as we had feared, but I could feel the sadness of such young and vibrant lives cut off abruptly and unexpectedly.

None of them had thought they would die in the cold of a lonely Manawatū paddock and end up in my mortuary when they set off from Auckland after their early breakfast that morning. That is, however, so often the way of it with unforeseen death. You just never know when it is your turn to visit the mortuary.

Three people had died when November Echo Yankee ploughed into the paddock, and in a curious symmetry they were matched by the three sheep who had simultaneously been slaughtered by flying debris. I suppose these ovine casualties are not too surprising; many folk around the world imagine rural New Zealand to be a place where you couldn't hit a paddock without hitting a sheep as well.

My task was now to describe and list all the injuries so that the forces causing them could be understood and the sequence of events could be established.

Both wings had been violently ripped from the fuselage, causing additional severe torsional forces where the wing spar was attached. This spar runs from seats 4 to 8, and it was the unlucky fate of both dead passengers to be seated in seats 6G and 7B.

'These marks on the chest and abdominal wall are interesting.' I had noticed a series of parallel abrasions spread over the upper abdomen and lower chest wall of one victim, a male passenger, 43 years of age, who had been recovered still strapped to his seat. The floor mountings had failed, and he had flown into the seats ahead. Literally flown, I mean, at pretty much the speed at which the aeroplane was flying at the time. Say 100 knots, allowing for the loss of energy involved in ripping the floor mounts out; that means around 185 kilometres per hour.

Hard landings

Ever try doing that speed in your car? Don't even think about it. It's terrifyingly fast and you'll probably kill yourself.

'What's the cause of them, doc?' The mortuary assistants were always curious about everything and picked up a lot. I reckon some of them knew as much as any experienced pathologist. The police photographers were also there. This was a serious case, of course, and they had to document everything for the investigation. They tend to be less inquisitive and more focused on their speciality of picturing everything to measured perfection.

'Porpoising marks, I think they're called. They're made when your body slides forward under the seat belt. Your body sort of jumps up and down like a porpoise as it passes under the lap belt, which unbelievably also stretches in the collision.' I made an undulating movement with my hand to demonstrate the motion.

'What do they mean?'

'Not too much, really,' I admitted. 'I guess it shows at least he was actually wearing his belt at the time, though. More usually you jack-knife over the top of a lap belt rather than porpoise under it. Maybe he was asleep when it happened? You know, lying low in the seat, legs out under the seat in front, and if that were so, you might instead slide under the belt as the plane decelerates?' I was guessing; I did not really know if that was the case.

The internal injuries were much more significant. There was a flail chest; that alone is enough to be fatal.

'It's when several of your ribs break in two places, and that stops that part of your chest wall moving in and out when you breathe. It's a pretty bad thing, as the air just can't get into your lungs,' I explained to the assistants, 'and you die of asphyxia.

'A flail chest can be caused by a shoulder seat belt, but he only had a passenger's lap belt, so that's out. His chest wall probably hit a forward seat at over a hundred kilometres per hour to fracture his chest wall like this.'

I considered. 'The only other possible thing that could have hit him was the wing root ripping through the cabin.' I shook my head. 'No — a force like that would have cut him in two, for sure. This must be a contact injury from being thrown forward into the aircraft's seating.'

Further evidence soon followed. His scalp was carefully peeled back, exposing the glistening dome of skull bone beneath. A few rivulets of blood trickled from the margins, running gently over the ivory orb.

I inspected the dome. There were no fractures.

'Open him up,' I quietly asked my assistant and stood aside waiting, watching carefully.

The assistant pulled a Perspex-fronted mask over his face, picked up the circular saw and began cutting through the skull as if he were lifting the top off a boiled egg. Round the skull he moved the motorised saw, sensing the give as he penetrated the cranium and then moving skilfully around to completely 'tap open' the top of the egg.

This is delicate and skilful surgery. If your cut is not deep enough, the cap of the skull will not lift off and you cannot see the brain contents. Too deep and you will tear into the linings of the brain, if not the brain itself, much to the anger of the pathologist, who prefers to examine the organs undamaged by the autopsy procedure.

Hard landings

Just right is how our assistants do it every single time. Not too shallow, not too deep, just right. I've tried to do their job, but it's an art that must be learnt. These days I just leave the task to their superior knowledge and experience. No one wants to have to see and put up with my ragged amateur cuts.

He jiggled the flat, flared blade of the skull key into the cut and turned it, levering up the top of the skull with a sucking wrench as the air met the brain for the very first time. The skull cap was gently eased off and I could examine his brain. My eyes were the first ever to see the magical hidden shore of it.

It was unsullied by haemorrhage, by trauma, by stroke or by tumour. Gently we pulled off the tough surrounding membranes. This was the dura mater or 'tough mother'. Below was the glistening, transparent pia mater, Latin for the 'tender mother', delicately covering the mysterious, moist hills and valleys of the convoluted sulci and gyri of the brain, wherein lies embedded everything from our intelligence to our humanity, from our piano lessons and childhood memories to our very souls.

I don't pretend to understand the workings of the brain at all. I leave all that to the psychologists and psychiatrists, who apparently know something of the connections within and what they might mean. I am competent only to look for the big breaks in its structure that account for its failure.

I could see none here. His brain looked perfect from the top side.

Gently, we eased the brain out of its cradle to see what lay underneath. And there it was: the cause of death. A fractured base of skull.

This is a fatal wound, known only too well to pathologists. It is also known to neurosurgeons, who may see some patients who survive this sort of trauma, but not all that many. Most are instantly dead. These fractures can reach from ear to ear across the densest and deepest part of your skull.

The problem is that these fractures impact on your brainstem in a big way. The brainstem is the slim tube at the brain's base where your heart's and lungs' working computers are kept. Stuff them up and you're dead, which is exactly what usually happens in this type of skull fracture.

This was a complex base of skull fracture. And it was right across the whole skull, passing through the foramen magnum, the 'big hole' through which the internet of the delicate spinal cord passes down into the body. I thought it was his most significant injury and was without doubt the cause of death.

'He has the same injury I often see in high-speed car and motorbike accidents. It's surely because of a head-on impact with something hard. And that's important here.' I thought for a few moments as I dragged my thoughts around the specifics of aircraft accidents. Assistants and photographers watched on in their usual relaxed mode as I did my best to explain.

'This is not a "ring fracture" of the base of skull, which happens when a plane hits the ground hard vertically and drives the spine upwards into the brain, like a spear thrust bursting the skull base. This is quite a different pattern to that.'

As I spoke, they looked down at the bloodied fracture site, an ugly zigzag of displaced bone across the empty middle fossa of the cranium.

'This fracture, I reckon, is due to blunt-force trauma,

from being thrown at speed into something ahead. It's not a burst-force trauma from hitting the ground.'

I pointed around at the empty tables in the mortuary. 'If they had hit the ground with the sort of force needed to cause a burst fracture in this man, I reckon we would have twenty-one casualties in here with the same injury, not just our three.'

I thought that pretty well decided this man's story, and eventually this was found to fit with what the investigators found. Their final reconstruction suggested that his seat had detached from the floor and had been thrown forward to impact with the fuselage.

The other passenger had similar injuries, with minor variations. His autopsy added nothing to what I had already discovered and to our understanding of what had happened.

Life is endlessly flipping a coin, isn't it? Heads you live, or tails you die. We all face this unwittingly every day. Inevitably someday, some time it will be tails for you, as indeed it will be for us all. Chance or luck, though, will play a part in deciding whether on this occasion you will be among the quick or the dead.

Your allocated seat on an aeroplane may well be the decider. That is exactly what happened on Flight 703.

'I was sitting up towards the front, in seat 3A, watching the stewardess talking to the couple in front of me. I remember it was cloudy outside.' Paul Cameron is a Manawatū farmer, and he told me of what happened to him on that day. 'Then the next thing I knew, I was looking at grass in a paddock. I couldn't make any sense of it at all'. I don't know how I got out. All I got were bruises, but later I noticed my foot was sore when it flapped around in my gumboots on the farm.

I had an X-ray and it showed I had broken my little toe. And that was it. That was all I got.'

My first patient had been sitting in seat 7B, and he was killed instantly. The passenger next to him in seat 7A was sitting millimetres from the wing root when it was violently ripped from the fuselage. He suffered only a broken ankle and index finger. These were surprising and disproportionately trivial injuries given the speed of the impact, and he was able to hobble out of the wreck. He survived by sheer chance, due to a random seat allocation made by a computer back at Auckland Airport.

It is sobering to think the selection of who is to die entirely depends on a few split seconds that determine your place in the queue at the ticket counter. Lingering a few seconds over that last sip of coffee could change everything, and you might get the ill-fated seat 7B and not the lucky 7A.

'A throw of the dice will never abolish chance' — so wrote the poet Stéphane Mallarmé in 1897.

* * *

The autopsies on our three dead were the end of my professional duties for the moment. However, we were sad to hear of a fourth death several days later, when Reg Dixon died of the terrible burns he had sustained to 80 per cent of his body in a flash fire coming from the right engine. That fire suddenly erupted, raging around him while he was trying to rescue others trapped in the wreckage. He was posthumously awarded a well-deserved New Zealand Cross for his bravery on that day.

The dying was now over; the dead had been cared for to

the utmost of our abilities; the slow recoveries of the living were only beginning.

The mighty law now stirred and began to consider the options. The law grinds slowly, ever so slowly, but it grinds surely.

Was there a case to answer? People had died, many were injured. Who would protect the people from this assault on the public weal? Was this an accident, no fault of any man? Or was it something else? Could this even be culpable homicide?

There was an immense wrangle about all of this. My story is not about that. I had already seen the sorrowful human consequences of this crash, but this is how I see the aftermath.

The police and Crown prosecutors, as defenders of the public interest, have an obligation to look at whether criminal charges should be brought. I personally thought charging a pilot with manslaughter was wrong, and I asked prosecutor Ben Vanderkolk about it.

'Why would you do it? The pilot always knows he is the very first to arrive at the scene of an accident. Surely it is hard to argue some sort of careless negligence when you are the first up for the consequence, especially when that is sudden death. Wouldn't Nature make you always do your utmost for yourself and therefore also for your passengers?'

That was how I saw the situation, and also what I believe to be the social contract between myself as trusting passenger and an aircraft's pilots.

Ben explained that his hands were tied by the legal definition that manslaughter was the omission to perform your legal duty without a reasonable excuse. And this sad collision apparently fitted that definition. Competent airline pilots like Michael Guerin, who wrote a book analysing all the technicalities of this accident, agreed wholeheartedly with what the law then decided to do.

I did not agree. This prosecution case just didn't seem right to me.

The case took years to come to court. The aviation authorities in Canada and Australia, the Air Line Pilots' Association and virtually all individual pilots refused to help the prosecution or to testify. No one would help Detective Dennis O'Rourke, who had been put in charge of the investigation by Detective Inspector Doug Brew, the head of the local CIB. All local and international doors were slammed shut and the experts turned their faces away. I was not too surprised.

I believe they did so because of a profound understanding of the enormous personal pressures of bringing an aircraft in blind, never mind with the added complication of a malfunctioning wheel. In the light of that understanding they probably saw a prosecution as unfounded.

There were arguments about whether voice cockpit recorders could even be legally used as evidence, which had international implications far beyond the New Zealand skies. There were many other legal matters, too.

In the end there was a thoroughly heard court case lasting six weeks. Captain Gary Southeran, now thankfully recovered from his head injury, was put on trial for four counts of manslaughter and three representative charges of injuring passengers.

The jury, after careful discussion for 22 hours, agreed on a verdict: 'Not guilty.'

Twelve men and women good and true. They are the backbone of our civilised law system. Good on you — I personally believe that this was the only fair verdict.

Hard landings

* * *

There is one question that still bothers me. It is purely a technical and not a pathological one.

Much was made of the ground-proximity warning instrument. It was designed to give its raucous alert a full 17 seconds before impact, which would easily have given enough time to feed in power to the engines and pull hard up and clear those hills.

The theory of what this instrument does and how it is designed to perform are easy to follow. The device was carefully tested in a laboratory after the crash and was reported as working perfectly, exactly as it was supposed to.

But how can that be true? Why does the actual flight recorder information show that this same device, working to its exact design specification — so we are assured — was only able to give Gary Southeran a brief 4.8 seconds' warning on that fatal day?

November Echo Yankee's radar altimeter antenna was later found to be carefully painted, including over the prominently embossed words 'Do Not Paint', but that was apparently not judged to be a problem. So much for that.

Some asked whether a cell phone call could have deranged the instruments. Investigations showed there was absolutely no likelihood of this happening. The technical avenues of possible reasons for a malfunction were closed off, item by item. But the fundamental puzzle to me remains the question of why the ground-proximity warning system didn't work to its specifications on the day of the crash.

There is talk amongst local fliers of unexpected and fierce downdrafts where the Manawatū Gorge punctures through the ranges. That was put forward by Gary Southeran, too, in his defence. But it was not accepted by the aviation authorities, and we fly in on that Tararua approach to Runway 25 even today.

In the end it was put down to a failure of what these days is cumbersomely termed 'cockpit resource management'. It was called 'human factors' before that, but I still prefer the even earlier term used when I first learnt to fly. That term was 'airmanship', which is what it had been called since long before the Second World War.

'Airmanship' is what we were taught. This is a simple word and a simple concept. Aviate. Navigate. Communicate. Ignore any of the golden rules to your utter peril and to your everlasting sadness.

The dead from that sad day in the Manawatū have already been long at rest, but I remember you all, and with sorrow, even now. None of you deserved this.

9 June 1995
Karen Anne Gallagher
David Alan White
Jonathan Peter Keall

23 June 1995
Reg Dixon

Requiescat in pace

Doubt grows with knowledge.
— Goethe, 1826

CHAPTER 6

Deliver us from evil

Pathologists' office, 3 p.m.

I always think of 3 to 4 p.m. as being the dog hour, to be endured until that final hour begins to run to close off the day. Only one hour it may well be, but to a dog, one human hour is said to feel the same as seven hours to us, and that is exactly how I feel about the mid-afternoon.

I was weary, with my spuddled brain brittle and on the edge of calling it quits, but with two hours yet to go until home time there was no way out. The bulk of the day's routine work had been done, but the deferred problem-diagnoses from the morning and from the day before and, terrible to tell, even earlier remained gnawing at me. As always, I was aware there were patients out there sitting on the edge of their beds anxiously waiting to hear what their future would bring.

The specimen slides of special stains and investigations ordered in the freshness of the morning started to flow back from the scientists for me to examine. I needed my wits and my eyes and mind alert if I was to find the light where all has been diagnostic darkness.

The Final Diagnosis

Maybe another coffee? I thought. But no, my mouth was already acrid and bitter from too many mugs throughout the day. To go make another would only be a displacement activity with which to cut a small chunk from this vapid hour. I sighed and tried to rub the concentration frown from my forehead.

The phone rang.

I snatched it in relief. Answering the phone surely could not be classified as a displacement activity?

'TC, Les Adams here. Are you free to talk?'

Les was an experienced gynaecologist and obstetrician. It was not a daily occurrence for general hospital pathologists to hear from gynaecologists, so something unusual was evidently afoot.

It must be about some patient of his with a cancer, I thought, as that was his usual reason to call. My mind flicked through my recent cases to see if I could work out who it might be. There are not a huge number of gynaecological cancers of the uterus or ovaries, so I usually have the most recent patients and their unusual diagnoses prominently in the forefront of my mind. But I could think of none at the time.

'We've had a maternal death, I am sorry to say.' I could now detect the strain in his voice.

'No!' Now I was shocked, too, and it takes something out of the ordinary to do that to a pathologist. The dog hour ennui was gone.

Maternal deaths — the death of a mother during pregnancy — are thankfully very, very rare, almost in the rocking-horse shit, or more politely perhaps hen's teeth category of unhappy events.

'I'm afraid so. Everyone is in a bit of a panic here. All very shocked, as you can imagine.'

I could. Normally delivery suites are joyous places, full of affirming life and the happiest in any hospital most of the time. Their staff live and breathe that warm and happy atmosphere. Disasters are rare and the doctors, nurses and midwives are not hardened veterans to horror and disaster, as are we in the mortuary.

'What happened?'

'We just have no idea. Theresa is — er, was — a thirty-two-year-old para two, gravida three, at term. She presented in relatively early labour with her cervix only one centimetre dilated. Her previous two deliveries were straightforward, so we decided to induce her with a prostaglandin E gel.'

Les paused. So far, through all his obstetric jargon it all sounded a standard story. An experienced mum, already with two healthy babies from normal deliveries under her belt. A whiff of a hormonal paste to ripen up the cervix and get things moving. All this happened a thousand times a day, all around the world.

'I was called from the gynae ward to the delivery suite as she seemed in quite a bit of pain. More they reckoned than she should be with her uncomplicated history. I thought so, too.'

There was a silence.

'And?' I prompted. 'What happened?'

My mind was racing through horrible scenes of catastrophic haemorrhage, of a ruptured uterus, of dead babies. Air embolism maybe? Sometimes air was sucked into the large veins around the vagina and uterus and raced to the heart, which then churned uselessly, making a hideous frothy shake pumping useless air but little blood out to the waiting brain and body. It was just like an unprimed pump.

Les's voice came down the line, uneven and emotional.

'She died. She just died, while I was standing there looking down at her deciding what to do.'

'Nothing else happened?' This was odd. 'No bleeding?'

I could almost see the negative shake of his head.

'No. Nothing. Her heart just stopped. And nothing we could do made any difference. Even the ICU team came down to help. But she didn't respond at all. Her ECG just flat-lined.'

'Hm,' I pondered. 'And her baby?'

'She's OK, thank God. APGAR ten out of ten—' Les naturally lapsed back into his birthing jargon: the little girl was pink and breathing and moving normally is what he meant — 'so that's at least something that worked out of this frigging mess.'

It was a sign of his stress that usually gentile and urbane Les was swearing, even mildly.

I thought this surely must be an air embolism. That was the commonest cause of sudden death during a delivery. And it is a bugger. The fatal ones are usually big — more than a Coke can of air — but even one as little as the size of the dregs in your coffee mug can kill you if you're very unlucky.

'Her placenta was still attached,' Les went on, getting a grip on himself again, 'so I delivered it because I didn't want her bleeding to death from that if she made it through the cardiac arrest.'

'Have you kept it for me? You never know, the clue as to what has happened might be there.' I knew we could leave no stone unturned to find the cause of Theresa's death.

'Yep. Got it in a bucket here in the sluice room.'

'I'll come right on up and pick it up now.' I did not need to go myself, and no doubt a porter would pick it up and deliver it to the lab eventually. But my investigative hackles were up. I wanted to see the scene for myself, to find out what the hell had caused this tragedy.

This was also a chance to escape the afternoon tedium. The dog hour still had forty minutes to run.

Les was waiting in the office of the delivery suite. The bucket and placenta were on the floor in a clear plastic bag, with a label attached around the neck. I bent over and twisted the label around.

Theresa Maria Arthur, I read. *KRD4421. DOB 26.09.1978. Placenta.*

A chilling sadness sunk into my soul when I saw this first palpable sign of the tragedy. That does not happen often to me, as I am used to disaster and suffering. It must have been the thought of Theresa coming in here to this place full of joy and life and the promise of a new baby only a few hours earlier. Now she was dead and would never see or hold her baby. She had walked in but would only ever be wheeled out dead, alongside her placenta in a bucket labelled with her cold clinical details.

Life can be a real shit, that's for sure. And this death must rank amongst the worst.

'When can you do the autopsy? I called the coroner, and he has authorised one.' Len looked anxiously at me, a man in torment.

'I'll do it today, though it will only be tonight some time. But it's important to find out the cause as soon as we can.'

He nodded gratefully. 'I'd appreciate that. I don't think I'll be sleeping much tonight myself.'

The shocked family, now unexpectedly caring for the orphaned infant, would need to know. The devastated midwives and the delivery staff were in turmoil, too. We all just needed to know the reason why.

Air embolism was the first thing I had thought of and needed to investigate, but it's not easy to prove.

'We have to arrange a CT scan as soon as possible,' I told Pat, the head of the mortuary staff. 'It's the only way to see air embolism. You can see the bubbles in the vessels around the uterus as well as in the right side of the heart, and if we can see them the job's done, and an open autopsy may even become unnecessary.'

The radiology staff, though overwhelmed most nights with patients from the Emergency Department and the admission wards, were as helpful as always. They squeezed us into the earliest possible slot when there was a gap in the urgent cases lining up in the corridor outside.

I chatted to the young, enthusiastic and newly minted radiologist Joe Singh as we watched the CT scanner throbbing its magic eye around the blue-bagged body. Theresa was alone in there for the moment, but she would soon come back to our watchful care.

'Thanks for doing this so quickly, Joe,' I said. 'I'm especially looking for air embolism. This was almost impossible to diagnose without your help back in the old days.'

'How did you find it before CT scans?' Joe asked.

'We had to open the patient's body underwater to look for the bubbles of air escaping. That was really the only reliable way. Messy and difficult, too. The blood stained the water so heavily you couldn't see where the bubbles were even coming from. It was a pretty random and ineffective procedure.'

'I have seen air embolism once before,' Joe told me. 'That one was easy, but that was in a neurological case, not obstetrics.'

I nodded. Brain surgery was a well-known cause of embolisms, where air got sucked into the venous sinuses on the brain's surface inside the opened skull.

'It's usually during induction of labour, isn't it,' asked Joe, 'and usually when they're using forceps and things?'

I nodded again. My eyes were glued to the images on the screen in front of us, willing bubbles of air to appear and solve the mystery. Joe was also keeping a desultory eye open, but he was clearly intent on having a yarn while we waited. I guessed he had not had much company during his long shift.

'And now there's oral sex, too. I mean, as a cause.'

'What?' That caught my attention. I snapped my eyes away from the gleaming right heart ventricle and stared at Joe.

'Yep.' Joe looked satisfied at having some knowledge to share. Young consultants fresh from their final college exams are a wealth of information gleaned from hundreds of hours studying the medical journals — much of it useful, some interesting, some weird and some just useless.

'There have been a couple of cases reported of oral sex during pregnancy causing air embolism.'

'Come on, Joe! Surely that's bullshit?'

'Not at all. In one reported case in a journal, a man blew air into his partner's vagina, and it went through the cervix and between the uterus and foetal membranes into the placental veins. They saved her and the baby by putting them into a hyperbaric chamber — you know, like they use for

The Final Diagnosis

deep-sea divers with the bends — and pressuring her until the bubbles of air shrunk down and were absorbed.

'They said it was important to be aware of the possibility to make the right diagnosis and start the right treatment! How could you even ask a patient that with a straight face?' Joe laughed.

I shook my head in disbelief and turned back to our task, gesturing at Theresa's images. 'Nothing there, is there?'

'No, no air in there at all,' Joe agreed.

Theresa's CT scan was pristine, perfect in every way. The womb swollen from the pregnancy was the only sign of her recent history.

'Thanks, Joe. Definitely not air embolism, then. We'll get on down to the mortuary and see if we can find what did this.'

* * *

It was late by now, and I pondered other possibilities as Pat and I pushed the trolley on its last sombre journey along the dim, deserted corridors, into the empty lift and down to the mortuary for Theresa's final examination.

'Could be a pulmonary embolism,' I mused. Pat was used to my bouncing ideas around. It helped me think better. He had seen it all before many times, from plane crashes to pulmonary emboli and everything in between.

'Bit young, isn't she, doc?'

'Yep, not usual, but you can get clots in the veins in the pelvis from the pressure of the pregnant uterus. They can get to be really big and if they break off and end up in the lung, it can easily be enough to kill you. I reckon after air embolism that would be my next best guess. We'll just have to see.'

The mortuary is noticeably quieter during our night-time autopsies. By day there are interruptions from the police with their papers, suavely dressed and scented undertakers from all over the North Island, and slow-moving orderlies clashing their steel trolleys and slamming the heavy fridge doors as they bring the deceased bodies down from the ward. But at night the occasional orderly was often the only sign of the hospital resting in semi-repose. Sometimes I used to hear these orderlies being paged on their intercom phones as they pushed their burdens along the corridors.

'Oscar Base to Orderly. Pick up patient Jackson from Ward 23 by trolley to go to Ward 13.'

Ward 13 was the orderlies' euphemistic code for the mortuary. I would smile to myself and shake my head. The circle of life was closing indeed: another patient on their way into my care.

But tonight it was silent and empty, the only sound a low hum of some background machinery not noticeable by day. I looked speculatively at Theresa and sighed. We began.

'I'll do her lungs and heart first. If it's a big pulmonary embolism, it'll be obvious, and we'll have the answer quickly.'

Her lungs were spongy, pink and pristine. No cigarette smoke had ever been in here, for sure. The trachea and bronchus on each side were smooth and glistening but sadly silent now, no whistle and waft of passing air for the first time in her 32 years.

I picked up the long dissecting knife, noting with satisfaction its finely honed, gleaming blade. Pat always made sure our instruments were razor-sharp and ready to go. I sliced the right lung through the hilum, releasing it from its bronchus and the attached heart in its pericardial sac. Blood ran darkly over the blade and splashed onto the bench. Into the scale went the lung: 384 grams. Normal. I repeated the operation on the left lung: 315 grams. Normal.

Now the hard part. With the dissecting scissors, honed to sharpness as diligently as the knife had been, I opened the myriad branches of the large arteries that run blood from the heart to the lungs, searching all along the opening channels for that old enemy, the dreaded pulmonary embolism.

Theresa had died very suddenly and unexpectedly before Les Adams' shocked eyes, so I knew if there was an embolism there to be found it would be a big clot that I couldn't possibly miss. But an hour's meticulous dissection of both lungs right down to the small arteries at the very edges showed absolutely nothing.

'Bugger! No embolism here.'

Pat looked at me sympathetically, then I caught him glancing up at the clock. Quarter to eleven. The night was passing quickly, and I had nothing yet to show for my efforts.

'Ticker job?' Pat questioned helpfully.

'Sure, that's possible. I'll do the heart next but if it is an arrhythmia, we won't find anything of course. Maybe she's got a prolonged QT?'

I muttered the last bit to myself. Increasingly we were finding patients with an inherited ECG abnormality related to long QT syndrome, a heart-signalling disorder that can cause fast, chaotic heartbeats. This often only revealed itself by sudden, unexplained death, confirmed by a genetic diagnosis by the Cardiac Inherited Disease Service in Auckland.

Deliver us from evil

I had become interested in this condition when it was revealed as the cause of death in the homicide of Barbara Miller by Basil Mist back in 2002. I was not particularly surprised to find that I, too, have a long QT. I have had several nasty, cardiac-type blackouts during which I collapsed and went quite blue before spontaneously recovering. I also once began feeling quite uneasy and panicky while swimming in the sea in Fiji; as I later found out, these QT-type attacks are often brought on by swimming. Two of Barbara Miller's brothers had also died of the same condition while swimming in school galas, a year apart from each other!

The arrhythmias arising in prolonged QT syndrome are sometimes rather exotically called torsades de pointes. This sounds rather like a Portuguese bullfight to me, but it is actually a chaotic outage of the heart's electrics and is frequently fatal.

This was a genetic possibility that I had to remember to check for in Theresa's blood. There is no other way to detect it, as it leaves no sign in the afflicted heart.

By midnight I was finished with my autopsy, as well as mentally and physically. Pat still had a couple of hours to go, replacing Theresa's organs and sewing up her body, cleaning and dressing her before placing her in the fridge for the undertakers to collect and return her to her grieving family. They, too, would surely not be sleeping much on this first night.

Pat then had to label and pack up all the specimens I had taken: blood, stomach contents, sample tissues of all of her organs to prepare for me to look at under my microscope. All had to be directed correctly to different laboratories; the blood to the ESR lab for Fentanyl and tryptase levels, to look for anaphylaxis, and of course to Auckland for the cardiac QT genetic studies. The mortuary needed to be sluiced down and cleaned and the instruments washed, checked and sharpened for an 8 a.m. start on our next patient. Finally, the paperwork I had left filled in on the office table had to be faxed to the coroner in the morning.

Poor Pat; I would be fast asleep in bed by the time he was finished up here. And yet I always marvelled that he would be there, smiling, at 8 a.m. sharp the next day, ready to do it all again.

And me? Well, I had found nothing at all. No cause of death to report to her family, to Les and the obstetric staff. No way for the healing to begin.

Obscure natural causes, I wrote bleakly in the space on the coroner's form. This was no bloody use to anyone.

* * *

A week later, results from the ESR laboratory in Johnsonville arrived. It was 7 a.m. and I was sitting at my desk with my first steaming coffee of the day. I relished these early, uninterrupted hours to get everything ready before the day of rushing demands began.

I slit open the thick envelope and pulled out the folded sheets of test data and commentary from the forensic scientists. The results were surprising.

The mast cell tryptase level was very high. Her immunoglobulin E (IgE) level was up a tad, too.

I stared at the results. These were markers of anaphylaxis. That's a fancy Greek word meaning 'no protection', but it is less simple and much, much worse than that. We all know about anaphylaxis in these days of lethal peanut allergies and bee stings, as well as reactions to all sorts of other things. It is the body's allergic shock reaction to anything it doesn't recognise and decides is foreign. And it can be and often is a killer.

Raised IgE goes with this bizarre body storm, too. Both tryptase and immunoglobulin E are released when white cells called mast cells basically vomit their granular contents into the blood, fuelling the anger of the wild allergic blaze.

What's caused this anaphylaxis? I wondered to myself. It was still a little too early in the morning to fully engage my brain.

I saw Theresa had low levels of Fentanyl in her blood, but that was often given in the delivery suite as a painkiller, so I was not sure how it might be relevant. Fentanyl is a very effective painkiller, as it is a hundred times stronger than morphine and fifty times stronger than heroin. I know some anaesthetists suck air between their teeth and shake their heads about its use in pregnancy, but it is given pretty well everywhere these days.

But anaphylaxis? Could Fentanyl do this? Theresa's blood Fentanyl levels were lowish, but allergy doesn't need much of a dose to kick it off.

My mind was full of various news reports of Fentanyl causing celebrity deaths. There was Tom Petty and Prince for starters. These were all hearsay stories, I reminded myself. Don't get sucked in to confusing proven science with internet chatter. Still, it made me think and, just possibly, it could be the answer.

'Can you process the slides from Autopsy 245 from last Thursday night as a priority, please?' I called the scientists in

The Final Diagnosis

the Histology lab. They were already beavering away after their early 6.30 a.m. start, getting the patients' biopsies ready for the pathologists to start work on at their 8 a.m. kick-off. It was bad form for me to move an autopsy case up the queue in front of the living patients, but I was so consumed with curiosity about Theresa, I just had to find out. And naturally her family and doctors were still fretting anxiously in the wings.

The slides came later that morning. I picked up a section of the lung. It looked perfectly normal to me. My eyes went straight to the blood vessels: were they blocked with blood clots? Were there minute emboli everywhere, too small for me to see the previous Thursday night? Were there any cancer cells in there, embolising and blocking the arteries? I had seen such an event once as a young pathologist. A pregnant Xhosa woman in Cape Town presented with a puzzling lung condition, and the respiratory physician, Mike Hayhurst, took a biopsy through a bronchoscope. I discovered chunks of a rare type of cancer had caused lots of little emboli to plug up her arteries. Her cancer was a choriocarcinoma, and very oddly it had formed in her placenta and was flicking millions of malignant cells into her lungs. Death had rapidly followed.

No, not this time, though. Theresa's blood vessels were empty.

I studied slide after slide of Theresa's lung, and they all looked fine.

Or did they?

Slowly my unconscious brain began to stir. Something was not right but I hadn't got it yet. And suddenly I saw it. And once I had seen it, it was as plain as day.

Deliver us from evil

The arteries were not empty at all: they were full. Sure, they looked empty at first sight, but they were in fact bloated with a fine, granular material, almost completely camouflaged by the pinkness of the surrounding stained lung. It was hard to be sure, but I got the impression the material was lightly pigmented brown.

'It couldn't be!' I breathed slowly out.

But it was. I knew what it was.

It was amniotic fluid in the arteries. This was the rare amniotic fluid embolism.

This was said to happen maybe as rarely as once every 20,000 births. Some say only one in 80,000. I shouldn't even see one of these in a working lifetime as a pathologist, but here it was ...

Why it happens we do not know, but hair, bits of shed skin, debris and fluid from within the sac around the baby leaks into the mum's veins, with catastrophic consequences. The grungy fluid blocks the small vessels in the lungs, so the mother's blood can't get to the life-preserving oxygen in the air sacs. What may be even more deadly is that the skin cells and other detritus are foreign and, if you haven't already guessed it, they light the pyre of anaphylaxis and shock as well.

Together the effects are deadly. They are often so sudden and massive that little can be done to help. As indeed had been the case with Theresa.

'It is just extraordinary,' I explained to the registrars. 'We don't know the cause. I don't expect to see another case like Theresa again, and you young pathologists may never see one in your careers. At least, let's hope you don't. None of us wants this to happen again.'

The Final Diagnosis

* * *

Then it did.

'You are not going to believe this.' Les Adams was on the phone to me barely two weeks later. Once more it was unexpected, once more the line crackled with barely supressed emotion. The only difference from Theresa's case was it was mid-morning. There would be no burning of the midnight oil this time.

'Sitella was a Samoan lady, para three, gravida four, a bit post-term at forty-two weeks so we induced her this morning. All seemed to be going fine and then she just dropped dead. Oh God—' Les paused with the emotion.

I knew what had happened, of course. Otherwise Les wouldn't be ringing me, would he?

'What happened, Les?' I asked gently.

'I had to do a postmortem Caesar. Sitella was already dead. The baby was still alive. At least I thought he was.'

There was a long pause.

'And then ...?' I prompted.

'There were no suitable instruments in the delivery suite. They had to get them from theatre. By the time I got the baby out, he was dead, too. I was too late.'

Another shit story. It truly was a ghastly, Groundhog Day experience in every way. It just shouldn't have happened again, not when it is only supposed to occur once every 20,000 births.

From the application of the prostaglandin gel to ripen the cervix and start the labour, to the raised anaphylactoid tryptase, the Fentanyl and the plugged arteries lying forlornly under my microscope lens, it was identical. The only difference this time was there was no living child to hand to Sitella's family. Only two cold bodies united forever in death.

Why this happened twice in quick succession was a complete mystery. Nothing seemed untoward, and identical labour procedures were progressing to happy live births in delivery suites all around the world. Why us? Why here? Why now?

There was an enquiry, of course. It was my sombre task to tell the story to the coroner, to Les and the other medical staff and, of course, ultimately to the family. The coroner had questions; the family had questions. Even *I* had questions, but I knew intuitively the answers would not to be found in a court full of lawyers.

I was questioned by the Medical Protection Society lawyer.

'In your experience, was this a serious, that is to say a significant, embolism?'

I looked at him, puzzled. The legal mind could sometimes be obtuse.

'She is dead, so I would have to say yes, it was a serious embolism.'

I saw the coroner smile at the silliness of the question.

'What I meant is, was it large in comparison with other such events you have seen?'

'I've never seen an amniotic fluid embolism before, but as there is also anaphylaxis, size is certainly less significant than in, say, a simple blood clot.'

None of this legal questioning achieved any sort of fundamental answer, nor I suspect did it help with closure for any of us.

The Final Diagnosis

For some years I thought about how they say lightning never strikes the same place twice, because that was how I eventually came to see the coincidence of Theresa's and Sitella's deaths in the same fortnight. Can lightning in fact strike the same place twice in a single storm? The phrase is used to reassure people that bad things are not repeated, though surely the same also is true for good things, like winning Lotto. Tall buildings sure do get hit more than once; the Empire State Building in New York probably gets hit every time there is a storm, which is about 25 times a year. An American park ranger, Roy Sullivan, has apparently survived seven different hits over the years.

The saying clearly isn't true. Lightning can and does strike twice, and that is what I thought must have happened with Theresa and Sitella.

* * *

In 2015, I read a medical journal reporting on a study of 120 women with amniotic fluid embolism in the United Kingdom. Since Theresa's and Sitella's deaths I had been interested in this condition and followed up any new developments that I came across.

They discovered that women who were given prostaglandins to induce labour had their odds of getting amniotic fluid embolism go up by a whopping six times! Was that the cause then?

Could the prostaglandin gel have been the small pebble that started the deadly amniotic avalanche? That is something I often ponder, though nothing like those terrible events has ever happened hereabouts again. I guess I'll never know for sure.

Deliver us from evil

Flow down, cold rivulet, to the sea,
Thy tribute wave deliver:
No more by thee my steps shall be,
For ever and for ever.
— Alfred, Lord Tennyson, 'A Farewell', 1842

CHAPTER 7

What on earth have you been eating?: part I

'Doctor, I've been feeling unwell for the past two to three months. Nothing in particular, just tiredness and a feeling that something serious may be the matter.'

Gaynor Glendale was an immaculately groomed lady in her early eighties. As always, she was beautifully attired, this time, in recognition of her appointment with the doctor, in a cream lace embroidered blouse, a knitted cardigan ornamented with a pearl flower brooch and matching earrings, long skirt and flat black brogues. She clasped the head of her walking stick commandingly.

This consultation with her general practitioner was probably identical to many thousands that occur daily throughout New Zealand. Most do not reveal anything seriously wrong and simply reflect problems caused by advancing age or the hectic pace of our modern social-media-driven world — or maybe both. Most merely require an examination, a soothing chat and maybe a few simple blood tests for the lab to check out.

A wise GP once confided in me, 'Most of my patients are seeking reassurance or need me to certify that they are not

What on earth have you been eating?: part I

going to die. Mostly they are well and aren't going to die — at least not just yet, as far as I can tell, anyway.

'You have to dig an awful lot of dirt to find a little gold in this life. The skill lies in finding that gold. It's too easy to miss the real illness amongst all these worried well.'

It is the same with our lab blood tests. The yield is surprisingly low, with most being boringly normal or showing trivial changes at most.

Until they don't. And that is what happened to Gaynor Glendale.

'Mrs Glendale, good evening to you. It is Dr Dell speaking. I am sorry to call you so late in the day, but I have the blood result from the lab here.'

'What is it showing, doctor?'

'It's very odd. Your creatinine is sky high. I am afraid you have renal failure.'

'Renal failure?'

'Your kidneys. They've stopped working properly.'

'My kidneys have always functioned perfectly well in the past. What is the matter with them?'

'That I do not know,' admitted Arthur Dell. 'But I want you to go up to the hospital tomorrow morning. Dr Gear is the physician on call, and he will see you. We'll have to see what he says and take it from there.'

* * *

The cause of her renal failure proved elusive, and Gaynor was referred to the renal physicians for a super-specialist opinion.

'Her urine is unimpressively bland,' Marilyn Aday told me.

The Final Diagnosis

She had come to the lab to tell me a renal biopsy was coming shortly, and more importantly to tell me Mrs Glendale's history and what had been discovered so far.

A kidney biopsy is a highly invasive procedure, in which a needle is stuck deeply through the back into the rear of the abdominal cavity. You want to do it only as a last resort, chasing an elusive diagnosis. Like the investigation of a murder, the pathologist must be in on the investigation from the start, so all the known facts can be brought together to find the truth.

'There is no blood and no red cell casts in her urine, and only a few white cells. It does not look like an active glomerulonephritis and anyway, the tests for hidden infections or the usual types of vasculitis are all negative.' I listened intently for any clues.

'It sounds like an interstitial nephritis caused by drugs, doesn't it? Has she been popping any pills lately?' Often the elderly and the not-so-elderly fall into failure after thrashing their kidneys with some new medication.

Marilyn nodded. 'I also thought of drugs first, most likely due to one of her medicines. But she is on only a few drugs, like an ipratropium inhaler and omeprazole.'

'Everyone in the universe seems to be on omeprazole, so that's not a problem. The inhalers are OK, too. What about anti-inflammatories? Is she perhaps taking those for her aches and pains?'

We all do that — I certainly do. In this modern age any muscle spasm or joint discomfort is to be medically massaged away forthwith, and there's nothing like ibuprofen or Voltaren to do the job. I sometimes wonder what our ancestors would have thought about our sensitivity to these most trivial of pains.

What on earth have you been eating?: part I

'No, I specifically asked her about painkillers. She's surprisingly well for her age. There really is nothing. I even asked about alternative medicines. But no, nothing.'

I nodded. Along with over-the-counter painkillers and other more conventional medicines, a sizeable segment of our society has fallen in love with alternative medicines. These are completely uncontrolled by any competent agency and some of them can be seriously toxic, even causing death in extreme circumstances.

I once struggled with diagnosing a mysterious skin rash that made the patient look like a boiled lobster. We were worried about a malignant lymphoma of the skin, which can do exactly this, but I was convinced the rash was due to some drug or chemical. It was only after a substantial number of punitive biopsies that the man sheepishly admitted to secretly taking bee-venom extract. Not only was it very expensive to buy, but it was proving seriously toxic to his skin.

Many of these potions, philtres and poisons can certainly cause kidney failure. Not this time, apparently. Mrs Glendale indignantly denied any such behaviour.

'The biopsy will have to tell us the answer, then. I can't think of anything else. We will just have to wait. The slides will be ready this afternoon.'

* * *

We peered down the microscope. The kidney biopsy slides had arrived hot off the processing press and the renal physicians, and the medical and pathology registrars all crowded around, jostling for a place at the multi-header.

The Final Diagnosis

I rotated the focusing dial and the kidney image crisply swam into our view. It looked entirely normal. There were rounded glomeruli, tubules lined by plump cells and pristine blood vessels: all the God-given apparatus required to filter the blood into urine, but no soupçon of a flaw to catch our eye at all.

'There goes the theory of an interstitial nephritis,' I said. 'It doesn't look as if she's been sneakily taking any nasty drugs.'

So what was it? Everyone was frowning in puzzlement, looking intently down the eyepieces, willing an answer to appear. I shrugged and looked again. Still nothing, nothing, nothing to see as I panned over the kidney at a higher magnification — and then I saw it.

'Oh no! Not again! I don't believe it! This just can't happen twice.' Everyone was now staring at me, still puzzled.

'Look, I'll show you.' I swung a lens into the apparatus to polarise the beam from the illumination bulb. This meant the light beam was now vibrating in one direction only, so the field went dark, but the bright, shining, jagged crystals plugging every tubule in the kidney shone like beacons. They were like the lights on a tree early on a dark Christmas morning.

'They're oxalate crystals! The kidney's tubules are totally plugged up with oxalate crystals. No wonder she's in failure. The urine just can't get past them. It's exactly the same as your kitchen sink drain blocking up and backwashing.'

'What's the cause? I mean, in Mrs Glendale's case?'

'I had an identical case once before. It's really rare and to now see a second case ... just unbelievable!' I was ecstatic at this amazing find.

What on earth have you been eating?: part I

'That first patient was a Massey professor who was taking industrial doses of vitamin C. I think he did it to prevent cancer, or maybe it was to slow down aging. Anyway, he doped himself up daily on supplements from the health shop and gummed up his kidneys exactly like this. He only admitted it on his death bed in ICU.

'Excessive vitamin C is a potent cause of oxalosis in the blood and will cause kidney failure. It's dollars to donuts that'll be what she's been doing. It may be hard to get her to admit it, though. The professor was very secretive about it all, right to the end.'

'Could it be anything else?' one of the registrars asked.

'Well, the most well-known cause that is always talked about is drinking ethylene glycol, or antifreeze. It's a chemically complex alcohol that's either drunk accidentally or, as legend has it, as a cheap substitute for booze. I have my doubts about that — the stuff is positively lethal, and surely not even a hardened alcoholic would touch it? Anyway, drinking antifreeze is quite improbable in an eighty-year-old Palmerston North retiree. But you never know, so it always pays to check.'

Marilyn smiled. 'Not Mrs Glendale. You should see her — very gentile. It's quite unimaginable for a lady like her to be a secret alcoholic and then topping it up with antifreeze.'

'It can rarely occur with Crohn's disease, but no sign of that, I assume?'

The medical registrars had taken her history and examined her, and they were shaking their heads even before I'd finished my question. A chronic gut ailment like Crohn's was hardly likely to be overlooked in 84 years of life.

'OK, then, she must be taking vitamin C on the sly. It's up to you to prove it.'

But time went by and that just wasn't the case. Mrs Glendale was perplexed at the line of questioning.

'Young lady, I have no idea why you keep pestering me about vitamin C. I have a very healthy diet and I've certainly never taken such a thing in my life. Why, I am not even sure where one might find it in the first place. I suppose it's the sort of thing the chemist shop might keep.'

'I believe her absolutely,' Marilyn told me. 'She is not taking vitamin C. Or antifreeze, for that matter. It must be something else. I am just going to have to take a complete history of everything she eats.'

'And of what she does, too,' I added. 'It might be an accidental contamination from some weird hobby, though God only knows what that could be. You get ethylene glycol in brake fluid, too. I don't suppose she rebuilds vintage cars or something …?'

Merilyn smiled, shaking her head as my voice trailed off. All this was just so improbable. What could Gaynor Glendale be doing to plug her kidneys with this crystalline gunk? It had to be something she was eating or drinking. There is no other way for the oxalate to enter her body.

* * *

'I'm going to research this and see what plants are full of oxalates. It must be something like that,' I told Marilyn.

My starting point was the plant oxalis. This was something nostalgic from my youth. Wood sorrel grows prolifically in Africa, and as kids we would pull the clover-like plant

What on earth have you been eating?: part I

from the ground and nibble at the soft, slender roots. It was deliciously sour, because of all the oxalic acid in it.

I suddenly stopped sampling the oxalis roots one day when my older brother Lawrence saw me sucking at these delectable treats. To me they were just as good as sour worm lollies are to me today.

'That's a disgusting thing to do. Don't you know why it tastes so sour?'

I shook my head, wide-eyed. I believed everything my brother told me. Of course I did — he was an unfathomable six years older than me.

'They will only grow where a dog has pissed. Didn't you know that? You're eating dog piss.' He smirked at me.

His story was rubbish, but I never touched it again. People do eat it though, apparently. As it is also rich in vitamin C, eating wood sorrel could be a double hit, plugging the kidneys with oxalate crystals — although no one has yet noticed it causing kidney failure.

There are hundreds of different types of oxalis plants, and many have been cultivated to grow in our gardens. The vets say these domestic plants can poison dogs and cats, but humans seem OK eating them. Still, wood sorrel seemed out of the game for Gaynor.

There is one other common food rich in oxalates and that is rhubarb. I always hated rhubarb as a child, despite grownups guffawing at me about how delicious it was. I had also heard that this poisonous plant will not be eaten by cattle. What intelligent beasts they are! My dislike may be because Nature is trying to tell me something, as it is so toxic. I don't mean the stewed stems served with custard (yuck) or rhubarb and apple crumble (marginally better but still no thanks), but the plant's leaves. Most veggie gardens have a rhubarb plant or two, with its depressingly prolific leaves and unlovely lumpen, bruised flowers.

Rhubarb leaves have long caused disease and death. In 1917, as the world was gripped by war, the German Navy launched what they hoped would be the decisive blow by unleashing unrestricted U-boat warfare against all shipping coming to the British Isles.

The idea was to starve Britain into surrender, and it came quite close. To maximise the food supply, the Ministry of Food issued an edict saying that rhubarb leaves were as nutritious as cabbage leaves and should not be discarded. A recipe was included on how best to prepare them.

The consequences were grave.

An inquest held on the body of the Rev. W.R. Colville, Minister of St Paul's Presbyterian Church at Enfield, before the coroner A.M. Forbes on 4 May 1917 tells us what happened.

'Have you formed an opinion of the actual cause of death?' the coroner asked Dr Bernard Spilsbury, the Home Office pathologist.

'Yes, indeed,' answered Dr Spilsbury. 'There was fatty degeneration of the heart and liver, entirely due to the oxalic acid contained in the rhubarb leaves.'

The coroner declared in summing up: 'I hope the press makes it clear that there was nothing in this case which might cause the public to have any alarm or prevent them from using the stalks of rhubarb as a fruit.'

Thanks for that sage advice, Mr Coroner, but for me, no thanks.

There were numerous admissions to hospitals throughout Britain in 1917 and several more deaths before the Ministry

What on earth have you been eating?: part I

rescinded the notice and put out a warning. The mini epidemic ended. These deaths by rhubarb were ultimately the only major success of Germany's U-boat campaign.

On the other hand, star fruit or carambola is delicious, though it is also full of oxalates. It is a tropical fruit that you can get in Australia quite easily but not in Palmerston North, so that seemed out of contention, too.

My line of inquiry was stumped. Many plants contain oxalates, but nothing I looked at seemed to be a likely villain.

* * *

It was Marilyn who solved the riddle.

'I've got it!' she exclaimed, flushed with excitement. 'It's peanuts!'

'Peanuts?'

'Yes, peanuts are a big source of oxalates, and guess what she does? I went through her day, hour by hour, looking for something, anything at all. The day was fine food-wise, but when we reached the evening …'

When Marilyn had talked through her day with Mrs Glendale, the truth had come out. 'My husband and I always have our drink and a snack to accompany it,' Mrs Glendale said. 'That would be at six o'clock, when we watch the TV One News broadcast.'

'What do you drink? Is it always the same?'

She nodded. 'We always have a gin and tonic. A Spanish gin and tonic, as a matter of fact. Walter makes it the same way every night.'

'Do you know how it's made — I mean, what goes into it?'

'Of course I do. You use one ounce of Bombay Sapphire gin with four ounces of tonic water on crushed ice. Walter adds a peel of orange and a few juniper berries. Sometime a sprig of mint if we have it.'

Marilyn had checked out juniper berries, but they were OK. So she asked her about what snacks they had with their tipple.

'I always have peanuts. A packet of roasted peanuts. I do like roasted peanuts.'

'How big is this packet?'

'Usually it's the big packet — that's about 200 grams, I believe. Sometimes I buy them in a jar. I think that may be nearly half a kilogram?'

'Do you share that with Walter?'

'Oh no, he loathes peanuts or any snacks. He prefers to wait for his dinner. I eat them myself. Sometimes we do have more than one gin and tonic, though. On special occasions.'

'Guess what else I found out?' Marilyn told me excitedly. 'There are over 300 micrograms of oxalates in each packet, and that's more than enough to cause kidney trouble. But there's more. The reports say that oxalate toxicity is made worse if taken with alcohol.

'If you take a little alcohol, then that's quite good, as that flushes the crystals out. The problem is too much alcohol, because if you get dehydrated then the crystals just solidify into a sludge.'

'One G and T sounds modest to me, though. I suppose it depends on how frequently the "special occasions" come around.'

Marilyn laughed. 'I think many nights may become special occasions.'

What on earth have you been eating?: part I

I nodded. 'Tell her the gin and tonics are OK, just drop the peanuts, and she'll be right.'

Sadly, that was not to be. Gaynor's recovery was complicated, as she developed a stubborn colitis from a bacterium she picked up in the hospital. After several difficult admissions she died several months later. Gaynor was arguably a victim, albeit an indirect one, of roasted peanuts and their oxalic acid.

Gaynor Glendale became very ill, ultimately because of what she ate. The world contains a huge variety of plants. Some are eatable and delicious; others are edible but don't do much either taste- or nutrition-wise; and then there are those that are simply toxic. Not all edible plants are free of toxins, as Gaynor discovered, but usually we have no idea what is in the plants we eat each day.

Gin and tonic. Booze and peanuts. Both are iconic and generally safe recreational enjoyments. No one in their right mind would think of banning them or regulating them because of such a rare risk, but in the right — or rather in the wrong — circumstances they can hurt you.

I often smile at the current fad of saying a food is 'natural' or 'organic' or 'plant-based', as if that is some sort of a magic stairway to health. Sometimes it may be and sometimes it isn't, though either way it is often accompanied by a very pricey label.

* * *

I have always kept a pathological eye out for poisonous plants causing disease and death but have only come across two or three cases, so it is not common in our safely sanitised society.

The Final Diagnosis

The oxalates in peanuts were a surprise out of left field for me, but I have known of several common plants that are somewhat, or really, poisonous. I have been on the lookout for one particular plant as a cause of death for decades, but surprisingly have not yet seen it.

All over Palmerston North and in the gardens of other towns and cities around New Zealand I see oleander growing and blooming. They are a beautiful plant and are easy to grow in salt spray and drought, which is why they are so popular here.

Yet I wonder at their profusion every time I see one, for they are deadly poisonous. Every single part is deadly, from the flowers, stalks and roots to the smoke from burning its wood, even to the honey that bees make from it.

They were the favourite flower of Vincent van Gogh. Not only did he paint *Oleanders*, a wonderful still-life of the flowers in a vase, but he also described them as 'joyous, life-affirming flowers that would bloom inexhaustibly'. Van Gogh was undoubtedly a great artist, but his enthusiasm for their beneficial effects on people clearly did not take into account their inherent toxicity. In this, as in his lopping off of his own ear, his judgement was woefully misplaced.

Dogbane plants, of which oleander is one, contain up to 30 different chemicals, all of which are severely toxic to your heart. One Italian couple succumbed to an escargot stew made of snails they collected from their own garden. Sadly and quite unknown to them, the snails had been feasting off oleander leaves. The poisons were found in man and wife as well as in the snail's bodies recovered from the kitchen pot.

In the cold winter of 2004, the wasted bodies of a young man and woman were found lying beside a forester's storehouse in

What on earth have you been eating?: part I

an Italian pine forest. They were thinly clad in light summer clothing and were severely emaciated, both weighing in at a paltry 38 kilograms despite being 170 centimetres tall. This is a BMI of 13; the WHO classifies 16 as severely underweight! They were clearly homeless, and as there were no injuries it was thought they must have died of cold.

At autopsy, they both indeed showed signs of death from cold. Their stomachs contained vegetable matter, with spotty points of haemorrhage in the gastric lining. Both also had haemorrhage into their pancreas. These features are exactly what is seen in death due to extreme cold.

The applecart was upset when the toxicology came back. Digoxin was found in lethal amounts in both of their blood. That was ridiculous. How could two homeless forest folk have overdosed on a prescription-only cardiac drug like digoxin? It was quite implausible.

Digoxin is a cardiac active glycoside, famously first discovered by William Withering in 1785. Oleanedrine is a similar glycoside, found in oleander. The two cross-react in lab tests and can be mistaken for each other. That is what happened in this case. The vegetable remnants in their stomachs were the leaves of oleander, which was found to be common throughout the pine forest.

The victims were identified only four years later, when a Belgian couple were watching a television show about missing people. To their horror they recognised photographs of the wasted woman as their 26-year-old daughter. She had run away from home with a friend in the summer of 2004 and joined an extreme vegan movement.

They were living off, or perhaps more accurately slowly dying of, raw vegetation garnered in their wanderings. One day they decided to harvest oleander leaves. It was to be the death of them.

Not a particularly appetising last meal, either.

* * *

Though it may be a surprise that there are potentially dangerous chemicals occurring naturally in plants we have eaten for millennia, such as we discovered of the peanuts, it cannot be news that insects have always been quite plentiful in our food. They are generally harmless to eat, and actually may do us a lot of good.

Just before the first Covid lockdown, I bought two sacks of basmati rice. The first sack seemed to go on forever, despite my cooking rice four or five times a week, and it would be more than two years before I got around to opening the second sack.

I cooked up a pot for dinner and was appalled when a scum of jet-black weevils floated to the surface. I killed them by freezing the rice for a couple of weeks, and I thought it would still be fine for my dogs. I boiled up a large stockpot for them, which bubbled away with its thick flotsam of weevil carcasses.

The Labradors didn't seem to mind after the rice had been mixed in with chicken livers and mixed vegetables. I suppose it was just more yummy protein to them. I even flirted with the thought that it would be fine for humans, too, but that was firmly vetoed.

There's nothing wrong with eating most insects other than the creepy-crawly thought of it. That is just our conditioning.

What on earth have you been eating?: part I

The great thing about eating insects is they're crammed full of vitamin B12, as are most animals. In many largely vegetarian countries like India these hidden creatures in the grains, rice and veggies are usually the only source of this vitamin.

Vitamin B12 is critical for brain function and for making blood, and death from its deficiency is well known. The food-dwelling insects' B12 is lifesaving to millions of people, even if they don't know it. The cure for the lethal pernicious anaemia discovered last century was to eat a daily half-pound raw liver sandwich to get your vitamin B12. I think I would probably find food seasoned with concealed insects more appetising, though I suppose a half pound of creepy crawlies might be a bit of a mouthful.

Strict vegans in developed countries, by contrast, can easily run into problems with a vitamin B12 deficiency, as the endless washing of produce and the packaging in airtight plastic keeps the insects out. It would be better to chew a few concealed caterpillars and keep your blood thick and your cognitive function sharp. Alternatively, you could ditch the veggies and try beef and lamb, which would be my preference.

* * *

We had all settled into our seats for our weekly meeting with the surgeons, where we look at the pathology of our current patients and talk about how they presented, what was found and how they should be managed. It is a place where there is a crossover between management of patients and furthering the education of all of us. Today we had a surprise.

Mike Young took the floor. 'Hey, I've had a most amazing colonoscopy experience.'

I half-expected someone to innocently ask 'Oh, who did it to you?' or 'Did you do it on yourself?', because these meetings are quite often informal and sometimes funny, too. But that was an old joke and there were no offenders today.

'I had gone through the colon and was in the caecum and it all looked fine. I thought I would push through and have a look at the terminal ileum, too. It looked OK and so I turned to have a dekko at the appendix opening.

'"My God!" I said to the patient. "You've got a crab sitting in your appendix!"'

We all stared at Mike.

'What sort of crab?' I asked. My pathological mind was a blank. I could not compute 'crab' with 'appendix' and come up with anything meaningful.

'Here, I'll show you!' Mike was grinning as he pulled his phone out of his pocket. We crowded around as he held up the screen.

It was a photograph of a crab. A conventional crab, with eight legs and two claws and eyes sticking out on stalks. It could easily be imagined on a beach or in a rock pool anywhere in the world. Except that it was miniature. I knew that because it was sitting on the appendiceal orifice, which I had seen thousands of times and knew to be a couple of millimetres across. It wasn't quite covering the opening, so it would be even smaller than that.

'It didn't *move*, did it?' I asked. 'Surely it couldn't be alive after passing through the bowel with all the digestive enzymes having a go?'

'No,' Mike confirmed. 'It was dead.'

What on earth have you been eating?: part I

'Did you take it out for us to have a look at in the lab? And where the hell did it come from? Surely no one eats crabs that small?'

Mike shook his head. 'No, I left it there. But the patient knew exactly what it was.'

The patient was sedated but conscious through the colonoscopy, so he was able to explain Mike's surprising discovery. 'It's a pea crab,' he told Mike. 'I've been down in the Sounds last week and we were pulling dozens of mussels off the rocks every day. We ate the last of them a day or two ago. Pea crabs are small crabs that live inside the mussels.'

'Apparently it's true.' Mike saw the disbelief on my face. 'Most mussels in this country have them, apparently, but the crabs do no harm. Every time you eat a green-lipped mussel, you're probably eating some of these crabs, too.'

I found it hard to believe, but I did some research. These wee crabs take up residence inside the mussel's shell, where they are protected from both the seawater and predators, and they live off food stolen from the mollusc's gills. They are parasites — they do no good to the mussel, and their thievery can stop the shellfish from growing plump. (Though I wonder if being a runt-sized mussel is a distinct advantage, as people may be more likely to leave them on the rocks. Perhaps their failure to thrive because of the relationship with the crabs is ultimately their best protection from ending up in the cooking pot.)

Some gourmets consider these pea crabs a delicacy in their own right, but it must be hard to get a decent mouthful, because there is only one crab living in each mussel. I do wonder how the pea crabs manage romantically with their solitary quarters, but I suppose they must have some conjugal visiting arrangement or they wouldn't still be around.

Green-lipped mussels and crabs: yes, I can live with that parasitic combo very easily. Sounds to me a bit like frutti di mare, that mixed seafood salad so beloved of Italians, and crabs are infinitely more palatable mentally than bugs.

Other than the yuck factor, insects in food are fine by me, and the hygiene theory says a little exposure is good for your immune system. In Canada, health authorities accept up to 30 insect parts per 100 grams in peanut butter as inevitable, and it is not regarded as a contaminant!

What the hell anyway — the oxalates in peanuts may put you at greater risk than a few crunchy cockroach carapaces in your peanut butter.

Enjoy!

The normal food of man is vegetable.
— Charles Darwin

CHAPTER 8

What on earth have you been eating?: part II

'Hey, paths! Registrars! Come up and have a look! What do you reckon this is?'

Richard Coutts held a pottle and shook it vigorously. There was no formalin inside, and whatever it was rattled against the sides and lid. Clearly it was not the usual biopsy tissue sample.

I took it from him and squinted at the contents. It was a translucent spicule — definitely not a soft-tissue biopsy, then.

'Where's it from?' I had to ask the question. *Always get the full history before you commit yourself*, I heard the ghostly voices of generations of past pathologists whispering their hard-won experience in my ear. That was especially wise with Richard, as he has this habit of being involved in unconventional things.

'It's an interesting story — I'll tell you what happened,' he said. 'This man, Peter Clareburt, originally came in with kidney cancer. John Chrisp whipped it out, so that wasn't a problem. Then we found the cancer had flung a few metastases into his adrenal glands, so I said I would winkle them both out for him.'

The Final Diagnosis

We listened, fascinated. Richard's tales always took some tangled twist. Operating to take out cancer metastases is usually fruitless, but kidney cancers are odd and can pitch up as singletons in distant parts of the body, which can be successfully plucked one by one.

My old friend Ron Raymond, airline captain and Vietnam War veteran, had kidney metastases taken from his thyroid gland, stomach and the humerus of his right arm over many years. He remained hale and hearty throughout, and I used his slides as mysterious exam cases for the pathology registrars for years.

'Peter settled down nicely, but then he got another lump in his pancreas. We settled that by getting the whole pancreas out. But it looked like we had run out of luck this time.'

I was not surprised. The Whipple operation to remove the pancreas and duodenum is about the biggest there is in the book. It's one of those ones where it seems Nature holds up her hand and says, 'Whoa! You're going too far this time.' Complications and a long stay in ICU following the surgery are common.

'He was OK for a bit — got out and about, went up to Hamilton to watch his boy rowing. He and his wife stopped off for fish and chips on the way back. By the time they reached Bulls he was really crook with a gut ache.

'They decided he had better divert to Palmy Hospital and get it checked out. It looked like an infection, but we couldn't figure out where it was. After a Whipple any damn thing can happen though, so I suppose it wasn't too surprising. Eventually we got a CT scan done.

'Bingo! There was a mass in the lower abdomen, and they could see a foreign body stuck in it. The radiologist thought

What on earth have you been eating?: part II

it was a drain that had got left behind at surgery — that was the most likely thing.'

'Why would you have a drain right down there after a Whipple? Is that usual?'

Richard nodded. 'There'd be several intra-abdominal drains to clear out any ooze after the surgery. There can be quite a lot of fluid and blood. It's possible a drain had detached and fallen in there, although that doesn't happen often. The other thing they thought that it could be is a stitch abscess or granuloma.'

I knew that sutures quite often got some infection around them, creating an irritated and painful spot that would not clear up. The only real option is to cut them out.

'Peter's wife was not impressed about us leaving a drain behind — and I don't blame her, after what he had been through.'

Cancer surgery is a stressful business for surgeon, patient and for their suffering families. It's lousy news when you hear that to top it off, there's a problem due to medical misadventure.

'I took him to theatre to have a look,' Richard continued, 'popped in a laparoscope, and there was this thick phlegmon of pus and granulation tissue coating the gut. It was quite far from the Whipple site though, which was a surprise. The mat of muck was coating a few coils of small bowel. Sticking out the top of this crud there was this quivering antenna, standing proud. I couldn't recognise what it was — maybe a suture, though how it got down there beats me.

'I grabbed the tip of it and pulled. It slid out smoothly, but it seemed to go on and on. I thought it could be a drain, maybe? Here it is.' Once more he rattled the pot. 'So, what is it?'

It was two centimetres long, a slender, pellucid spicule.

'A fish bone?'

Richard nodded energetically. 'Yes, it's a fish bone. But extra points if you can tell me the type of fish.'

'A big one?' ventured a young registrar.

'It would have to be, looking at the size of this bone,' I said. 'It was good news, anyway, that it wasn't a drain or a surgical suture. No one can blame us for a fish bone.'

'Yes, that's right. When I showed him and told him what it was, he admitted it readily. I said to him, "Peter, this is a fish bone, and that's what punctured your gut and leaked into your abdomen. That's what's been making you so crook." He looked at it a bit embarrassed and then smiled. "Yep, it was a big bit of fish we bought. I thought I might have swallowed a bone but thought she'll be right. My wife did tell me not to swallow it." It should clear up nicely now that's gone, and the leak will just plug over.'

'What did Peter's wife say?'

'She was good, if a bit surprised. She couldn't blame us, as it wasn't our fault — he had done this to himself.'

'Even my grandmother knew that swallowing fish bones was dangerous,' I said reflectively, 'and as in Peter's case it usually creates a local inflammatory mass, not a generalised peritonitis.

'When I was a young pathologist, I heard of another fish bone story from the famous Professor Symmers,' I added. Everyone looked at me expectantly, so I began.

A well-known London socialite was pregnant and visited her obstetrician for a routine check. He saw this small red spot just beside her umbilicus, and asked her, 'Do you know what this mark is?'

What on earth have you been eating?: part II

'No, I haven't noticed it before,' she replied.

'Well, it probably isn't anything important. We'll just keep an eye on it. Let me know if anything changes.'

A few weeks later the lady called him back. 'There has been a development. The spot is still there but I can now feel a hard ridge alongside it.'

He examined her and found it was exactly as the lady had said. He reassured her.

'I feel sure this is a thrombosed superficial vein, which is why it is so hard. It is nothing to worry about.'

Soon the patient was oozing blood and fluid from her belly button, so things were beginning to look more serious. A general surgeon was consulted, and after her confinement was duly over, he carried out a diagnostic laparotomy.

I thought I had better explain this to the young doctors, many of whom were late Gen X and Millennials.

'In the middle of last century, when I was a young doctor, we had our hands, our stethoscopes and plain X-rays to help us with diagnostic dilemmas in the abdomen. There were no CT scans or MRIs, and even ultrasounds were primitive pictures that only obstetricians frowned over. Flexible endoscopes and keyhole surgery were still in the realms of science fiction.

'It was not rare to open up the abdomen in a puzzling case and have a direct look at all the organs to make a diagnosis. You would repair what you could if you found the problem, but like Forrest Gump's box of chocolates, you just never knew what you were going to get. If it sounds primitive, I guess it was, but it was all we had.'

So the London surgeon opened her belly to have his look around. He found nothing amiss at all. There was only the inflamed lump in the skin beside her umbilicus, so he excised the whole lesion and sent it off to the pathologists to find out what it was.

'I suppose he might have charged her a hundred guineas for the operation back then, which would be an archaic payment for an archaic operation. The guinea was twenty-one shillings, and was another oddity used by doctors and lawyers to charge their fees back then.' I thought I had also better explain the pre-decimal currency to the youngsters.

Part of the answer came from the pathologists. They discovered that there was a fish bone embedded in the middle of the inflamed abdominal wall. With some research they ascertained it was a salmon bone.

'How had it got there? You would guess it would have worked its way up there by puncturing the small bowel wall and stabbing its way to the surface, but the normal findings inside the belly at surgery made that quite improbable,' I continued.

The socialite was able to provide the answer, however. 'My husband and I were guests of honour at a public banquet recently. All eyes were on us seated at the top table, sitting alongside *le monde*. One course was of Scottish salmon, and as soon as I had taken a mouthful, I knew I had made a mistake, as it included a prominent and quite hard bone.

'I tucked the bone away on one side of my mouth and chewed with the other while I considered what to do next. I knew swallowing it might be dangerous, but how to retrieve it with dignity before hundreds of watching eyes seemed an impossible task.

'I waited until I thought the general attention was elsewhere and surreptitiously brought my serviette to my

What on earth have you been eating?: part II

lips, intending to hide it therein. But it fell and went down the front of my dress. I was wearing a chevron-necked gown and it fell between my breasts. At least it was conveniently concealed, and I could remove it later. I thought I had solved my dilemma.'

It may have been out of sight, but a mystery arose. For when the lady was finally home and was undressing, there was absolutely no sign of the fish bone. She naturally thought it must have worked its way down the front of her gown and eventually fallen to the floor. She thought no more of it, until this apparently similar bone seemingly materialised from within her belly button.

'How did it get in there? Surely she would have felt it going in?' one of the registrars asked.

'Professor Symmers thought that it must have become embedded in the umbilical pit and worked its way, sharp end first, into the skin. He said the umbilical skin is relatively poorly supplied with nerves, and so is resistant to pain.' I looked at Richard for confirmation. 'Is that right? I have looked it up and it is true the belly button is actually just a scar, so the skin there is relatively insensitive.'

I chuckled. 'Madonna's belly button is the exception, according to Google. She says hers is a button that literally sends sex tingles up and down her spine.' Google had directed my anatomical research into territory never to be found within my well-thumbed copy of *Gray's Anatomy*.

'I'm not sure about the nerve supply of the belly button, but the body can trick you. Do you remember Mrs Gane? You know, farms up near Taihape? I did her dad's bowel cancer yonks ago. Anyway, do you remember her breast cancer?'

I could sense Richard was now into his own story-telling mode. We all settled back expectantly. This could take some time.

'She had a cancer in her right breast. It was quite lateral, almost in her armpit, and was still small. The radiologists banged in a hookwire and taped a dressing over it, and she came to theatre a couple of days later for me to do a wide local excision.'

In my fifty-year career, breast cancer treatment had changed beyond recognition. We used to treat every case by performing a radical mastectomy, taking off the entire breast and fleecing the armpit of every single lymph gland. That was it really; your chances of survival hinged on getting it all out early. It was a big operation, and complications such as the arm swelling up with lymph fluid was often a problem.

Nowadays, a hookwire is inserted into the middle of the cancer, and the surgeon excises generously around the wire tip to get the diseased lump out cleanly. The rest of the normal breast is left behind. There are still other treatments to be done, such as radiotherapy and chemotherapy and hormone therapies, but it is all much less disfiguring and usually works out really well.

The hookwire literally has a hook, rather like a fishhook, on one end, so when it has been inserted into the cancer it is snared there and cannot be easily pulled out. The surgeon then cuts out a cone around the wire, right up to the skin, and we get the tissue and cancer with the wire in place sent through to us in the lab. As in the case of Mrs Gane, the wires are often put in place a couple of days before the surgery, then covered with a dressing.

Richard continued. 'I got her on the table and took the

What on earth have you been eating?: part II

dressing off to feel the cancer and make sure of what I was going to do. But it wasn't there. The wire had gone.'

'Had it fallen out?' I knew that did not happen very often.

Richard shook his head. 'I didn't know. The dressing was still there where the radiologist had put it, but the wire was gone. I thought, she's yanked it out and it must be in the changing room, where she put on her theatre gown. So, I went through there to find it. I hunted around, and I found the eyelet that the wire goes through, lying on the floor.

'That proved it to me — I was sure now that she had pulled it out in the changing room. But where had she hidden it? There are not many places a patient can hide things in there, and I couldn't find it. I was convinced she had ripped it out, though.'

Patients do some very odd things, so I also thought Richard's story was a plausible explanation.

'I challenged her about it in theatre. She was adamant she hadn't touched it. "I would never interfere with what you're doing! I have never even seen this wire of yours. And I certainly haven't pulled it out."

'Quite frankly, I didn't believe her. I called Johnny Goulden from Radiology up here to the theatre and he did an ultrasound to see if the wire had slipped inside. Nix. But he put another one in as a replacement.'

The operation went ahead and was all OK. There were no problems afterwards either, until about two weeks later. Mrs Gane developed severe pain and swelling in her left shoulder.

'It's so bad that her husband drives her through to ED. They reckon it's nothing to do with the breast surgery, which all looks fine — and anyway, was on the opposite, right side of her chest.

'The ED doc thinks he can feel an abscess pointing just beneath the skin at the left shoulder tip, so he cuts down onto it. There's something hard in there so he grabs it with forceps and tugs. Out comes the whole length of her missing hookwire!'

We were all shaking our heads in disbelief.

'Somehow it had crawled right across her right breast, her sternum, her left breast and then up to her shoulder tip without her feeling a single thing or being aware of it in any way until it surfaced in ED.

'So yes, after seeing this, I can well believe a burrowing salmon bone could easily end up next to the belly button without her knowing.'

> 'When the beautiful Princess Alicia consents to partake of the salmon — as I think she will — you will find she will leave a fish-bone on her plate. Tell her to dry it, and to rub it, and to polish it till it shines like mother-of-pearl, and to take care of it as a present from me.'
> — Charles Dickens, *The Magic Fishbone*, 1867

* * *

The inadvertent eating of plants harbouring potentially deadly chemicals is one problem, but the equally lethal effects of an overdose of our normal, non-toxic food diet is entirely another. Deaths from overindulgence in our usual daily food now vastly outnumber fatalities from poisonings.

'Doc, we're ready for you now.' Pat sounded unusually subdued to me. I hung up the phone and went down to the mortuary.

What on earth have you been eating?: part II

Pat and Simone were waiting for me with a 'does he know what we know?' sort of look on their faces. All I had been briefed on was that my patient for the day was a 26-year-old woman, who had died at home after being bedridden for some years.

The exact nature of her illness was not revealed. I assumed that I would discover her relevant history as I went through her Pol 47 police report, which records all the relevant information from her doctor, the hospital, her family and any other source they thought useful. Pat would also have fetched her medical files from the Clinical Records department, so I would have everything I needed to know before carrying out my autopsy examination.

'Morning, Pat; morning, Simone.' I looked back at them guardedly. 'What have you got for me today?'

'She weighs a hundred and thirty-five kilograms,' Pat said flatly. 'We haven't taken her off the trolley yet. We thought we'd wait and see what you wanted to do.'

Ouch — 135 kilograms! This would be exhausting and very time-consuming, too.

I sighed and sat down to read her huge pile of medical files precariously heaped on the mortuary desk.

Jacqueline's story was bleak. At high school she had become tired at first, and then this became exhaustion even on any minor exertion. No physical cause was found, though some sort of hormone problem, possibly with her thyroid gland, was top of the list. Yet all her blood tests were plumb normal.

A variety of diagnoses followed. A recurrent glandular fever was first up, and then chronic fatigue syndrome was also diagnosed at one time. Many doctors, psychologists and specialists were consulted but without any noticeable relief. Then someone thought it might be a juvenile form of depression.

Jacqueline had been eating steadily though not spectacularly throughout this dark time in her life. It was not particularly noticed by the host of different doctors consulted by her family in their desperation, but her weight was slowly creeping up, year by year.

She was started on a variety of anti-depressant medications, which chopped and changed as they either had unpleasant side-effects or did nothing at all to help. Whether it was a side-effect of these medicines or just the nature of her affliction, Jacqueline now really began to eat in earnest. Just as teenagers become trenchermen as they hit their growth spurt, her food disappeared readily and never seemed to touch the sides.

It did not help that Jacqueline was inactive, preferring to stay quietly at home with her mum rather than be out and about doing sport or any high-energy teenage activities such as skateboarding or dancing at gigs. The inevitable happened and her weight bloomed uncontrollably upwards.

There was a ray of happiness in her life, for at the age of 22, she married. Her husband, Ratu, was a lovely young man, and he was devoted to her. He moved into the family home and gave up his job so he could help with her care.

Jacqueline needed plenty of that. She was bedridden and unable to get herself up and to the toilet, onto which she probably would not have fitted anyway. All her personal needs had to be performed for her at the bedside by her husband, her mother and father.

She developed sleep apnoea as a complication of her weight. Fat gets deposited around the neck as well as

What on earth have you been eating?: part II

elsewhere and compresses the pharynx. When all the tissues relax while the person is asleep, the passage into the lungs collapses. Jacqueline would awaken suddenly and horribly, her brain so starved of oxygen that she must have felt as if she were drowning. She had to sleep with nasal prongs delivering oxygen under pressure to keep her airways open. It all made for restless and uncomfortable nights.

One night Jacqueline succumbed in her sleep, and was found at peace by her mother, the oxygen still hissing gently from her nostrils. The coroner had requested that I do an autopsy.

'Phew!' I said. 'That is one very heavy story.' I did not mean the weight of the files, either.

Pat was sitting patiently by, waiting for me to finish reading so we could start. 'It's hard to believe this poor girl is only twenty-six years old.'

* * *

Jacqueline was too wide for the trolley. Her shoulders protruded well over the steel edges and her arms hung loosely down. They were too large, and her chest too tall, for us to be able to fold them across her chest.

I was shocked. It takes a lot to do this to me, but the physical effect of Jacqueline's mass was beyond my imagining from a reading of the notes. Pat, Simone and I stood in silence at the head of the trolley, looking down. This was sad in so many ways.

'How do you get so big?' Simone asked quietly.

'Eating too much,' Pat said. His usual smile was still there, walrus moustache quivering, but he, too, was more sombre today.

I nodded. 'It's a difficult one to answer. We learnt DoME and ELF at medical school.' They looked at me quizzically. 'Do More Exercise and Eat Less Food,' I answered briefly.

But then I shook my head. 'Too easy an answer, I reckon. You have to be a super-specialist in all sorts of things to know about massive obesity these days. Sure, some cases are from just eating, like the documentary *Super Size Me*, where the bloke ate the equivalent of ten Big Macs a day. But there are also "fat genes" in some people, and there's even a theory that the obesity epidemic is because of Adenovirus-36 spreading around the world.

'We used to talk about people with "nervous stomachs", who "ate their feelings" when they were sad. So who really knows what it's all about? Don't ask a simple pathologist.'

We still had our problem of how to do this autopsy, however.

'It'll be too hard to move her onto the table, so we'll open her up on the trolley. How did you get her onto this trolley, anyway?'

'Took eight of us to lift her out of the hearse and onto the trolley. It's impossible to roll her onto a sheet, and it may not take her weight anyway. The undertakers are already scratching their heads about how they're going to get a big enough casket for her.'

I examined Jacqueline from top to toe. She was 163 centimetres tall, which meant her BMI was more than 50. A 'healthy' BMI has always been touted as about 18 up to 25, though those folk always look very skinny to me and not so healthy either. I am probably right, because it is an odd fact that people in the 'overweight' group with a BMI

What on earth have you been eating?: part II

of up to 30 actually live longer than the lighter 'normals', according to the statistics!

A BMI of 50 is quite different, however. Imagine wrapping a 50-kilogram parcel of meat in a standard bath towel and you can get an idea of the problem the body has. There are a host of diseases and complications, from diabetes to death, at this level of obesity.

'What's this, doc?' Simone asked, pointing at Jacqueline's abdomen. A thick, pendulous flap lay to halfway down her thighs.

'It's a fat apron,' I explained. 'Like a beer belly, but much bigger.'

'No, I know that — I've seen those before. But what's that horrible-looking stuff on her skin?'

I looked at the apron again, and my stomach gave an involuntary churn. Though I had seen this before, somehow I just couldn't help myself flinching. I felt sick. The skin looked like a warty shag rug, with a shocking papillomatous eruption over what by rights should be satin-smooth skin. It had a rank and evil appearance and it stank of sweat and keratin and decay.

I swallowed my saliva and fought my stomach for control. I won.

'It's called elephantiasis nostras verrucosa — a bit of a mouthful to say.'

'How does it happen?'

'It's because of long-standing swelling of the skin, as the fluid cannot drain away. It's a bit like a blocked drain — the skin gets all cobblestoned and warty because of the irritation. I guess it's because she just wouldn't or couldn't move, so it just stagnated there.'

Pat sliced through the gibbous chest down through nearly 20 centimetres of fat to the bone of the sternum. 'With that amount of fat compressing the chest, it would be very difficult to breathe in and out without an effort,' I commented.

Pat opened the chest cavity, deftly detached the larynx and trachea deep in the cavity, and then, with an effort and a sucking squelch, drew out the heart and lungs. He placed them on my wooden dissecting board, and I began working.

I always have a sponge close to hand to mop blood and fluid off the part of the organ I am dissecting. I like to have a clean field to see everything as it is exposed. All pathologists have different habits, and I am the only one I have seen do this. Others use continuously running water to clear the blood, while the majority have developed techniques for soldiering on through the gore and yet not missing a trick.

I always recall Professor Tiltman saying to me when I was a young registrar, 'Keep everything clean and free of blood. It is hard to do, but it is easier to see the organs and it looks better. Our colleagues all think we are nothing but butchers anyway, and when they come in here and see organs swimming in blood and a drenched pathologist behind, it just reinforces their prejudice.'

So that is what I do. I also think cleanliness is much more respectful to my patients.

'Here's the problem.' I held up the heart I had dissected from its attachments. 'It's very enlarged for a young woman. Weighs four hundred and twenty grams and the left ventricle is more than fifteen millimetres thick.' I peered closely at the opened organ. The edges of the mitral valve were thickened with fibrous tissue, too. Pat and Simone looked on with

What on earth have you been eating?: part II

interest as I turned the heart around in my hands to show the cavities.

'Jacqueline has a cardiomyopathy. That's not surprising, given her weight and history. The heart has to pump through a vast volume of tissue just to keep blood circulating. She may have had high blood pressure in both her body and lungs as well.'

'That enough to kill her, doc?'

'Yes, usually by an arrhythmia like ventricular fibrillation. She would be even more vulnerable with her low oxygen levels at night from her sleep apnoea. That's most probably what happened to her last night.'

Pat nodded, looking thoughtful. 'She died at home, right?' I nodded. 'What I don't get is how her family gave her food all the time. I mean, she was bedridden. Why didn't they just say, "No!" That's what I would have done if she had been my kid.'

It was an interesting question, and I had wondered about that, too.

I did not know the answer. I asked the psychiatrists who look after people in these situations and understand a bit about these things.

'It's a tricky situation for a parent to find themselves in,' I was told by Floriana, a very perceptive psychiatrist. 'All parents want their child's love and affection and to care for them, and that colours their view of life. Jacqueline's husband would face the same dilemma as her mum and dad.

'To give food and see your loved one's approval is a powerful stimulant for the release of oxytocin, the warm-fuzzy hormone that will egg on the love centres in your brain and get you addicted to the behaviour that produces it.'

The Final Diagnosis

'You mean they become addicted to feeding her?'

'In a general way, yes. They become enablers, providing for the dependent. It is easier by far to bring food rather than to refuse. In Jacqueline's case it was food, but more often it's drugs or alcohol the enablers provide.

'Food is not unusual, though, particularly in cultures where eating communally is important. Food is just a fuel for some people, but it is an important part of the social fabric of cultures like Pasifika peoples or Italians, for example.'

Jacqueline's short life and death was a huge sorrow to us all. I was able to work out what she died of, but we still had no clue why. Whatever was the complicated cause of her affliction I do not believe that it was her fault or that she was unintelligent, lazy, willingly ate too much or did this to herself. She deserved better and we could not give it to her.

The obesity pandemic is well publicised these days, and there are now more overweight than underweight people for the first time in the world's history. But there have been obese people around for centuries, even before plentiful processed food became available. Prince Hal calls Falstaff, the gluttonous knight, a 'huge hill of flesh' in Shakespeare's *Henry IV*. When told by Hal to lie down, Falstaff asks plaintively, 'Have you any levers to lift me up again?'

As Falstaff realised too well, lifting and moving the morbidly obese is a major problem both at home and when in hospital. In Palmerston North there is one hover mat and a hover bed to help. These behave like a hovercraft, with air blown beneath the base to lift the patient. They are very efficient, and using them, one person can easily shift a 150-kilogram patient if necessary.

What on earth have you been eating?: part II

There are also problems with fitting patients into the CT and MRI scanners. Jonathan, a radiologist from the United Kingdom, told me that at Birmingham Hospital they have an 'open' MRI, designed originally for patients with claustrophobia. It has now become the tool of choice for the obese, too.

Our mortuary is old, and our 19 fridges are all of 1960s vintage. That was the Age of Twiggy and a time of widespread leanness, but in recent years we have run into serious accommodation issues.

Our largest patient ever came to us a few days before Christmas. He weighed in at 285 kilograms, and we knew we had a problem on our hands. He could not by any manipulation be laid to rest in one of our small, archaic fridges. The refrigeration facilities at the undertakers in town were no better.

'Can't you just bury him?' we asked the undertaker as we stood around the body. Perforce, we had to lay him to rest on a tarpaulin in the passage, ice packs piled around him. It was not a particularly dignified place of repose, and well below the standard we expect of ourselves, but there was nowhere else for him to go. The mortuary dissecting room was busy with two bodies on the slab and, with the Christmas rush, looked likely to remain fully occupied for some days yet.

'We haven't got a casket nearly big enough,' he admitted. The undertakers were as unprepared as we were for the magnitude of this problem, or for their increasing number of super-sized customers. 'We've ordered a coffin to be made, but it will be ready only on Christmas Eve.' He peered at us anxiously.

Christmas Eve. That was still four days away — a long time out of the fridge in the height of summer. The problem is that the deepest innards of the body cannot be kept chilled by a few superficial ice packs. Even now the fermentation of decay would be bubbling within. And in four days' time it would be much further gone ...

'I can't see any option, unless we can source a refrigerated container or maybe a truck.'

'Tried that already,' said Pat. 'No way is it possible. They're food trucks. Sheep carcases are OK, but we can't use them to store human remains, apparently.'

'It seems we have no alternative to keeping him here, unpleasant as it may be.' I turned to the undertaker. 'Please see if you can hurry the casket up so we can give this patient a decent send-off.'

'I'll do my best. It has been a big difficulty for us all. Did you know we have had to find a double plot for his grave?'

I had not thought of that aspect, but I suppose these problems arise everywhere for these patients, from car seats to coffins.

Christmas Eve came and there was still no sign of the casket. Our guest on the floor was to spend Christmas with us. Pat was seething. The spirit of Christmas is about spreading joy and goodwill, but the exasperated mortuary staff could only spread ice packs and tarps in a losing battle to stop the place becoming noisome and noxious.

We were eventually able to discharge our patient just before the New Year. He checked out in an enormous coffin, carried with difficulty by eight strong men. Something had to be done for the future. Nothing could be surer than that this would happen again. It was quite unacceptable for our patients and reflected badly on our professional service.

What on earth have you been eating?: part II

Pat had two ordinary fridges ripped out of the wall and fitted one larger replacement, suitable for a morbidly obese patient. That will have to do for now, but I do wonder what we will do on the inevitable day when we have two such bodies arrive simultaneously.

On one memorable morning not long after this saga, we were confronted with a different but related difficult task. An obese patient had died in the ward, and was wheeled down to the mortuary in the middle of the night and placed in the designated fridge to await developments. She was nowhere as massive as our record-breaking gentleman, though she was still a snug fit in the new fridge.

Her undertakers arrived early the next morning and collected her for her burial, planned for the next day. This seemed like a routine body collection, just like hundreds of others, and everything was under control.

Unfortunately, there had been a mix-up in communications and the coroner had taken jurisdiction over her case and requested an autopsy. At first this was no problem. The undertakers were called and they brought her body back to us. They had prepared her beautifully and then placed her in her coffin for the viewing.

But that was where the problem arose. It was a standard large coffin and they had done an impressive job in fitting her into the available space. Now she wouldn't come out.

We stood around the coffin looking perplexedly down at our patient. Only her face remained recognisable, her eyes closed as in serene sleep The rest of her body was coffin-shaped and overflowing along the brim.

'How are we going to get her out?' I asked the obvious question.

'Dunno.' Pat was thoughtful. 'We've tried turning her on her side to see if her weight can help roll her out, but nothing has shifted.'

The undertaker shook his head. 'There's nowhere to get a grip on the body to pull her out. That's what's making it difficult.'

'Bring me a chainsaw — I'll cut the coffin off.' It was all I could think of.

Pat smiled. The undertaker looked aghast at me.

'You can't do that! Do you realise that coffin cost four thousand dollars? You'll destroy it completely. Who's going to pay for it?'

'We may have to break it open,' I said firmly. 'There is no way I can do an autopsy on her in there.'

We struggled for nearly an hour and eventually succeeded in extracting her, but only after accidentally breaking the headboard of the coffin.

We wheeled our patient into the dissecting room to do our job, leaving the undertaker mournfully fingering the broken pieces of his coffin and shaking his head.

'Sorry about that!' Pat told him cheerfully. 'I reckon you can get a new headboard run up pretty easily.'

* * *

Obesity to varying degrees is now so widespread that in some ways we have come to see it as the new normal. One in three Kiwis are overweight; in Nauru it is two in three. At some point the skinny person ambling around becomes the abnormal one!

What on earth have you been eating?: part II

Gross obesity has strangely even become a sexual fetish. There is a twenty-something couple in Queensland called Jeff and Rosie, who also go by the improbable names of Kalorie and Viktor Karbdashian, who are into 'feedism'. Jeff is the 'feeder' and Rosie the 'feedee', and Jeff stuffs food into Rosie in late-night sexual sessions. Jeff, who is of normal weight and works out in the gym several times a week, says these sessions and Rosie's consequent gain in weight 'floats his boat'.

The result of the midnight sensual feasts is that Rosie has expanded by 76 kilograms to an eyewatering 177 kilos since meeting Jeff. In the feedism parlance she has become an SSBW or super-sized beautiful woman. Jeff seems quite skinny beside her. The couple remind me of the nursery rhyme:

Jack Spratt could eat no fat,
His wife could eat no lean.
And so between them both, you see,
They licked the platter clean.

Rosie doesn't plan on gaining any more weight at this stage and says of herself: 'I feel more confident and sexy the more I weigh. I go out in a bikini to the beach like everyone else. I wear tight clothes like everyone else. I just feel comfortable in my own skin. If I was smaller, I wouldn't feel confident.'

Feedism as a fetish is something I would rank at the weirder end of human behaviour. There are thankfully only a few such folk who deliberately eat themselves up to size. But many people grow their weight while seeming to live an active life and eat what appears on the face of it to be a normal diet. A big factor that bedevils us all in the weight saga is the profusion of modern ultra-processed foods.

Food factories hammer our food crops into high-calorie and tasty ingredients such as turning corn into high fructose corn syrup and soya beans into partly digested vegetable protein. These basic building blocks taste yummy and are easily digested and absorbed compared with the old-fashioned, conventionally grown and cooked food my mum and grandma made.

In one trial people either ate the traditionally grown and prepared food — basically the 'meat and three veg' of yore — or they tucked into modern ultra-processed meals. Given a choice they ate much, much more of the processed food and so rapidly gained weight. The food is cheap, tastes just dandy and is quick to prepare, and these days more than half of our food is ultra-processed.

This is a social shift that realistically is here to stay, and we will be facing the consequences for decades to come. Diet and exercise can do a lot to thin you down, but depressingly the pounds pack back on sooner or later. The bright light on the horizon are the GLP-1 drugs like Wegovy, which have led to huge weight drops of 15 per cent and possibly more, with other new types on their way. These drugs are as good as major surgery and may yet turn the tide.

It is amazing to think that a combination of senolytic anti-aging and Wegovy-type weight-dropping drugs now coming online together could make us all young and skinny again!

In general, mankind, since the improvement of cookery, eats twice as much as nature requires.
— Benjamin Franklin, quoted in *Many Thoughts of Many Minds*, ed. Louis Klopsch, 1896

CHAPTER 9

Covid comes

'Is anybody talking about anything else? Everywhere I go, people are talking about nothing but this bloody coronavirus!'

It was the first week in March 2020, and a group of pathologists from Australia, the United States, Britain, Ireland, Germany, Switzerland, Belgium and New Zealand were on the phone together, trying to find out what on Earth was going on around the world. We were not getting any reliable information from the floundering officials other than a mix of panicky messages usually followed by blandly reassuring ones.

These were still the early days of the virus. 'Corona' was the name still commonly bruited about, although Covid-19 had appeared by some bureaucratic diktat in February. We had not yet discovered the delights of Zoom, so there we were, all on an obsolescent teleconference.

The whole world was about to experience a seismic social shift.

I was bemused, and maybe even slightly amused, by it all. I thought this was going to be another case of mass global hysteria and not much would happen. After all, I had seen SARS, MERS, Ebola, swine flu and bird flu all come into the limelight, only to not come to much, then disappear from the news without a trace. Nothing much seemed to happen in New Zealand infection-wise, and that was especially true here in Palmerston North.

'Nah, it won't amount to anything,' I told my colleagues and other people who were starting to anxiously look sideways at the unfolding events.

First there had been the problem in Wuhan. OK, but that was somewhere in China. Never even heard of it before, so not our problem, right? But then came Italy — that was different. We all knew people who had gone there and even some who were just about to go there on holiday. Lockdown? What was the hell was a lockdown? In Italy? How could that be?!

The World Health Organization was saying there wasn't a pandemic, and 'there was no reason for measures that unnecessarily interfere with international trade and travel'. They didn't recommend 'limiting trade and movement'. They had also said 'Well done!' to the Chinese government for their impressive transparency and honesty in effectively containing the new virus.

So, everything was all OK … or was it?

'We know how these viruses spread and so can knock them out at source,' I confidently told everyone. 'And it will only take a few months for the big pharmaceuticals to bang out a vaccine. Then it will all be over.'

Was I in for a shock! We were all in for a shock.

My colleague Evangelos from Berlin started my shockwave of doubt, announcing to the teleconference: 'Germany is in partial lockdown. All the schools are closed. Even the football is grounded, and that shows it's serious. You can't find a café or bar open. We think the shops are closing next and probably they're going to close the borders, even with other parts of Europe … it's just unbelievable. About a hundred of our staff are French and commute across the border to three of our labs. How are they going to get to work? How will we run our labs?'

'Surely they'll contain the spread of the virus quite quickly?' someone asked.

That's what I thought, too.

'No, it's far too late — it's escaped already, and it looks like its highly infectious.' This was from an expert in infectious diseases.

'With the borders closed, how will we get our lab supplies?'

'You had better get in stock now while you can, because soon nothing is going to get across the borders, even if the factories can keep on going. And that doesn't look likely at the moment.'

For the first time I heard about social distancing at work, about sending non-essential staff to work from home.

'There will be a huge loss of productivity, of course.'

'If you are not ready now you had better get ready fast. It may already be too late.'

After this shattering call, I sat and stared bleakly out my window. It was a beautiful, clear day, and I could see Mount Ruapehu on the horizon. On my left, an Air New Zealand ATR 72 full of happy travellers was on the final approach into the airport. All looked normal out there. It was unbelievable.

'What did they say?' Bruce van den Heever came back into our office. 'Any news?'

I spoke flatly. 'We're stuffed.'

He stared at me in disbelief. 'What?'

The Final Diagnosis

'We're completely stuffed,' I repeated. 'It's much worse than we've been told. Maybe worse than even the government knows or can yet imagine. Better get the heads of departments in. We've got a lot to do.'

* * *

'Why don't they just let the bloody thing rip until we've got herd immunity?' We were in a tense lab meeting, called to figure out what the hell we were supposed to do. The immunity question was a fair one, and a lot of people were asking exactly this. Anders Tegnall, the expert from Sweden, seemed to believe in herd immunity, and in Britain they were saying much the same.

'Yes, it could happen, but the experts reckon Covid's just too deadly for that. They say there'll be millions of deaths if we do that. Maybe even hundreds of millions.'

'What about testing for coronavirus? Do we need to set that up?'

'No,' Bruce answered. 'Fortunately, that's one thing we don't have to worry about. The Ministry of Health has said there will only be three testing labs for Covid. Lab+ in Auckland will do the upper North Island, and the rest of the country will go to Canterbury Health in Christchurch. The ESR lab will be a backup for any excess tests.

'All we have to do, thank God, is collect the swabs and send them off to Christchurch. The testing's not going to be our problem.'

These were to be famous last words.

'I've booked this weekend away in Sydney. What shall I do?' one scientist asked.

Covid comes

'I strongly advise you not to go.' I put it as firmly as I could. 'It's not only the danger of now catching Covid, but we reckon the border is soon going to close. You may not get back.'

People will be people, though.

Off to Sydney the scientist went, and that proved to be a very long weekend. The scientist was seen back in the lab only many weeks later.

The scientists and technicians were divided into teams who were not allowed to mix with each other either at work or socially. Social distancing had arrived with a vengeance. We could not afford to do otherwise.

When Covid struck, we would need enough people to carry out all the critical, lifesaving tests that our 24-hour, 7-day-a-week medical service demanded. After all, people would still fall sick and need critical care for all the other diseases and accidents, too.

Our IT department went out and bought a pile of laptops, and we began moving our pathologists and everyone who absolutely didn't need to be in the lab to workstations at home. It was a massive undertaking.

I went shopping for myself, too. I stopped off on my way home that night at Moshims, the local Indian shop, and bought two very large sacks of their finest basmati rice.

* * *

A week later Pat and I were standing in the Heretaunga Street car park next to a roller door. This was the discreet entrance to the underground mortuary bay through which our endless daily supply of bodies was unloaded into the fridges to await their appointment with the pathologist. Beside us on the tar seal was a large refrigerated container, easily big enough to fit the contents of two three-bedroom houses and then some.

'Do you reckon it'll do the job?' I looked uncertainly at the metal box. It looked big, spread over a couple of parks. It was positioned under the windows looking out from the upstairs hospital cafeteria, and I could see the lunchers at their tables looking out with perplexed interest at this novel sight.

They could have no idea what these were for. Nothing much was happening hereabouts Covid-wise. We heard with interest on the news about the few positive cases: people from the World Hereford Conference in Queenstown, the Marist schoolkids, the *Ruby Princess* cruise ship and the guests at the Wellington wedding. 'Bummer, eh, getting it at a wedding?' folk were saying, but to us Covid always seemed to be happening somewhere else and to someone else.

'Yep,' Pat answered, patting the container side. 'We'll get pallets made up to put all the bodies on.'

'Who's making the pallets?'

We had ordered two containers to store the Covid dead in: one container for Palmerston and one for Whanganui. We figured the undertakers might still be operational, but they would probably close when things got really bad. We would nevertheless have to store the dead respectfully, until they could be decently buried. I just hoped it wouldn't come to mass communal graves, but in those early days who knew where we were headed.

'I've got the wood to make them on appro. It's all stacked up inside the container,' Pat explained. 'Got a template made up and Noel says he can knock them up in an afternoon. We'll only make them up if we have to. Bunnings say they'll take the wood back if we don't need it.'

Covid comes

'The bodies will be infectious, you know that?'

Pat nodded. 'We'll double-bag them. Got the warning labels, too. Here, I'll show you.' He pulled out two large plastic labels, one red and one blue. The red one said 'COVID POSITIVE' in large black letters, the blue 'COVID NEGATIVE'. I took one and fingered it, puzzled. They looked familiar but they weren't your usual toe tag.

'Where did you get these from?'

'They're ear tags for cattle.' He grinned at me. 'Got a thousand printed up, ready to go. They're in boxes right beside all the body bags.'

We were as ready as we could be. But then for days nothing happened. Thousands of doctors signed a petition calling for immediate lockdown. We looked at each other, perplexed.

'Have we got this wrong?' Bruce asked.

But we knew we hadn't. It was coming. We were like athletes on the starting block, waiting for the gun.

Jacinda Ardern finally fired the lockdown gun on 23 March, to our relief. But our troubles were only just beginning. There were thousands of Kiwis trapped abroad. Winston Peters warned everyone that the window to return was almost closed, as international air hubs like Singapore shut down. 'We are reaching a point where the best option for most New Zealanders offshore is to shelter in place, by preparing to safely stay where they are.'

At least we were relatively safe and would be playing it out on home ground.

* * *

The Final Diagnosis

As many people now know, swabs are a simple device you can stick up your own nose into your throat and mop up any snot or saliva to look for the Covid virus. We had a small stock of swabs to hand for the few dozen stray viruses we were asked to hunt down each year. But our stock was never going to be enough for the tens of thousands of Covid cases we were expecting.

'How many swabs can the lab supply?' I was at a District Health Board Covid crisis management meeting and the CEO, Kathryn Cook, was asking the question.

'Thirteen,' I answered.

'Thirteen?'

I nodded. 'Yes. Thirteen.'

'Is that boxes of swabs, or what?'

'No. Thirteen, as in one more than twelve.'

The room had gone totally silent.

'Why don't you order more?'

I thought I had better explain the problem. 'There are only a few thousand available, scattered here and there throughout the country. Everyone is in the same boat. The suppliers are promising to do what they can, but they just don't carry the stocks either. No one has got very many anywhere, not even in Australia.'

'Can't they bring more in?'

'They're trying to. The problem is, the swabs are made in a factory in northern Italy. Italy has closed its borders and is in lockdown. The usual supply-line has collapsed.'

The public health officer looked at me, aghast.

'How the hell can we manage a pandemic when you cannot even identify who has the virus?' he asked. I could see this thought was going through every mind around that table.

Covid comes

'I have also heard that the American government has bought all the existing stock, plus all production for the next couple of years, so our chances are not good, even if ships were sailing and the aircraft flying. Which they're not,' I pointed out, perhaps unnecessarily.

We were saved only by a stroke of luck. One of our scientists had mistakenly ordered a couple of thousand swabs instead of the few dozen he intended, and he had hidden them in a cupboard instead of confessing his mistake. He deserved a medal, because his mistake kept us abreast of the surging demand over the next few days until we could beg or borrow a few more.

The swab-supply solution proved simple in the end, and there is a lesson in this for us all. Our stores supervisor found a company in Auckland that said they could make the swabs. Their quality was superb, and they checked out, capturing the virus easily when tested in action. Even better, they cost a fraction of the price of the Italian ones. Talk about from famine to feast — we could now get all we wanted.

'The Yanks can keep those flash Italian ones, and they're welcome to them,' I said smugly.

Kiwis can make all sorts of things really well. I don't know why we think whatever is made overseas in those exotic places, where the rich go for their holidays, is always better — because it's not.

* * *

'We've got a real problem.' Bruce came in, looking anxious. It was late on Friday afternoon. There were now only three of us left in the office; all the other pathologists were now working from home. Despite Covid and lockdown, there were still patients out there whose diagnoses needed to be made. I turned from my microscope.

'Air New Zealand have cancelled all domestic flights from tonight. The airways are closed, apparently. We can't get our swabs down to Christchurch this weekend.'

'How many are there? Can't we send them to the ESR lab? We can drive to Johnsonville.'

Bruce shook his head. 'We've already tried that. There are too many for ESR, and they can only start processing them on Monday anyway. We must have today's swab results by early tomorrow to be of any use. We've got all the swabs from Whanganui as well as Tairāwhiti waiting here to go, too.'

Everywhere was in lockdown. The tests were urgent. We had to find a solution. We did not want to be the one place and the one lab that failed everyone and let the virus out into New Zealand.

'Too late to find a charter flight, I suppose?'

'Tried that. Everywhere is closed. There are only answerphones out there, no people answering at all.'

'Can we drive them to Auckland?'

'It's a possibility. We would have to do it again on Sunday morning to get Saturday's swab results back, too.'

'What happens on Monday? Is this going to happen every day?'

'There's the 737 freighter that lands here at eleven every night during the week and then flies on to Christchurch. So that's OK to cover the week, then. Though the turnaround time for the results is not good ...' Bruce's voice trailed off and he shook his head doubtfully.

Covid comes

I thought hard. 'We could ask Dave Baldwin to fly them. Why don't I give him a call?'

Dave Baldwin is a legend in the Manawatū, the Rangitikei and far beyond. Dave is a GP who built and runs the outstanding medical practice in Bulls. He is also the country's Flying Doctor and is to be found all over the South Island, flying his Cessna Skyhawk into rough strips to run aviation clinics.

I had known Dave since he was a highly enthusiastic young registrar in Palmy Hospital. He was renowned for telling us all how he once started CPR on a patient with rigor mortis in the darkened back of an ambulance. The pathologists were impressed that he was so driven to learn from autopsies that one year he single-handedly doubled the hospital's autopsy rate. Dave even managed, while on a far-off holiday, to arrange the welter of paperwork and family consents for us to autopsy one of his patients who had unexpectedly died. That is the only time that I have ever seen such an event.

'Sure thing, buddy,' said Dave. 'I can fly them down for you. That's easy.'

It was such a relief to find someone out there with a solution and not a problem. We had more than enough of those to go around.

'We need them down there on Sunday, too — is that possible?'

'I've had a look. There's a front coming up from the south, but it'll only come through later Sunday. It's the Kaikouras I've got to get over, they're the problem. I'll need thirteen thousand feet. But yep, I'll fly them both days.'

'That's awesome, mate.'

Saturday morning found me outside Dave's hangar, helping wheel Romeo Juliet Golf out onto the hardstand. The chilly-bin of swabs was strapped beside him in the passenger seat and Really Jolly Good, as Dave always called her, was soon airborne and climbing hard towards the South Island ranges.

'The airways are closed, you know?' Dave had told me. 'But I told Civil Aviation why and that I was going anyway. They said OK then, you can go.'

This was Kiwi pragmatism at its best.

'Christchurch International are being a pain, so I'm landing her on a farm strip near Rangiora. That OK?'

I swallowed hard. Every solution had its own problem but, of course, it had to be OK.

I called my daughter Charlotte in Christchurch and explained our predicament.

'Sure, we can go and get them. But aren't we supposed to be in lockdown? What if we get caught?'

'Better to ask forgiveness than permission. Just go. I'll send you an official-looking letter on lab paper authorising you to travel on emergency grounds. That'll probably do it, even if it's unofficial.'

I knew the New Zealand Police were also a pragmatic bunch and that we shouldn't have too much trouble.

It all worked perfectly both days, and the samples were soon running hot on the instruments in the Christchurch Hospital laboratory.

Dave refused any payment. 'No buddy, we're all in this together.' He is an awesome man.

Despite the difficulties, Covid was an amazing time, too, for how people came together in so many ways.

Covid comes

* * *

There was a precipitous edge to the precarious pathway we were treading through these early chaotic months, and things did not always go as well for our patients as they might in normal times. Early in lockdown I went down the stairs to the foyer one afternoon and stopped, staring at what I saw. The main door was now almost impenetrable. Like a mediaeval castle, the gates were closed against random visitors and fortified with nurses and security guards. Only close family were allowed in, even when the patient was dying. Compassion was officially off limits. It was a hard thing to see.

The wards had been emptied as much as possible in anticipation of the droves of dying that were expected daily. After all, we had seen the scale of the disaster on the TV, harrowing scenes from India and elsewhere; even in London we saw a temporary hospital, RAF Nightingale, with 4000 beds being set up at London City Airport, to take the pressure off the NHS hospitals. We believed the deadly Covid wave was coming. It was just a matter of time.

As I stared at the unfamiliar gate guardians, I noticed an elderly couple sitting inside, all alone in the seats along the outer window. Those seats were normally full of people and patients.

The woman looked unwell, and I could see her abdomen was markedly swollen. I supposed it was cancer. They looked up at me hopefully, almost pleadingly. I shook my head slightly. I was not coming for them. They looked down despondently. Their ordeal was still ongoing.

I felt guilty about just walking past them and heading off home, so I stopped to talk to Shelly, the receptionist in the foyer. She was hidden behind a mask, as we all were.

'What's the story with that couple sitting out here? They looked pretty anxious to me, and she doesn't look too good.'

'That's Maria and her husband. They've been there since midday.' It was now after three o'clock.

'Why? What are they waiting for?'

'She says she's here to have her stomach drained. It gets full of fluid, and it must be drained. They were told before lockdown that they had to come in today, but there's nobody here who knows anything about her. They have all gone home for lockdown.'

'Didn't they phone her? I mean, with lockdown changing everything. Only emergency cases are being admitted, to keep the beds clear, aren't they?'

'Yes, that's right. I told her that and they wanted to just go home, but I stopped them. Of course she needs to be seen and treated, and I made them sit there and wait. Maria reminds me of my mum. My mum had that swelling of fluid, too, and she nearly died from it, so I know it is important to get her treatment.'

'Is someone coming to see her? If it's a cancer that's so advanced, maybe the hospice would be able to help?'

Shelly shook her head. 'I don't think it is. Her husband told me she was waiting for a liver transplant. He was crying. It was so sad. I've already phoned everywhere, and no one knows anything. Her consultant is somewhere in lockdown, and they can't find him. But I did get hold of a charge nurse. I told her Maria has a humongous lump in her stomach. She's been really helpful and apparently, even though she can't find

Covid comes

anything in their lists about Maria, she says she is going to find her a bed. Someone will see her.'

I had to be content with that. I tried to nod encouragingly at them as I left. There wasn't really anything else I could do.

* * *

'Why can't you do the Covid tests here? This 24- and 48-hour turnaround time from Christchurch is just bloody hopeless. We can't manage our urgent admissions like this.'

Since that first frantic weekend we had found a new, tortuous but reliable, trail to the South Island, so we no longer needed Dave boldly criss-crossing the strait, keeping one eye on looming weather fronts. The swabs now flowed southwards, and the results came back up north.

But that took time. The process was cumbersome and slow at best.

We discovered that even with the best will in the world this was not going to work. People ill in the community had to have a rapid result in hours. Those coming into hospital needed theirs even faster. Isolation to stop the spread of the virus and take care of the ill in special Covid wards just wasn't possible without immediate results. A 24-hour turnaround was useless to us all.

Richard Coutts was enraged. 'We've got a man here with a big brain haemorrhage that needs urgent draining. I've teed up the neuro team in Wellington to crack his nut and we're supposed to fly him down right away. But the air ambo says they won't take him unless he's got a negative Covid test.'

The fastest we could get a result from Christchurch was by the following night. The patient would be dead long before then.

'If he is Covid positive, what happens then? Will they not fly him down?'

'Dunno,' answered Richard. 'I suppose he will be driven down, but that's not good enough.'

In the end the air ambulance did take him to Wellington, but valuable hours had been lost. We were happy to learn his surgery was successful.

It certainly was a bad time to be a patient. But the dead were being inconvenienced as well as the living.

Our receptionist phoned in a panic one afternoon. 'TC, you must come down here at once. There are people everywhere in the corridor and there are two Māori men who are really upset.'

I grabbed a mask and rushed down. A corridor full of people sounded quite wrong. After all we were in lockdown. Everyone was supposed to be staying at home in their bubble, being kind to each other.

Two very angry faces, sans masks, were waiting outside for me. They started shouting as I came out of the locked door. They were clearly in no mood to be kind.

I persuaded everyone to move from the corridor in front of the lab to the waiting area on the next-door mezzanine floor. The rest of their whānau were all gathered there. There wasn't a mask in sight. I reluctantly pulled mine off and stuffed it in my pocket.

'I hear you have a family member who is here for an autopsy?' That much I had gathered from the outpouring of anger in the corridor. 'Tell me what has happened, and I'll see how we can fix things.'

Gradually calm was restored. The women took the initiative and told me what was happening. The men were still livid, fuelled up on rage.

'Our brother, he died in Waipukurau, and the coroner says we have to have an autopsy. We agreed because they said we could take him home today. But now they say we can't, because of Covid. Why?'

'Did your brother die of Covid? Maybe that is the problem? Maybe they don't want him infecting your whānau?'

'No, he was a suicide. Someone said maybe he had Covid, but I don't think he was even sick. They said they had to check for Covid first. They said we must go home, and it would be days before we can have the body.'

'Who told you that?'

'The man in the mortuary gave us the coroner's number and they told us. But we are not going without him. Then the hospital security came and told us to go, or they would call the police. So we came around to the front of the hospital to find someone and they told us to go to the lab.'

This was not good news at all. 'Wait here, and I'll go and find out exactly what's going on. I can't promise you anything, but I'll do my best.'

This was looking bad. I could see this family were not going to just capitulate and trek back to Hawke's Bay. I called the coroner first and explained the tense situation.

'There's nothing more I can do,' I was told. 'My advice is that he may have Covid and will need a negative test before an autopsy can be carried out. I've already explained that to the family. Hospital security has had to clear them out once already. You need to tell them that they're breaking the lockdown regulations. They need to go home and just wait until we are ready.'

Go home and wait. Hmmm ... well, that was not going to fly, that much I knew for sure.

I called the duty forensic pathologist. She was cheerful and helpful. Pathologists usually are, even in difficult times. We are used to seeing adversity.

'I don't think there's any real chance of him having Covid. It's these damn safety protocols they've foisted on us. They say we need a negative PCR. I've taken the swab this morning but it's only going away to Christchurch tonight. God knows when we'll get the result.'

'What are we going to tell the whānau?'

'Tell you what, bugger the rules! I'll just do it without the test. But it'll be tomorrow morning before everything is done and the coroner can release the body.'

I went in trepidation back to the crowded mezzanine floor to tell the family the news. I need not have worried; they were delighted that he was coming home, even if it was to be tomorrow. A woman threw her arms around me and hugged me. 'Thank you so much for listening!'

Social distancing may have been broken, but there are times when our social fabric is more important than capricious rules.

Some rules are stupid anyway, and are just made to be broken.

I realised one thing for sure. We needed to carry out Covid tests here and now in Palmy, for the sake of both the living and the dead.

Covid comes

* * *

'We've got no option, have we?' I asked our team. 'We have to set up PCR testing for Covid here and now. The only question is how.'

'That's not going to be easy.'

'Why?'

To be honest, I had no clear idea then how Covid testing was done other than that it was this sophisticated, sexy DNA method called the Polymerase Chain Reaction or PCR. The PCR technique was patiently explained to me.

The basic idea is that it's like that Indian legend where the god Krishna challenges a local king to a game of chess. The king generously allows the god to choose the winner's prize. Krishna says, 'I am a modest man, with few wants. All I ask is that if I win you give me a few grains of rice. I will explain to you how.

'You must put one grain on the first square of the chess board, two grains on the second, four on the third, eight on the fourth and so on until all sixty-four squares have been so filled.'

The king happily agrees to the deal. He loses the game and starts to fulfil his side of the bargain, but soon the extent of the problem becomes apparent. The first few squares are easy to fill with a few rice grains, but by the time you reach the sixty-fourth square, more than eighteen quadrillion grains are needed. And that amounts to trillions of tons of rice — much more than the entire world produces in years and years.

What's this fable got to do with PCR? The principle of doubling the rice grains on each square is what the PCR test does with the virus. If there is only a single copy of Covid DNA from your nasal swab, two are copied by the instrument in the first cycle, four in the second, eight in the third and so on, just like Krishna's fabled grains of rice. We keep on doubling any possible DNA for 40 cycles before accepting that there's nothing there. If it's there, even in the minutest amount, we'll find it. We were all amazed when a single case of Covid, tucked away in isolation, could be detected in millions of litres of a city's sewage, but that just shows the extraordinary detection power of the test.

'Where in hell's name can we get the instruments, the space and the scientific expertise to run a PCR lab?' I asked. We had never done anything remotely like this before.

'God only knows,' answered Bruce. 'All I know is that it can't go on like this.'

We racked our brains for several stressful days. The real anguish pouring out from the clinical side was a powerful motivator, but no solution presented itself.

Then suddenly it did, and the darkness lifted, and all was OK.

Serendipity: that means to find by fortunate chance. We were lucky and found the solution by that fortunate chance. For out there in the community, someone held up her hand.

Rebecca Lucas-Roxburgh had been a scientist in our lab before heading off to do a PhD at Massey University, where she investigated the role of human papilloma viruses in cancers of the head and neck. Rebecca had become expert in the PCR technique, and now she readily joined us to set up our Covid testing service. We 'borrowed' the PCR instrument at the Hopkirk Research Institute on the Massey University campus that had been set up to test the national

Covid comes

dairy herds for *Mycoplasma bovis*, for over the previous few years our nation's cattle had experienced a devasting epidemic storm of their very own.

The Mycoplasma testing had to go on; Covid was bad, but we did not need, nor could we afford, a massive hit on our dairy herds. The institute scientists tested Mycoplasma by day, then our teams arrived at four, sat themselves on their still-warm chairs and worked through the night until all the Covid testing was finished. The patients' results from the hospital, and those from the community testing centres, came hot off the press and were ready from late evening. The positives were called through at midnight to sleep-dazed hospital specialists and public health doctors.

The turnaround times were now great. The system at last was working well.

* * *

There were moments of humour to lighten our journey. Pathology is a serious profession, and it could not in all honesty be described as joyful, as you might say of delivering babies or curing children. However, we rely a lot on our humour, which is usually black or irreverent, or both, to keep our spirits up.

Our reporting room is a quietish place where clinicians tend to come together out of the hurly-burly to discuss their patients. Stories always seem to collect around us for this reason.

Richard Coutts came through the door late one morning.

'Hey paths, here's a question for you! Can you get Covid through your eye?'

The Final Diagnosis

We looked at each other, puzzled. Everyone was masked against infecting others or getting the dreaded bot ourselves. The practice was observed with a very variable degree of enthusiasm and integrity, though. Our most diligent pathologists climbed out of their cars at work wearing the tightly fitting N95 masks in the morning and returned the same way in the evening. Those of us who did this found an evening headache was the usual reward, due to the buildup of carbon dioxide in our blood from re-breathing. We just hoped its toxicity was not enough to disrupt our diagnostic thought processes.

Others were more cavalier. Richard, for example, was wearing his simple paper surgical mask around the bottom of his chin, rather like a beard. While this may have given him the advantage of access to fresh air and unmuffled speech, it made its anti-viral efficacy moot. It also suggested that his question about eye entry was more philosophical than practical.

'It's a good question,' I replied, 'and one we have talked about. If the virus is in an aerosol of droplets, why couldn't some of those settle in your eye? It's then a simple trek down the lacrimal duct into the nose, and it's home and away!'

Richard nodded. 'I asked the ophthalmology boys if that happened, but they just laughed at me,' he said rather morosely.

'Why are you asking? Do you think we should wear goggles, too? How about trying a proper mask first? Just as a gesture?' I pointed at his mask; I was chaffing him now.

'I've already been hit,' he explained. 'This morning. I reckon I've got the bug now.'

'What happened?'

Covid comes

Richard, always the inveterate storyteller, settled into his tale.

'I was doing a colonoscopy on this woman. She's under the gynaes for endometriosis and she's now come in with a "maybe" subacute bowel obstruction. So they asked me to have a dekko. She's just had Covid but is over it, so I wasn't worried, as I've got my mask here.

'I put the scope in and spotted the sigmoid was a bit narrowed but should be passable. I thought she probably had some endometriosis in the bowel, and I could whip that out for her later — no hurry right now.

'As I was coming out, this huge haemorrhoid bulged out at me. "I can sclerose that up for you," I told her. We were all keen, so I had a syringe of sclerosant drawn up and given to me.'

This was typical of Richard, always on the lookout for some bodily malfunction to repair surgically. I remember him taking out a difficult stuck-down gallbladder once. It took a long time — much, much longer than anticipated. Richard claimed that when it came out, the theatre staff gave a cheer. He added, 'Her appendix looked a bit odd, so I whipped that out as an encore!'

'Anyway,' he continued, 'I bent over and lifted the quivering haemorrhoid. I looked closely and found the spot I wanted. I was just about to plunge the needle into it when a stream of shit shot out of her anus right into my eye.'

We all laughed. Richard looked at us sadly. 'That's what everyone does, just laughs. But is there Covid in shit? Can you get it like that?'

'You sure can. They can find the virus in sewage, and we all know what that's full of, don't we?'

The Final Diagnosis

* * *

There was humour, but there was a bit of stupidity, too. Hindsight is great, but it can make you cringe.

A movement grew that we all had to be 'fitted' with N95 masks. Everyone was doing it and it was said to be 'unsafe' not to do so. Despite our lab staff having used masks for years, we hired a company to show us how to put them on. They showed us how the mask was held onto the face by its two elastic bands. Any child who has put on a face mask knows how it works.

It was laughable really, but everyone took it very seriously. The mask bands were of either blue or red elastic.

I went into the testing room we had set aside for the ceremonial fitting. My blood pressure was taken. It was my usual 140/75.

'That's very high!' the young woman testing me said. That should have warned me that something was amiss, as that level is quite normal.

The mask was held to my face and the bands were ostentatiously pulled over my head. This so far was exactly as I myself had done thousands of times throughout my medical career. I put my head in a plastic cabinet and a mist of spray was squirted in. That was novel.

'Do you smell anything?'

'No,' I said. I did not tell her that I have no sense of smell anyway.

'That's fine, then. It fits.'

'What if I did smell something? What would you do?'

'We would use the other size of mask. You've got the blue-banded one, so we would try the red-banded one. That usually works.'

Covid comes

This exercise cost us $35,000, so it wasn't cheap. I later found out that the red- and blue-banded masks were identical in every other way, including size. The blue ones came from the company's factory in Singapore, the red ones from its China operation.

When I hear the Ministry of Health has spent $45 million to store $150 million of unwanted RAT tests, all about to expire, I tut-tut along with everyone else, but when I think of our mask farce I am reminded that we all did some pretty idiotic things during Covid.

As my old dad used to say: 'A fool and his money are soon parted.' More contemporarily, Forrest Gump had the perfect pitch for this occasion: 'Mama always used to say, "Stupid is as stupid does".'

* * *

Our worldwide laboratory teleconferences soon graduated to Zoom. I am sure computers are like dogs and can smell fear, as they usually play up and ambush me at every turn. It was a pleasant surprise, though, how simple Zoom was, and for me it worked every time. Our conferences kept us up to speed with all the latest news.

The vaccine was coming, so they said, but it still needed more testing before they could finally release it to the suffering world. But when? We were so sick of lockdown already.

'How much longer is this damned virus going to last?' I had called to ask my flamboyant virologist friend Jon, from South Africa. He is an expert in everything viral. His hobby is to find out just how organisms have affected and altered history, and he has some brilliant yarns about how bacteria were so much more deadly than bullets in the Great War.

'Covid-19 is just one blip in the human story, and it isn't the first time a coronavirus has done this to us either.' Jon chuckled. 'There have been massive pandemics perhaps four times already in our history but, people being people, we've forgotten all about them.'

'You mean pandemics like the 1918 'flu?'

'No, I mean actual real coronavirus pandemics.'

That was a surprise. 'When?'

'The last biggie was the Russian 'flu in 1889. It wasn't really influenza, though. It killed the old, spared the young, caused loss of smell and taste, and spread around the world in waves, killing five million people. It was never proven but it sounds like the same combo as Covid, doesn't it?'

I had to agree.

'After a couple of years, it became a tame pussycat and is now just one of the common cold coronaviruses, called Alpha. Guess when Alpha mutated and "jumped" into humans from cattle? About a hundred and thirty years ago. The timing is spot-on for the Russian pandemic.'

'So, you reckon Covid-19 will do the same and just lose its virulence? Maybe become just like another cold?'

'That's most likely what'll happen. There probably was a pandemic before the Russian one, too, about six hundred years ago, say about the 1350s. That would be about the same time the Black Death reached Europe and killed a third of the people. Some of us reckon there was a Covid pandemic mixed up with the plague, at about the same time. The poor bastards wouldn't have had a clue what was what, though.

Covid comes

No way to know back then. The social effects were pretty impressive, though.

'The feudal system of owning serfs collapsed, the Viking settlement of North America fell over, and even the French and English declared a truce in their endless wars. But that fourteenth-century virus is now also just another common cold, called Beta.

'So, these two Covid pandemic tigers became two pussycat minor colds in the head. There's also Delta and Gamma pussycats, and I think they're probably going to be from other, even earlier pandemics, lost in the mists of time.'

'So you think one day maybe there'll be another corona pandemic?'

'Nothing could be surer!' said Jon cheerfully. 'Want to bet we'll have forgotten everything by then and won't be ready? Just like this time?'

'Interesting but dammed depressing about waiting it out for five years. Not sure how any of us are going to last that long if we have to keep sitting around until it turns into a pussycat cold.'

* * *

All the labs worldwide had problems with the supplies needed to do the Covid PCR tests. The major manufacturers were all German, and they also made the instruments that could churn through thousands of the PCR tests each day. They were 'closed' systems, designed so you had to only use, and pay for, the test kits the manufacturers provided. The various governments took control of these supplies and said they would not be available for other countries until their own

The Final Diagnosis

needs were met. Fair enough, I suppose, but I do wonder what became of the 'brotherhood of man'.

We at the utmost and insignificant ends of the Earth were at the back end of the broken supply chain. One supplier I was talking to told me, 'I'd love to be able to help but I've got nothing to offer. I'm afraid our stock has all been impounded in Australia and is released only for their labs. New Zealand is very much sucking the hind tit in that regard.'

We were again saved by Rebecca, because she chose an instrument that was 'open', meaning it could use any suitable reagent. And guess what? We didn't need the big German manufacturer with their jealously impounded reagents at all. We found this great little Kiwi company called dnature in Gisborne!

It was the swab story all over again. dnature could make as much reagent as we could use, and it was all ready to go right now. Kiwis can do it along with the best in the world.

The supply chain? We ran our own lab courier each day from Gisborne to Palmerston, carrying our usual hospital samples, and the crucial Covid reagents just went along for the daily ride.

Soon we were doing thousands of tests a day on our swabs as well as helping out with Auckland's overflow from the tens of thousands of tests that were overwhelming their testing centres.

We improvised, borrowed and eventually came through the time of Covid better than we dared hope. The refrigerated containers in time went back unopened and certainly unmourned, and the wood was returned unused. Our worst nightmares never happened, and the mass graves were not needed. We later got a lovely certificate and a badge from the Prime Minister to say thanks for everything.

We were just so relieved the worst was over, even though we keep hearing that it isn't. The tiger is not quite yet a pussycat, but it seems much tamer than it was. We have returned to a normal life. Jon is right, too, I suspect: we have already started forgetting all about it.

These so-called bleak times are necessary to go through
in order to get to a much, much better place.
— David Lynch, interview with *Dazed*, 2020

PART III

Murder most foul

CHAPTER 10

Musings on murder: part I

Murder: a word that causes a distinct feeling of unease.

It is wrong, we know that. Cain knew it when he invented it, murdering his brother Abel in a jealous rage because God preferred his brother's sacrificial offering to his own.

We punish the deed severely, in fact to the utmost extent allowed by our law. After the messy hanging of Ray Bolton, a Whanganui farmer, back in February 1957, New Zealand no longer executes murderers, but it still commonly happens in many countries around the world. We do jail them, though, and for many, many years. Often most of their remaining lives. We do take it quite seriously.

God punished Cain for his deed by banishing him from the settled lands for ever. Having started the fashion, Cain apparently became paranoid that he, too, could be murdered by someone else. I presume that he must have been thinking of a younger brother (or sister, for that matter), since the proliferation of humanity had barely begun from Adam and Eve back then, and the list of persons of interest would be limited to a small group of close family members. That is still often the case in many homicides today.

Interestingly, this also tells us that having discovered the homicide process, Cain must have realised that it was now here to stay. And that this was a bad thing.

Cain and Abel's story has some critical elements common to all murders. There must always be a victim and at least one murderer. A body is usually desirable, to prove that there has indeed been a murder, though this is not an absolute prerequisite. There are also the important evidential things that the police, and the pathologists who help with the forensic story, always need to bear in mind.

The perpetrator and the victim need to be linked, so they are both at the scene at the same time. Alternatively, from a defence point of view, an alibi is needed by the murderer. Basically 'alibi' comes from the Latin meaning 'somewhere else', which pretty much gives you the idea of why you would need one in the circumstances.

A motive is important, too. Admittedly, disagreement over the quality and acceptability of sacrifices to God would be an unusual one to see today, though it was obviously important to Cain. Fashions do change down the years, of course. Today the motives are usually more prosaic, if not downright boring: jealousy, rage, swiping a bit of chump change and just plain orneriness are the usual suspects.

The human fascination with murder is profound. I have spent my professional life in pathology involved with the most fascinating diseases and diagnoses, many quite unbelievable. But at dinner parties and during question times at the meetings and lectures I give it is always the murder cases that people want to talk about.

The cases I have been involved with have all had a satisfactory outcome and the murderer has been held to

Musings on murder: part I

account. Those are naturally the cases I write about and present. Yet I am often asked, 'But have you ever seen someone get away with murder?'

'If I have, how would I know?' I answer. 'Surely if it were a perfect murder, no one would even know a murder had even been committed.'

It seems a simple question, and my answer is OK at a presentation session, but it is not quite true, for I first came across a perfect murder at quite a young age.

Like most families, mine has a few skeletons in the cupboard. As a youngster of about ten years old, I remember quietly crouching against the outside wall, eavesdropping through an open window on my father talking to a visiting uncle about the death of a female relative. Children were not permitted to sit with grownups inside the lounge back in the early '60s, so illicit listening was my only option. This young woman had, I gathered, died at the hands of her husband.

'He kept a pistol in a drawer in their bedroom,' my father was saying. 'It was there in case they had a burglar break in.'

This was in Africa, where the social fabric is somewhat different from New Zealand, and robberies under the cover of darkness were not uncommon.

'His story is that Dorothy was sitting at her mirror doing her hair, while he was getting dressed. She asked him, "Do you still keep that gun in the bedroom?" He said he did, went to the drawer, opened it and took the gun out. Now, why would she ask that in the first place, and why would he take it out?' I could hear the disbelief in my father's voice.

'He walked over to her, with the gun in the palm of his hand. "Here it is," he said, and passed it towards her. It went off, and the bullet went into her head, killing her instantly.'

The Final Diagnosis

There was a silence as they digested this information. I was enthralled. The yet-to-be pathologist in me was assimilating this: my very first real-life, unnatural death.

'Why didn't the police become suspicious?' my uncle asked.

'He was very clever about it. He was a doctor, you know? He phoned for the police and for an ambulance immediately, though he told them on the phone that he was a doctor and that she was dead.

'The police did charge him in the end, and he was brought to trial. He stuck to his story and played the dreadfully upset husband, who could never forgive himself for what happened.'

I could easily visualise the killer. Dark-haired, swarthy but clean-shaven, a dark striped suit, patent leather shoes. A typical murderer, I imagined, though I now realise that in my fevered, naive imagination I was basing him on the only other doctor I knew: our gentle Irish family GP, Dr O'Brien, who definitely was not a murderer.

My father went on. 'He was well known, a respected doctor in the town. The jury quickly gave him the benefit of the doubt, and he was found not guilty.'

I felt cheated somehow. The baddies always got their punishment in the TV programmes and films back in those days. That was the expectation of society in the '60s.

'Then a few months later the bastard up and marries his receptionist. She was pregnant, you know. The baby arrived soon afterwards.'

I could tell Dad was outraged, for I had never heard him use bad language before. This gave me my first inkling of the role of motive in a murder, though in those innocent days,

Musings on murder: part I

I would have had only the vaguest idea of what the social mores of an extramarital pregnancy meant.

But what I did understand was that the murderer had got off! It was too ghastly to think about. I was outraged, too.

'Less than a year later, he got cancer. He had the new baby, but by then people had turned against him. The cancer finished him off in a few months.' I could sense Dad's satisfaction at this just outcome.

Mine, too. I didn't really know back then what cancer meant either, only that it must be bad. Anyway, the baddie was dead and, by the lights of my ten-year-old view, it jolly well served him right.

But you must admit, it was a near-perfect murder.

* * *

So, when people ask me how you might commit the perfect murder, in which the crime remains undetected, I'm not able to tell them. Apart from having no hands-on personal experience to share, my opinion would probably piss off the CIB, and be very dubious from an ethical point of view. The Medical Council would certainly disapprove.

My attention has always been on the murders in which I have been closely involved in a professional capacity, for they are usually complex and take years to pass through the various court and appeal processes. But in recent years I have turned my interest to study several other murders that have occurred elsewhere in New Zealand. I am always professionally interested to see how and why they happened, how they were investigated, what was found and, most importantly, what became of the murderers.

This interest is shared by many Kiwis. The events surrounding these murders are all publicly well known, which means that by definition they could never be candidates for 'the perfect murder'. But even if I cannot tell you how to get away with murder, I can talk about what went wrong for the perpetrators of some of these murders. These cases are the opposite of the perfect murder, and are rather a look at what *not* to do.

Murderers usually do get caught. That is the first lesson to heed.

Inspector Doug Brew once told me, 'All murderers make at least three mistakes. That is why thick shits like me can catch them.'

Doug was never thick, but he was certainly right about their mistakes. Let's look at what went wrong for some infamous murderers.

* * *

While we all were recovering from our Millennium celebrations and congratulating ourselves on not being wiped out by the Y2K apocalypse, Dr Colin Bouwer was busy murdering his wife, Annette.

Colin was a psychiatrist by profession, and by all accounts was good at his job. He was clearly intelligent — you do not become head of psychiatry at the Otago Medical School unless you are — and could presumably compute the odds of his getting away with this deadly deed.

Annette had a very difficult year with which to end the last century. She had been bedevilled with an odd and debilitating illness, in which her blood glucose levels

Musings on murder: part I

periodically plunged to low and potentially lethal levels. Colin was the attentive and solicitous husband throughout her ordeal and made sure she had the finest and most sophisticated tests available. He suggested all her symptoms could be due to an insulinoma hidden within her pancreas. This is a rare tumour that produces insulin and causes exactly the sort of devastating blood-sugar collapses that Annette was experiencing.

Most of Annette's pancreas was removed to get rid of the hidden tumour. Colin was naturally encouraging and supportive of this massive operation. However, no such tumour was found by the pathologists.

The attacks continued unabated, with multiple hospital admissions to rescue her from her repeated and devastatingly low glucose levels. Annette finally succumbed, dying at home in bed on 5 January 2000.

Her physician wisely asked for an autopsy. Her cause of death, her bizarre medical history and the desire to find that elusive insulinoma all demanded that it be done. However, Colin tried to head off this examination with a weird take on Annette's religion.

'She is Orthodox Jewish and has to be cremated within forty-eight hours,' he claimed, so an autopsy was therefore not possible.

Annette was known to be a practising Christian.

Two full autopsies were eventually carried out. No insulinoma was found, putting that particular theory to bed. Crucially, Annette's blood was taken on each occasion and was sent for a toxicology analysis.

The surprise was that a significant cocktail of drugs was found in her blood. They should not have been there.

The Final Diagnosis

There was glipizide and glibencamide and metformin, all anti-diabetic drugs used to lower blood glucose. Some experts questioned why the two bloods taken showed different levels of the drugs, but this does not worry me. This is common in autopsy blood, because the levels can differ depending on the site from which it is collected. This is because of a phenomenon known as 'postmortem drug redistribution', which is well known, at least to the forensic boffins.

But crucially, Annette was not and never had been a diabetic. And there was no possible way these drugs could have accidentally got into her system.

The police were called.

* * *

'Dunedin is the perfect place to get away with murder as the police are not sophisticated enough to catch anyone in a complicated case.' Colin Bouwer had sent such an email to his sister-in-law in South Africa, giving his opinion of New Zealand's investigative ability. He was clearly confident that he could outsmart the local constabulary. Alas, hubris has been the undoing of many a murderer. Colin left a cornucopia of circumstantial evidence to mark his journey, and the Dunedin CIB had little trouble spotting the clues he had scattered behind him.

In most murders it is the partner who does it, so that is where the police tend to start. What could be his motive?

There was an insurance policy on Annette's life, for $260,000. A tidy sum but hardly enough to push a high earner such as Dr Bouwer to commit an elaborate murder, surely?

Musings on murder: part I

'Cherchez la femme', novelist and playwright Alexandre Dumas wrote as far back as 1854, 'Look for the woman.' This has now become a byword in crime fiction, where a love interest is often at the root of a murder.

Colin Bouwer had become close friends with Anne Walshe, a colleague in his department. The two had travelled overseas together to a psychiatry conference in Copenhagen the year before. But it still seemed odd. Colin had already been divorced once, so surely if he entertained an idea of making Anne the third Mrs Bouwer, that would be a simpler way forward? He wouldn't choose to murder Annette, you would have thought.

Then there were his tutorials to the medical students. You might assume that when a psychiatrist takes a group of students for a teaching tutorial, it will be on the subject of mental health and psychiatry. You would normally be correct, but that is not what Colin talked about.

Colin taught the students about anti-diabetic drugs and how they might be used to carry out an undetected and presumably undetectable murder. This included a proposal to inject insulin between the victim's toes. Presumably his thinking was the pathologist would not notice the injection site in such an obscure spot.

This is a topic a long, long way from psychiatry, and you can only wonder why on Earth he would even be thinking about such matters, let alone teaching it to aspiring doctors.

Police discovered that eleven separate prescriptions had been written by Dr Bouwer, each for a medley of anti-diabetic drugs. I understand he used the identities of real people, which he filched from his own patients' records. Unfortunately for Colin, none of them was diabetic and none would ever have been prescribed such drugs. None of them personally collected any of these prescriptions, which were all filled at a variety of different pharmacies scattered around Dunedin.

The volume of anti-diabetic drugs so harvested was vast, verging almost on an industrial scale. Awkwardly for Colin's defence team, he was the prescribing physician for each, his own signature embellishing each smoking gun.

To complete the loop, the same drugs were discovered hidden in the Bouwers' garage, as was a pestle and mortar containing the powdered remnants of the offending agents.

Then there were the emails. Colin contacted at least one medical expert in Australia in which he posed as a pathologist called to court for a forensic opinion. He needed to know, he said, whether an autopsy could discover insulin and the other anti-diabetic drugs in the patient's system.

The evidence was all circumstantial, but it was substantial, and the jury had no doubts, rapidly returning a guilty verdict.

Colin Bouwer made many more than three mistakes. In fact, it is hard to find anything at all that he did with any competence. It would not be an exaggeration to look upon this case as an example of how *not* to commit the perfect murder.

* * *

But you should not believe all is lost just because you made a few mistakes, got caught and sent to jail. Welcome to the support group.

Many, if not most, high-profile murderers in New Zealand develop a support group. It has become almost a rite of passage. It would be easily comprehended if the group consisted solely of the murderer's close family members — after all, blood is thicker than water. Usually, however, they are started and fronted by unrelated people. And as they grow, the aim seems to be to relitigate some or even all aspects of the evidence. The aim is to undermine the public confidence in at least one point of evidence and thereby attempt to undermine the entire investigation and portray the trial as ineptly bungled.

Basically, they take a piece of evidence, reverse the conclusion 180 degrees, and then cast around for some other new expert for support. The ultimate goal is an appeal to the Supreme Court of New Zealand or, in the old days, to the Privy Council in London. This hopefully leads to a new trial and a largely repetitive case but which — playing on the principle of double or quits — may lead to a different result the second time around.

Your support group needs mana to be attractive to the press. Ideally you want it fronted by an articulate sporting celebrity or a high-profile journalist or author, who mines the thin seam of murders for a living; a prominent businessman will do at a pinch. What is essential, though, is a profound and unwavering disbelief in any, indeed, *all* the evidence that relates to your conviction. No argument or analysis should be able to convince the public of any interpretation other than that you are innocent.

Colin Bouwer, despite what on the face of it appears a particularly unpromising field to farrow, was fortunate to find such an advocate. Rather, the advocate found him.

Professor Vincent Marks was an internationally recognised expert in diabetes, hypoglycaemia and related medical issues.

The Final Diagnosis

He was the author of a book entitled *Insulin Murders*, as well as many erudite medical publications. He was called as an expert witness by Colin's legal team, and he eventually included the story of Annette's murder in his book.

By chance, he sold his house in Guildford in the UK to a well-spoken and highly competent business analyst named Peter Filmer. The professor gave Peter a copy of his book, in which Peter read about the Bouwer case. He decided they had got it all wrong.

Peter believed he had spotted a medical misdiagnosis of Annette, and this had in turn resulted in a miscarriage of justice. Peter had made his own diagnosis of myasthenia gravis, a relatively rare neurological disease, based on her having a benign thymoma in her chest cavity, found at autopsy. He had some knowledge of myasthenia because he, too, had been afflicted by this condition, so he was able to relate her symptoms to those he had himself suffered.

Peter took his thesis to Dr Rudy Capildeo, a consultant neurologist and internationally renowned expert in myasthenia gravis. Peter was persuasive and convinced the good doctor in the rightness of his observations and his alternative cause of Annette's death. Dr Capildeo wrote an expert opinion to this effect.

Bingo! This is exactly what you need for the Privy Council.

The Privy Council and the New Zealand Supreme Court will not let your team just rehash the old evidence. You are not permitted to cruise the academic swamps of the world seeking out another (but different) opinion on the same old stuff. You must convince the court that you have found 'fresh' evidence, unknown and unheard at the original trial,

Musings on murder: part I

if you want them to hear your appeal. Dr Capildeo's affidavit fitted the bill perfectly.

Peter Filmer was elated and flew forthwith to New Zealand to tell Colin in person that it was all now over bar the shouting. Colin was incarcerated in Rolleston Prison, and Peter went there as soon as he arrived, the crucial affidavit clutched in his hot little hand.

You can imagine how this played out when they met there in the prison. The excitement, the elation, the glimpse of a promised freedom to follow!

No, it didn't quite happen like that. Colin Bouwer was reading from a completely different script.

He admitted killing Annette. He told Filmer how he gave her small doses of the anti-diabetic drugs to get her into hospital. He told of mixing the drugs and giving them to her dissolved in water. He then came back later, once she was unconscious, and injected her with a lethal dose of insulin. Insulin had been in the last of his eleven fraudulent prescriptions.

Peter Filmer departed back to Guildford, defeated.

In general, I have found that no evidence, however strong, will rock the foundations of a support group. Peter was a particularly thoughtful man. I would have loved to have sat next to him on that flight home and heard his thoughts after receiving Colin's confession.

* * *

Colin Bouwer had romantic motives for murdering Annette, so the police had good cause to look much more closely at him. But what if a murder apparently has no motive at all?

The Final Diagnosis

That makes everything so much harder, for motive often ties a murderer to their victim almost as powerfully as their having no alibi for the time of death. A perfect murder ideally would have no discernible motive to direct the police investigation towards the murderer.

Lack of a motive was a problem in the murders of Ted Ferguson and Margaret Waldin on the night of 27 May 2005. Ted and Margaret lived in Feilding, a pretty Manawatū town that has won the New Zealand's Most Beautiful Large Town Award on dozens of occasions. Ted was 73 and Margaret 76, and they were best friends. Margaret usually spent one or two nights a week staying over in Ted's pensioner flat.

The pair had spent the evening chatting with friends over their drinks in the Manchester Tavern, which was their usual watering hole. Ted left first, while Margaret finished her drink.

'I'll leave the door open for you,' he said, and headed off into the night.

Margaret followed half an hour later. Neither was ever seen alive again.

The next day, neighbours noticed the door of Ted's flat was open and were surprised that he was not to be seen up and about. The police were called.

Both were found dead, with multiple stab wounds. Ted had 25, Margaret nine deep wounds. Both had been stabbed through the heart.

Margaret appeared to have been killed as she arrived at the flat, as the groceries she had been carrying were not even unpacked. Ted was murdered after he had got up out of bed, possibly after hearing the commotion of the attack on Margaret.

Musings on murder: part I

The problem was, there was no one who might have a motive to kill them. They had no enemies and were popular in the tavern. There had been no obvious robbery. Where to go next?

Remember, this was 2005 and a new technology was just surfacing that was going to change the face of crime detection completely. The tavern had put up one of these new-fangled security cameras, and because of this David Konia became a person of interest to the police. He was seen to be seated close to Ted and Margaret's table, and he got up and followed Margaret out when she left.

David had a sad story. He was a schizophrenic who had been sent out to live in the community, part of the flotsam and jetsam of patients released when Lake Alice Psychiatric Hospital near Whanganui was closed down. He was never really well and suffered from hallucinations. He ultimately confessed to the murders, and his explanation of why he murdered Ted and Margaret really defies belief.

Apparently, he had had a stroke of luck some weeks before with a nice little win at the pokies. David shouted the folk in the Manchester Tavern a drink on the strength of his winnings.

Some weeks later, and being a bit down on his luck, he started brooding on why his hospitality had not been reciprocated. It might have been only a little thing, but it loomed large in his fevered brain, and triggered a murderous response. David followed Margaret to Ted's flat, where he stabbed them both to death. He was sentenced to life imprisonment, and died of cancer in prison ten years later.

To me this story is not about David's culpability or competence or mental illness or motives, although all these interesting elements are there. But it illustrates one of two technical advances that have changed the way we used to do everything when investigating a murder. One is the use of DNA, of which I will talk more in a later chapter. The other is the vast numbers of security cameras now operating virtually everywhere in the big and not-so-big cities and towns of the world.

These two components are, I suspect, now the mainstays of almost all murder investigations. After a murder, all the footage from any surrounding cameras will be picked up and scrutinised. I doubt you can even pick your nose in public these days without it being recorded somewhere.

We were all aghast with equal measures of horror and fascination when we heard that Grace Millane, a 22-year-old British tourist, had been murdered by her Tinder date, Jesse Kempson, in the run-up to Christmas 2018. He was metaphorically done for, legally speaking, when CCTV footage showed Grace kissing Kempson, going into a hotel room with him and never coming out; then him hurriedly buying supermarket suitcases to bring back to the hotel; then wheeling the now heavy cases down in a lift on a porter's trolley. Grace's body was found within the same suitcases buried far away in the Waitākere Ranges.

Quod est demonstrandum, as the Romans said, or 'There you go, then', as a Kiwi joker might have even better put it.

This dreadful killing happened here in New Zealand, and sadly, equally terrible things happen elsewhere, too. In March 2021, Sarah Everard was kidnapped in Brixton Hill near Clapham Common by off-duty Metropolitan policeman Wayne Couzens. He raped and strangled her, then burnt her body. There was no previous association between them, and

Musings on murder: part I

in the old days this case would have remained a mystery — that is, unless or until he did it again and probably again and again, and the police eventually had a lucky break. Repeat performances seem to be the way of it with this type of murder.

But in 2021 it was different. Sarah and her abductor were caught twice on the CCTV footage of a passing bus.

One piece of video identified the pair standing beside a Vauxhall Couzens had hired, and the second gave the car's number plate. The car was also captured on footage in Hoad's Wood near Ashford, where Sarah's dismembered body was eventually discovered.

It's hard for murderers to explain video footage away, and we are all much better off these days because of the cameras. Sometimes having Big Brother watching is not all bad.

I do, however, confess to some nostalgia for the old days of the Sherlock Holmes-type of investigation — the excitement, the search for circumstantial clues, and the painstaking detective work triumphantly leading to an eventual dramatic arrest. Who could not fail to be moved by Sherlock's electrifying words? 'Come, Watson, come! The game is afoot. Not a word! Into your clothes and come!'

* * *

The absence of any sensible motive struck me right from the beginning in the unusual case of Peter Plumley-Walker, the cricket umpire, and Renée Chignall, the dominatrix, way back in 1989. Their tale has been told many times, but there are some instructive points in considering what makes a perfect murder, so it bears a little teasing out of the circumstances.

The Final Diagnosis

Peter Plumley-Walker's divorce was finalised that fateful day, 27 January 1989, and he decided to treat himself to a celebratory session with his favourite dominatrix. New Zealand was a very different place in those days, in many ways. The availability of such a service as Renée provided was not widely known. The prices were mouth-wateringly low by today's lights: her newspaper adult-section advert offered a medley of choices from Basic Bondage and Discipline at $130 to Slave Training at $140–480 and Cross Dressing for a mere $110. Peter opted for the Bondage and Caning package.

This all took place in Renée's Remuera townhouse, where she had a room in which she strapped Peter to the wall with shackles and a collar across his throat. After giving Peter a thrashing with a riding crop, Renée popped off for a break and to enjoy a coffee and a durry with her man, Neville Walker. It is very strange to reflect on what might be going on behind your neighbours' closed doors, but this must certainly rank right up there with the strangest.

Sadly, when she returned for another punishment session, Renée found Peter was dead. Blue, not breathing, heart stopped, and hanging from his straps. She called Neville and they took him down and laid him on the floor.

This is the point where Renée and Neville got it so wrong. So far what had happened was not murder or even manslaughter. It was an accidental death during sexual activity. It was entirely consensual and most certainly not in the 'rough sex' category that Kempson tried unsuccessfully to claim had occurred with Grace Millane.

A phone call to the police and an explanation of the circumstances would have been embarrassing, but I would

Musings on murder: part I

predict that would have been the end of it. Peter's sad death would have been just another occurring while using a prostitute. These deaths are not particularly uncommon, and I have told of an episode of this old story in 'In the Arms of Ecstasy' in my book *The Cause of Death*.

But as they panicked and argued about what to do next, the doorbell rang. It was Renée's mum. Parents can be damned inconvenient at times, but she meant well, and had popped around unannounced bearing a propitiatory meal of fish and chips for three.

It seems Mum may not have been aware of how Renée earned a crust, but in any event, she was not brought into the problem. There was nothing for it but for Renée and Neville to sit around the table with Mum chewing the fat, as well as their fish and chips, while Peter Plumley-Walker cooled down in the next room.

By the time Mum left it was late, apparently near midnight. Peter was by now cold and stiff, and that would surely prompt the police to ask some very awkward questions. The window of plausible deniability was now nearly closed.

In the end, they did some very stupid things. First, they decided to dispose of his body as far away from the house as possible. They hit on the Huka Falls, just outside Taupō. You could not choose a worse place to hide a body if you had thought about it for a full year.

Water is usually a bad choice, because bodies do float eventually. They are easy to see bobbing about on a flat and featureless body of water. People also go to water features for swimming and other water sports and pastimes. They have time on their hands to look around as they relax and enjoy the outdoors.

The Final Diagnosis

Added to this, Huka Falls is a place several thousand tourists visit on most days. They take boat rides below the falls as well as intensely studying and filming the boiling cauldron.

Peter's bloated corpse floated and was found a few days later, in early February.

The second unfortunate thing Renée and Neville did was tying Peter's hands together before chucking him in the 220,000-litre-per-second waterway. Bound hands were obviously going to make the police think of murder.

My involvement was peripheral, but interesting and informative. We hosted the annual conference of the Society of Pathologists in Palmerston North, and I had invited as a guest speaker my forensic pathology teacher from university days, Dr Kevin Lee. Kevin is a highly experienced and very entertaining pathologist, and he proved a great hit.

The autopsy on Peter Plumley-Walker had been carried out in Rotorua by David Taylor, and he had brought his findings along to ask for Kevin's opinion. Kevin was quite unequivocal.

'There is no evidence of drowning here at all. I think he had to be already dead when they put him in.'

David was a bit disconcerted by this. I gathered he had already told the police that the death was due to drowning.

'You can't justify that,' Kevin said. 'I certainly wouldn't support that in court.'

'What about his hands being tied behind his back?' David challenged. 'Why would they do that if he were already dead?'

It was a fair question. Kevin smiled. 'If he was already dead and had been lying there on the floor for five to six hours before they left Auckland, what would you have seen?'

Musings on murder: part I

David shook his head, puzzled. I was enjoying this, though, to be honest, I did not immediately twig onto the answer Kevin was after either.

'Think about it — he would have rigor mortis. It is very difficult to carry a body through doorways with the arms rigidly stretched out on both sides.'

It was true. Stiffening of the muscles after death, the so-called rigor mortis, is very well known by everyone in and out of pathology. It starts after death and is maximal by eight hours later, and often in less time if it is warm. We often have to use considerable force to straighten out leg and arm muscles in our patients in the mortuary before we can get them into a position where we are able to start their autopsy.

Kevin continued, 'If he had been lying there on the floor, arms outstretched in the crucified position in which he was strapped to the wall, then they would have to have forced his arms down, and they might well have tied his hands together to keep his arms tidily in place. Anyway, it's a reasonable explanation in the circumstances.'

David departed, looking very thoughtful.

For a variety of reasons, Renée and Neville went through three separate trials. They were found guilty in the first two, at which the jury accepted the murder narrative, but finally were acquitted when their story of an accidental death and a panicky reaction was finally thought to be so much more plausible.

I have always thought them innocent, too, simply because of the absolute lack of any reasonable motive. There was no robbery, no blackmail, no illicit love affair, no insurance scam and no inheritance expectations. Renée and Neville were not random serial killers preying on multiple elderly men. There were no mental health issues such as that which David Konia was suffering from.

This was just plain old tawdry sex between a willing buyer and a willing seller. He had paid good money before, had done so again on this occasion, and no doubt would return and pay again on other occasions. He would be the ideal satisfied repeat customer.

Why on God's green Earth would they want to murder a harmless if eccentric old man? It just defies any logic and reason.

Her blood is settled and her joints are stiff;
Life and these lips have long been separated:
Death lies on her like an untimely frost
Upon the sweetest flower of all the field.
— William Shakespeare, *Romeo and Juliet*,
Act IV Scene V, 1597

CHAPTER 11

Musings on murder: part II

On the night of 16 April 2020, most of us were relaxing, breathing sighs of relief that New Zealand's Covid lockdown was finally over. Not so Sandy Graham of Otautau, a small settlement in rural Southland. She had just shot her partner, Dale Watene, in the mouth and killed him, using a borrowed .22 calibre rifle.

While it was humorously quipped that many wives or partners could have murdered the man of the house after months of tedious lockdown together, Sandy said she had a clear motive. Apparently Dale had attacked her, and she feared for her life.

However, our interest in this murder is not about her motive or method, but rather Sandy's thought processes and actions around the disposal of Dale's body. Like Renée and Neville with Peter Plumley-Walker, Sandy decided not to call the police and explain the self-defensive nature of the shooting, but rather to hide Dale's body away forever. She presumably hoped that either no one would notice he had gone missing, or alternatively that they would not connect her in any way with his disappearance.

Many murderers seem to harbour this particular illusion. The scenario doesn't usually play out that way in real life, but murderers as a group seem — fortunately for the rest of us, perhaps — not to be able to learn from one another's mistakes.

Shifting a body, lugging it to a suitably remote spot and digging a grave is all hard work. Believe me, the dead weigh heavily and are very awkward to carry, not to mention the annoying rigidity of rigor mortis.

Sandy asked her good friend, a reliable and likable farm worker, George Hyde, for help. George appears to me to have been an uncomplicated soul and a pawn in this saga. It seems that Sandy exerted her feminine charms to encourage him to help her.

George agreed to help her dispose of Dale's body because, as he told the police, 'I did not want her to get into trouble for having an illegal firearm.' This is touching but suggests that perhaps George had a rather naive view of life, given that the trouble Sandy was heading for was rather more serious than a minor firearms misdemeanour.

Anyway, George and Sandy loaded Dale's body into the truck and drove off into the night to dispose of it. A month or so later, his grave was discovered in the remote Longwood Forest.

Detective Inspector Stu Harvey oversaw the investigation. He was interviewed by Blair Ensor on *Stuff*, and he tells us part of the tale:

'The Longwood Forest area is a really large block, well over 20,000 hectares. There are a number of access roads, but they are all dirt. It's a bit of a maze when you get into it and start driving around ...

Musings on murder: part II

'There are a number of roads and a number of turnoffs. There is an 800-metre very narrow track which ends in a turning bay ... You can't drive a car down it without getting it scratched and damaged ... It's not the sort of area you'd go into unless you had a specific reason ... The discovery of Dale's body there was a miracle.'

This is true. Southland is sparsely populated. Otautau is a small rural settlement 40 kilometres out of Invercargill, and the Longwood Forest is a good 20 minutes' drive beyond that, on winding, narrow roads. So why did the CIB go looking there for Dale, and why specifically down that rather unlikely dead-end road?

It reminds me of the old Irish story of a traveller who pulls up on a remote road and asks a local farm hand for directions.

'Is this the right road to Dublin that I'm travelling on here?'

'Ah,' replies the farm hand. 'If it's Dublin you wanting to go it's no use starting from here.'

Like our Irish buachaill, I would have thought it would have been of no use starting to look in the Longwood Forest if you wanted to find Dale Watene. You might have had more chance at winning that week's Lotto prize, which stood at $3.9 million.

Nor indeed would the police have ever looked there but for Sandy Graham's assistance.

Naturally, with Dale missing they went round to see what light she could throw on her missing partner. That much is standard procedure in these sort of cases.

'I last saw him in the Longwood Forest on the night of the sixteenth,' she told them. Sandy then identified the dead-end track as the place where she and Dale got stuck in their four-wheel-drive vehicle. Apparently, they were so stuck that they had to summon friends to get them free and moving again.

Detective Dougall Henderson takes up the story, again talking to Blair Ensor in the filmed *Stuff* interview, which also portrays the absolute isolation of the place.

'We were looking for an area where Dale and Sandy had got stuck in his vehicle on the last day she saw him alive. We came down the track and had a bit of a look around and it seemed pretty clear to us that they hadn't been stuck in here. But then we came to this area ...'

They had reached the turning bay right at the track's end. It all looked normal, but just off the track there was a curious sight. There was an area decorated with a scattering of bricks and builders' rubble, bits of metal flashing, a drum and an old car tyre.

What was this doing there? Fly-tipping is a problem in many parts of the world, but it is drawing a long bow to imagine that someone drove all the way out there to dump a rather meagre pile of building waste by the side of this track.

The rubbish marked the site of a shallow grave containing Dale's body. George Hyde had dug the grave next to the turning bay that fateful night and buried Dale within. The site was so remote, it could easily have worked out to be a perfect murder, and Dale's disappearance might have remained an unsolved mystery.

I personally think it would have been better to have buried him a few metres off the track, somewhere nondescript in the middle of its 800-metre length rather than at its turning bay

Musings on murder: part II

terminus, but the choice of that position was not necessarily their fatal mistake.

Their other errors defy reason, though, and compounded together they resulted in Sandy and George being caught. Once Sandy had fingered that particular track to the police as the last place Dale had been seen alive, they were in significant danger of discovery. Why she chose to do this is unknown. She could have chosen anywhere else in Southland, but she chose there, where otherwise no one would have thought to look.

George made discovery inevitable, though, by attempting to camouflage the grave with a veneer of bricks and other odd rubbish, for without that there was nothing particular to attract attention to the site of the grave. The building waste turned out to match that lying beside his house, which was also careless.

Sandy Graham was found guilty of Dale Watene's murder and was sentenced to life imprisonment. I was glad to see George Hyde received only eight months' home detention for being an accessory and helping dispose of the body.

* * *

After almost every talk I give, I am asked, 'What do you think of the Scott Watson case?' It is a huge question.

In common with so many Kiwis, I have read most of the books and press articles and watched the documentaries on the harrowing disappearance of Olivia Hope and Ben Smart from a New Year's Eve celebration at Furneaux Lodge in the Marlborough Sounds at the end of 1997. The story of rides in water taxis, the mysterious ketch to which they were delivered and of Scott Watson and his single-masted steel yacht *Blade* is so well known that it does not need repeating here.

So much has been written and re-enacted on TV that I can visualise the whole sad saga exactly as it is said to have happened. It is now so vivid in my mind that sometimes I even feel like an actual eyewitness.

And there lies the problem. Because I wasn't even close. I have only seen those TV re-enactments.

And this leads to the problem of the reliability of eyewitness testimony and memory.

There are two major components to the Watson trial evidence that stand out to me, and they both pose a problem. The first is the eyewitness testimony on which most of the case rests, and its credibility. The second is the detection of Olivia's DNA in hairs recovered from *Blade*. This was the only bit of scientific evidence offered, and it, too, raises questions.

Journalist Ian Wishart has written extensively on this case, and he has waded through 40,000 pages of police evidence, so his views are well researched and authoritative. I have not read the gargantuan police file, as he has. Life is much too short for that. Ian's 100-plus-page summary is, however, available online and is an informative read about a highly confusing series of events.

We all have memory failures, which is why we have desk diaries and make lists of all sorts of things. I have a secret diary in which I have written all my passwords to access services from Ticketek to Trade Me, as there is no way I can remember them all. Eyewitness evidence and people's memories of events are known to be a very unreliable source of evidence. That is why circumstantial evidence is so much

Musings on murder: part II

more robust, and why CCTV has been such a significant forensic development.

There are many theories about how memory works and why folk recall things differently from the way they happened. I am convinced that memory is like a Word file on your computer. Whatever you write can be saved, but call it up again and rewrite over it, and that will become the new and authoritative version that is saved.

If this theory is correct, then when we recall a memory, we are remembering the last time we remembered it and not the original event at all. What does this mean to eyewitnesses as they are repeatedly interviewed by police, journalists, filmmakers, friends and ultimately down the years by the ubiquitous murderer support groups?

Let us have a look at examples of the crucial eyewitness accounts of two people who were at Furneaux Lodge the night Ben and Olivia disappeared.

Reg McManaway was a boatie who had spent much of the night in the bar, where he was something of a regular. He told the police about what he had seen that day.

5 January 1998, five days since the disappearance

'I saw a guy come onto the deck of [the ketch] ...

'He was a male Caucasian, about 32 to 34 years old, six feet tall, brown-coloured hair ... a bit of a beard — looked a bit scruffy.

'I didn't see him ashore and I didn't see him in the bar ...

'I can't remember specific things about the boat [ketch] — it was tied bow-on to us.'

The Final Diagnosis

11 February 1998, 42 days since the disappearance, 37 days since his first statement
'I believe I saw [Ben and Olivia] ... I did notice there was a scruffy-looking male with them. He was the same male that I described from the yacht [presumably the ketch?].

'I have been shown the identikit pictures of the two males, they don't really look like the male I saw in the bar or on the yacht ...

'I do not recall seeing the yacht [Scott Watson's Blade*] from the photos at all.'*

2003, five years after the disappearance
This video interview by Reg with investigator Mike Kalaugher highlights a very different memory.

"'... that's when I passed the Blade*," says Reg, mug of tea on the kitchen table in front of him. "—the dinghy tied up alongside him and he was pulling his anchor up. I said to Scott, 'Don't worry, I won't hit your dinghy. I'm watching it.'*

"And he was still there at half-past seven [on New Year's morning], so I don't know how they got the story that he left at four o'clock."'

Hmmm — not very consistent, is it?

Guy Wallace was working as a barman at the Furneaux Lodge party, and had also driven the inflatable water taxi, called a Naiad, in which Ben and Olivia and the alleged murderer were carried to the mystery ketch. He was the most significant of the eyewitnesses, as it was his recollection that was the origin of the ketch in the narrative.

Below Guy describes the ketch to which he had delivered the three passengers.

Musings on murder: part II

January 1998, initial statements to police
'... what is surprising about this particular [boat] is the middle is not far out of the water ... there would be a lot of water coming aboard ... what they call a "wet" boat.

'When they stepped off from the Naiad it wasn't very far ... there was no strain at all.'

He would later go on to tell the Court: *'I am pretty vague about it. I actually couldn't be sure. A photographic memory would be nice to have.'*

2003, five years after the disappearance
Guy appears in the dramatised documentary Doubt: The Scott Watson Case. *He stands in the* Naiad, *his hand high above his head, holding on to the deck of what he calls a 'high-sided ketch', and describes this as exactly the type of high-sided boat on which he dropped Ben and Olivia.*

The low-slung 'wet' boat of January 1998 has evidently sailed out of his memory and into history. By 2003 I think Guy was reworking old memories, plausibly helped by seeing endless television footage related to the case.

There are other glaring examples of inconsistent eyewitness testimony in this case, but I am not at all critical of any of these witnesses. They are honest people and I have no doubt they are telling the truth as they recall it. They are certainly not lying to cover up a heinous crime.

But these examples do reflect the frailty of the human brain and its unreliable recall systems. We have all inherited them; they are what we have to work with and we must make do with them the best we can. The effect that the media and their numerous dramatisations have had on our collective memories must also influence their memories and make any retrial a real problem.

Neil deGrasse Tyson, in his brilliant book *Starry Messenger*, tells of how he was rejected for jury service in New York. The only evidence to be heard in this case was that of one solitary eyewitness, and pre-trial the judge questioned the prospective jurors on whether anyone would have a problem with that limited testimony. Tyson held up his hand and pointed out that eyewitness evidence was notoriously unreliable and by itself could surely not be regarded as sufficient for a conviction.

The judge then asked the other jurors, 'Does anyone else here feel they would need to have two eyewitnesses to hear the case?', before dismissing Tyson.

That is not at all what Tyson had said to the judge, or even meant. It is a telling point that even a judge trained in law and the meaning of language cannot reliably bear accurate witness and repeat what he has heard mere seconds before.

In this the judge is no different from the thousands of other eyewitnesses who appear daily before him and his brother and sister judges. These witnesses daily feed the justice system with the flawed 'evidence' of what they honestly but erroneously believe they have seen and heard.

As Tyson perceptively says: 'No matter what eyewitness testimony is in the court of law, it is the lowest form of evidence in the court of science.'

* * *

The psychology of transient and changing memory is an interesting topic, though rather removed from the pure

Musings on murder: part II

science of pathology. The DNA analysis of two long blonde hairs found amongst several hundred other short, dark hairs laboriously collected off an ornate tiger-motif blanket taken from on board *Blade* does, however, sit right in my bailiwick.

I have trouble with the statement about these blonde hairs having come from Olivia, her sister or her mother, which is a very odd way of presenting DNA evidence in my experience. There are other concerns about the ESR handling of the bag containing the hairs, and a thesis about possible contamination through a small cut in the bag which cloud that issue. I am not going to enter that particular fray.

It is the result of the DNA analysis on those hairs and its interpretation that interests me. The UK lab that did the workup evidently did not find Olivia's DNA profile in the cellular tissue attached to the hair shaft but did find some maternal DNA.

We all carry the unique DNA code for our genes in the nuclei of all our cells, and that is what makes us be us. It is also what forensic matches are generally about. This nuclear DNA is a mixed bag that we have inherited in roughly equal measures from our mums and dads.

Inside these cells there are also thousands of mitochondria, which are little energy packets. These are the batteries driving the business of living. They are different to nuclear DNA because they contain only DNA we got from our mothers. She got hers from her mum, who got it from her mum, and so on in a pure line down through the ages. It's not limited to girls; mums pass it on to both their sons and daughters equally. Of course, your dad is different, as he has only his own mum's DNA in his mitochondria.

The Final Diagnosis

The story of these mitochondria was told in a semi-fictional but easily followed book by Professor Brian Sykes called *The Seven Daughters of Eve*. There are seven (now possibly eight) ancestral women from whom virtually all people of European heritage are descended. Sykes gave each 'daughter' a name and a story to make them seem more real. There was Ursula from Greece, Tara from Ireland, as well as Helena, Xenia, Velda, Katrine and Jasmine.

I have had my DNA profiled and my ancestral mother is Jasmine. Jasmine, whom the scientists call by the unlovely name of Haplotype J, came into Europe 10,000 years ago from the area now known as Syria. About 17 per cent of both male and female Europeans share descent from Jasmine through their mothers. The other daughters cover different percentages such as Helena (40 per cent) and Ursula (11 per cent), so the seven or eight women cover every person of European descent alive.

I do not know which 'daughter of Eve' or haplotype Olivia Hope, her mother and sister were descended from. If it was Jasmine for instance, like me, then the matching long blonde hairs they found on the blanket could equally be mine, or come from about 17 per cent of all men and women of European ancestry. If it was Helena, then it would be even higher.

It is a match of sorts, but from the perspective of my armchair sleuthing it does not seem a particularly compelling one.

I do not know who killed Ben Smart and Olivia Hope and I cannot say to what, if any, degree of certainty it was or was not Scott Watson. The whole Sounds murders narrative is complex, confusing and completely contaminated by endless speculation. Readers will have to make up their own minds.

Musings on murder: part II

The unreliability and inconsistency of eyewitness testimony is hardly news and has been well known for decades. CCTV would have rapidly sorted out this mystery but it was not available back in 1998. DNA was available, but it is not a magic bullet, and needs expert interpretation to make sure of what it is telling us.

* * *

The Sounds mystery does not suggest any helpful components for carrying out a perfect murder, but it does show that even without a body, or even particularly compelling evidence, you might still be found guilty by your peers. Not so the sad murder of Marice McGregor.

Marice was a lovely, gentle, 45-year-old woman from a salt-of-the-Earth Kiwi farming background. Her parents were dead and had left her well provided for. She was rather shy socially and, anyway, it is not easy for a woman alone to go out to bars and clubs to meet and make friends. As has become quite conventional these days, Marice went online to meet men, and with some success.

Then she met Dean Mulligan on a dating site. Dean was a 43-year-old computer technician from Feilding. He lived there with his wife and two children, though he told Marice he was single, as one apparently does in these liaisons. She was told they could not meet up at his place because he had a female flatmate who was a bit of a virago and would freak out.

Dean had lost a leg but was perfectly mobile with his prosthesis. They became close. Marice had squirrelled away savings of $70,000 from her inheritance, but unfortunately

Dean got wind of it. Soon $51,000 had been withdrawn, which was quite out of character for the careful Marice.

Marice then disappeared and was reported to the police as missing by her brothers. The brothers in turn had been told that she was missing by none other than Dean. So, he seemed to be the first to know. But the trail was dry and for some time, while the police ground away in the background, there was no news of her at all.

It did not take them too long to open her computer, find the dating sites and get a list of men she had met in this way. Dean's name figured as the most recent, and it turned out that at least $20,000 of the recent cash withdrawals were directly traceable to him. The police decided to have a word with Dean and ask a few awkward questions.

Dean was quite forthcoming, which is not surprising. Denial would have looked very suspicious, and the stark facts were against him. In a homicide investigation, if the perpetrator tells a story that is so close to the truth that any investigation will not find any discrepancy, then the chances of getting away with the perfect murder are much improved. That is what happened with the 'accidental' gunshot that killed my relative, and it worked well in that case.

'Yes,' Dean confirmed, 'I met Katrina online.' Katrina was the name Marice had used for her dating persona. 'She did give me some money to help me set up a business. That's about it.'

No, Dean had not seen her recently. No, he had no idea where she had gone or might be.

There were emails from her, asking for repayment of her money. He freely acknowledged the loans and said he was

Musings on murder: part II

willing to repay her. In short, there were no contentious issues between them.

No body, plenty of motive — but where was she? Could she have headed off somewhere for a break and just not told anyone? It would be quite unusual for Marice and seemed unlikely.

Who knows how the investigation would have progressed if that was all the police had to go on. But Dean was now a person of interest, and big ears were listening. One evening Dean was enjoying some beers and having a yarn in his favourite watering hole with some mates and casual drop-ins.

'If you had to hide a body, where would you do it?' someone asked.

'I know a place,' Dean rushed to answer the question. 'About fifty ks up the road to New Plymouth there's a place called Whiskey Bend. Just past there is a place hidden away by the roadside. There's this ravine and a waterfall. No one knows it's there. It's the perfect place to hide a body.'

The police were soon on their way to check out Whiskey Bend. In the old days, a lorry carrying crates of whisky overturned here, and the local farmers were able to score a generous harvest of unbroken bottles for themselves.

Marice's body lay beside the secret waterfall, down the ravine and next to the road, exactly as described in the bar by Dean. She was dead from three blows to the head with an iron bar. A few hours before he murdered Marice, Dean had made several internet searches for 'hard hit to the head'.

It was all over. Dean confessed.

It is not relevant to my story, but it is interesting that Dean later withdrew his confession, removed his prosthesis and moved into a wheelchair, appearing for the purposes of the trial as a particularly weak and disabled invalid. It was not him, he told the court, but another man, and possibly even two men, who murdered her there over a cannabis sale gone wrong. He, too, was a victim, he claimed, for they had raped him as a warning. He was unable to identify the man, or possibly two men, involved. The jury had no trouble finding Dean Mulligan guilty of murder.

Silence is a source of great strength. Keep your mouth shut.

This is a good rule in life generally, but I would suggest doubly so if your intention is to carry out the perfect murder. Dean Mulligan did a poor job of concealing his tracks and getting caught was simply a matter of time, not chance.

His big mouth made it an inevitability.

* * *

Mark Lundy, like Scott Watson, fronts a murder that seems to have become part of the Kiwi psyche, and I get asked for my opinion on the story over and over. The Lundy murders still engage us, and there are frequent refresher episodes with various appeals to the courts, the Parole Board, the Royal Prerogative of Mercy and now the Criminal Cases Review Commission.

The basic components of the murder have been told many times over the years. Kitchen fittings salesman Mark Lundy clandestinely returned to Palmerston North from an overnight business trip to Lower Hutt and murdered his wife, Christine, and daughter, Amber. I have written about the internal lab-based intricacies of how we reached our evidential conclusions in my first book, *The Cause of Death*.

Musings on murder: part II

I will not revisit that all again, but it is interesting to look at the major mistakes that Lundy made that ultimately undid a plan he designed to be a perfect murder. There is a welter of confusing background evidence, from psychics to petrol pilfering, but the main circumstantial problems to consider are the staged break-in and robbery, the choice of the murder weapon, the late-night call-girl alibi, and finally the brain-matter contamination of his shirt. It was certainly nowhere near a perfect murder in any sense.

The penniless Mark Lundy had unwisely entered into an unconditional agreement to buy a Hawke's Bay vineyard, and the Crown's proffered motive for the murders was a $200,000 insurance policy on Christine's life. Evidence was left at the scene suggesting an alternative 'motive' of a common thief breaking in and swiping a clown-shaped wooden jewellery box. This is not a particularly compelling motive. Jewel thieves are not common in Palmerston North anyway, and the suburb and the Lundy home would not have been a particularly lucrative target. It is hard for us to comprehend a robber was prepared to commit a brutal double-murder of a mother and her child for a few simple, low-value pieces.

The window that was jimmied to suggest the conventional break-in had Christine's blood smeared on the *outside* of the frame, and that is impossible to explain unless the break-in was staged after her murder. The motive and break-in scene together just do not add up to a reasonable proposition.

The pathologists collected multiple orange and blue flecks of paint from within both Christine's and Amber's head injuries, and it is clear these came from the murder weapon. The flecks were of the same colour and chemical type of paint as that with which all of Mark Lundy's tools were painted. Mark had been a builder in an earlier career and had painted his tools to avoid confusion in the workplace.

Although it is certain an axe was the murder weapon, no axe was ever found amongst Mark's tools on the premises. This evidence is not in the 'gotcha' category, but a break-in by a random jewel-thief-cum-axe-murderer who happened to have an axe decorated with precisely the same paint as all of Mark's tools begins to sound like long odds indeed.

A careful thinker will find a puzzle, too, in Lundy's prostitute alibi. It is not a particularly robust one when examined in the cold light of 2024. Unless a call girl is hired for the entire night, then the alibi only works for the one to one-and-a-half hours that the working girls usually provide. 'Belinda' was with Mark from a quarter to twelve to twenty-three minutes to one, a total of fifty-two minutes. As Lord Hughes observed in the open interrogation in the Privy Council, the precise timing was never critical to the Crown's case. If the murder did not take place before the liaison, there would surely be ample time afterwards.

Mark Lundy must have known this, so why did he even choose the call girl as an alibi? He could never have predicted that Christine and Amber were to buy a McDonald's meal, that the timing of their murders would come to rely on the controversial pathological gastric-emptying clock, and that the prostitute alibi would become a crucial marker of time in his first trial. Or was it not even an alibi — was he just indulging himself, as he admitted he had on earlier occasions?

A McDonald's meal was bought by Christine at 5.38 p.m. on the evening of her and Amber's murders. Full stomachs containing the remnants of an undigested meal were discovered in both victims at autopsy. This was interpreted

Musings on murder: part II

to mean that the murders were committed an hour or so after the hamburger purchase. That timing had in turn meant that Mark would have had to make an infamously fast trip from Petone to Palmerston — a reasonable distance of some 134 kilometres, and at a busy time of evening.

The time needed to drive back home and execute a double-murder was barely doable with Lundy's call-girl alibi, so this was a rich field to exploit from a legal-defence perspective.

We heard long arguments about this in the Privy Council. I thought they were going nowhere, when Lord Hughes asked Cameron Mander, the Crown solicitor: 'Why is the Crown so concerned about proving when the murder was carried out? Surely the Crown has only to prove who carried it out and not when it was done?'

Lord Hughes of Ombersley had been vice-president of the criminal division of the Court of Appeal, so I reckon he knew his way around a murder or two. His were words of wisdom, and that is precisely the position the prosecution took in the retrial.

A firm 7 to 7.15 p.m. slot for the murders was chosen to account for the full stomachs in the first trial. In the retrial, this became some unidentifiable time between just before 7 p.m., when Christine was last on the phone to a friend, and 8.30 a.m. the next morning, when the mother's and daughter's bodies were first found.

This was a sensible approach, for the facts are that a review of the original stomach contents rules out McDonald's being the final meal prior to death. The photographs of these contents show a mixture of long, thick, straight fries, as well as very distinctive commercially available crinkle-cut potato chips. There is not a single shoestring fry or other portion of food to suggest the passage of a Macca's meal. What is seen there is a very different meal, which must have been cooked and eaten later in the evening.

It is interesting to speculate that the whole series of three trials may have been quite different if the correct significance of the type of gastric contents had been properly appreciated back in 2003, and no specific hour for the murders presented. The withdrawal of the incorrect 7 p.m. time slot in the second trial effectively rendered the call-girl alibi useless, as indeed it always had been.

* * *

The Privy Council was quite unlike the courts in which I had appeared as a witness over the years. The three Law Lords and Dame Sian Elias were presiding.

The Crown and defence counsel stood before the high judges and waxed lyrical, presenting their arguments. The fun then started, and the lords would ask the counsel questions and often make comments. This was a lively process and full of interesting content. I know most people, and the press, read only the final judgement written by one of the lords, reflecting their combined opinions, but there was much more to it than that.

For instance, at one point Dame Sian asked Cameron Mander, the Crown counsel, a question about a legal point in his presentation, and he gave her a rather good answer, I thought.

Dame Sian smiled at him. 'Isn't that a rather austere view?'

Austere. Hmm. That didn't sound like a good pass mark to my ear.

Musings on murder: part II

The inquisition and the relationship between the lords and counsel uncomfortably reminded me of the viva voce examinations we had suffered when studying anatomy as fledgling medical students.

'Mr Temple-Camp, would you please describe to me the medial relation of the left main bronchus?'

I could imagine Professor Whitting's steel pointer hovering above a tattered grey organ tucked in the dissected mediastinum of a dismembered cadaver in the Anatomy Department dissecting hall. And rather like the Chief Justice, he might well reward my laboured attempt with a raised eyebrow and a polite but terrifying reply.

'Isn't that a rather austere answer?'

I sat enthralled through the three-day Privy Council hearing in London. It was slow, but it was like a Netflix serial that you have got hooked into. You just sit there willing the next episode to come, to see what happens next.

The evidence of the two flecks of brain tissue found on Lundy's shirt was inevitably the centrepiece of all three trials, and ultimately was the critical evidence that Mark Lundy had to explain. We had been rather rocked when two Oxford University pathologists, Professor Kevin Gatter and Dr Waney Squier, had produced a report saying that the tissue present could not be identified as brain, though they did say that 'meat product containing animal brain (e.g. sausages, or hamburger) would also be consistent with the result observed'.

I took this to mean that the tissue did in fact *look* like brain, since animal and human brain tissues are microscopically identical. But their view was certainly a big surprise to all the pathologists involved in the first trial.

The Final Diagnosis

It was during this verbal give-and-take between the learned legal beagles that Lord Hughes made a comment that I thought got to the real root of the matter. His take on all this flimflam was succinct: 'The experts on both sides disagree. Do you really expect us to choose who is right? The experts for both Crown and defence need to be together in one laboratory and reach an agreement.'

These were again words of wisdom from Lord Hughes, and that is exactly what was done in the 2015 retrial of Mark Lundy. The experts representing both Crown and Lundy were Professor Colin Smith of Edinburgh and Dr Daniel du Plessis of Southampton. They examined the original slides we had worked upon, repeated the tests we had done, and added other tests such as those showing there were blood vessels within the tissue and looking at cellular structures under very high power using an electron microscope.

The two experts were in complete agreement, and in a memorable paragraph in his affidavit to the second Lundy trial, Dr Du Plessis said: 'The appearances of these samples can only be explained by it being brain tissue with no reasonable possibility that any other tissue might share similar varied and highly specific features. To still insist that this [the tissue not being brain] remains a reasonable prospect is the biological equivalent and of the same credibility as medieval alchemy.'

Daniel du Plessis presented these findings at the Royal College of Pathologists in Sydney in 2023, and his views remain as strong today as back in 2015.

This was professionally pleasing, but I am a scientist at heart, and I was troubled by how and why two Oxford academics could reach such vastly different conclusions on

Musings on murder: part II

the same material I had seen in provincial Palmerston North. After all, a crucial basis of our pathology profession is that there is substantial agreement between different observers in what we are seeing before we reach a diagnosis.

I decided to find out more, and I was surprised by what I discovered. The late Kevin Gatter was not actually a forensic or a neuro- or anatomical pathologist at all. He was a haematopathologist, a specialist in diseases of the blood, and no doubt was an eminent expert in that field. But brain tissue? In a murder case? He was surely pulling a long bow in having any opinion at all in this case.

Dr Waney Squier was different, as she had been practising as a forensic neuropathologist, but it transpired that she had had a troubled career in recent times. Dr Squier very publicly fell afoul of the British General Medical Council and in a judgement of the High Court of England in November 2016, it was found she had committed serious professional misconduct and was barred from giving evidence in court for three years.

I dropped my plans to contact her for an explanation of their report, as I thought she must be living in a difficult space, professionally speaking. I guess it is true that there is 'nowt so queer as folk', as the old North Country saying has it, meaning that indeed sometimes there just may be no rhyme or reason as to why people do or say things. And I don't mean only murderers — pathologists qualify, too.

* * *

Mark Lundy was again found guilty of the murder of his wife and child in his retrial, and was returned to prison to serve out his sentence.

The Final Diagnosis

The appeal from the 2015 trial to the Appeal and Supreme courts failed. I was interested to read that the primary ground of appeal was that scientific evidence relied on to link Lundy to the murders should not have been admitted. This concerned the presence of messenger RNA of human origin in the tissue, and was no longer focused on whether there was brain tissue on the shirt and whether the scientific techniques used to prove it were experimental. That at least had been laid to rest with the Du Plessis and Smith evidence, though I know the Lundy support group remain quite unconvinced, even today.

The appeal was that the scientific evidence should be dismissed as being too complicated to understand, and this rather jarred. Juries are smart. They have 700-plus years of collective life experience. We all live in a science-based society with remote controls, microwaves, computers and aeroplanes. We understand science, and while we may not know exactly how it works, we know it does. And it can be explained simply so we can follow it. It is not witchcraft, after all.

Christine's DNA was found in both flecks of tissue on Lundy's shirt. It was reported that the odds were one billion billion times to one more likely that the DNA was from Christine Lundy than from someone else unrelated to her, chosen at random from the New Zealand population.

This is a massive boost to the case against Lundy, and the statistical level of certainty shows how reliable DNA matching can be. These numbers are in stark contrast to those produced linking the blonde hairs from *Blade* to Olivia Hope.

The DNA belonged to Christine. The Oxford pathologists first brought up the idea of sausages and hamburgers as a

Musings on murder: part II

source of animal brain tissue, and that story gained some traction, as I still get asked about it from time to time. But Mark Lundy would have to be the unluckiest man in history to have got an accidental contamination with animal brain tissue from a hamburger, and then for that tissue also to contain DNA indistinguishable from his wife's.

All I can say is the DNA on his shirt is human and was of good quality. The tissue was brain, as the international experts have established, and I can say it was uncooked through microscopic histological examination. I see cooked meat and other foods histologically in my daily work, so I am confident of that.

How is that, you may ask? Where do pathologists see cooked food?

Patients having colonoscopies and gastropathies are supposed to undergo meticulous bowel preparation to purge all the food and faeces inside, to give the doctor a clear view. Those of us who have had a 'bowel prep' done will have sat up on the toilet all night as the purging laxative you are given charges through your gut, doing a washout. This has to be experienced to be believed. Even so, quite often fragments of cooked food remain stuck to the biopsies taken by the endoscopists along the way.

I often point out the muscle fibres of meat, as well as distinctive plant cells with their thick walls and multi-coloured contents. The effects of cooking are very obvious in the coagulative changes to the tissues. So I can say with authority that the brain tissue on the Lundy shirt had emphatically never been cooked.

It was science applied to the two deposits of brain tissue on Mark Lundy's shirt that put paid to his plans of getting away with murder. Lundy realistically could never have predicted and therefore planned for this accidental minute but unequivocal soiling of his shirt. That was his most significant mistake.

The perfect murder does exist, though by definition we will be unaware of it even if we are closely involved. Fortunately, I believe the police and other authorities are very skilled at recognising suspicious deaths. Pathologists and forensic scientists are good at their jobs, too, and nowadays CCTV coverage and the relatively easy detection of even minute amounts of DNA mean that the odds are you will be caught.

Better perhaps to take advice from the famous American lawyer Clarence Darrow: just sit back and wait, and watch Nature take your proposed victim for you in her own good time.

> *I have never killed a man, but I have read many obituaries with great pleasure.*
> — Clarence Darrow, *The Story of my Life*, 1932

CHAPTER 12

My age is against me

'I really don't see any point in doing this autopsy.' I was struggling to stay calm and use logic and reason to win this discussion. It was not going well.

'I can understand why you think that.' The urbane voice of the coroner floated out of the phone pressed against my ear. A registrar sat beside me, with nearly 20 diagnoses for me to check and hopefully to teach on. Another pile of slide trays stood accusingly beside my microscope. These were my cases to be worked up that morning. I also had a surgical meeting to prepare for that afternoon.

And now, to top off a hectic day, the coroner wanted me to do an autopsy, and I was not sure how I was going to fit everything in.

'She is nearly a hundred and one years old,' I pointed out. 'At her age I will find a multiplicity of things that might have caused her death. She is bound to have advanced coronary artery disease and senile emphysema of her lungs, cerebral atrophy and God knows what else. It'll be anyone's guess which one was responsible. "You pays your money and you takes your choice", as Mark Twain put it.'

The Final Diagnosis

'That quite probably will be the case, doctor, but I would feel much happier if we were able to assign a more precise cause of death, for the sake of the relatives.'

I made one last attempt. 'I understand that the lady's death is not at all suspicious. I understand she passed away in a rest home.'

'Yes, you are correct. She was in a rest home but living independently there in an apartment. The staff found her dead in bed when they went to check on her at eight-fifteen this morning. By all accounts she passed peacefully in her sleep.'

'Not a bad way to go, and a pretty good innings for her.' I had known all along that I would end up doing the autopsy, and despite the other calls on my time, I found myself looking forward to it with some interest. I had never done an autopsy on such an old patient before.

'Come on!' I said to the registrar. 'Put the colon biopsies away. We've got an unusual autopsy to do.'

'A murder? A suspicious death?' he asked hopefully.

I shook my head, smiling. The youngsters were always hot for the gore, though it was the unusual but natural deaths that taught the best lessons.

'A 101-year-old lady dead of obscure natural causes. Our job is to un-obscure those causes.' The registrar shrugged and yawned. It must have sounded dead boring to him. I felt he would rather head off for a coffee across the road than follow me down to the mortuary.

'I have never done one on so old a person. I would think early nineties would be as old as I have come across. But I have read of one on a 154-year-old man.'

That got his interest quickly enough. 'A hundred and fifty-four years? Impossible! Where was this?'

My age is against me

'William Harvey, physician to King Charles I of England, did it back in 1636. Harvey was the bloke who first figured out that blood goes round and round the body in arteries and veins. Everyone thought he was cracked at the time. He did a pretty fair autopsy, too, so the king ordered him to do one on Thomas Parr, who was known to be a hundred and fifty-four years old.' I laughed. 'I suppose being asked by the king is a bit like the coroner asking us to do this one today. It would not be a good idea to refuse the king in those days! Anyway, I've got a copy of his original report here.' I went to my filing cabinet and, after a bit of a rummage around, found the yellowing piece of paper. 'Listen to this.' I began to read from the paper. '"The appearance of the body was well nourished, the chest was hairy, and the hair on the forearms was still black although the shins were hairless and smooth.

'"The genital organs were in good condition, the penis was neither retracted nor thin — while the testicles were large and sound — so good in fact as not to give the lie to the story commonly told of him that, after reaching his hundredth year, he was actually convicted of fornication and punished. Moreover his wife, a widow, whom he had married in his one hundred and twentieth year, in reply to questions, could not deny that he had had intercourse with her exactly as other husbands do, and had kept up the practice to within twelve years of his death."'

I looked up. 'Dr Harvey and the king seem to have had a prurient interest in Thomas's sex life. These are certainly not the sort of enquiries pathologists are expected to make of the spouses of the dead in this day and age.

'Harvey goes on: "The chest was broad and full: his lungs were not spongy but, particularly on the right side, were attached to the ribs by fibrous bands. The lungs also were considerably distended with blood as is usual in Pulmonary consumption. To this cause too I attributed the bluish colour of the face, and a little before death, a difficulty in breathing and orthopnoea. As a result, the armpits and chest remained warm long after death."'

I eyeballed the registrar. 'What do you think Dr Harvey was seeing?'

'Sounds like a double pneumonia to me. The fibrous bands are just an old pleurisy scar and not relevant to his death.'

'And what about warm armpits? That's not a sign easily recognised by pathologists today, is it? Remember Harvey was a very accurate and careful observer. He wouldn't make anything up.'

'A sign of a high temperature just before death? Don't they get temperatures of forty-plus degrees in the crisis phase of pneumonia? I would guess this would suggest Parr's body had not cooled too far by the time Harvey got there.'

I nodded approvingly. He was listening and thinking about the possible diagnosis, something we pathologists must do all the time.

I turned the page and read on. 'Harvey went on to inform King Charles of his considered opinion. "To sum up, there were clearly visible in his dead body this and other signs customarily found in those dying of suffocation. I concluded that he was suffocated, and that death was due to inability to breathe, and a similar report was given to his most Serene Majesty by all the physicians present."

'Hmm ...' I frowned and thought about this assertion. 'Harvey is mixing up the mode of death, which was suffocation, which today we would call respiratory failure, with the *cause* of death, which was pulmonary consumption or pneumonia. Otherwise, it is quite modern in format and its contents similar to our reports to the coroner. I suppose we are really doing the same process as he did when we report to the coroner, who also ultimately represents the Crown.

'Now, what else does he say?' I scanned the document to find my place. 'Here we are. "When the sternum was dissected, the cartilages were not more osseous than in other men, but were flexible and soft. The intestines were in excellent condition, fleshy and vigorous: the stomach appeared the same, but had some ring-shaped constrictions due to the fact that frequently he ate any kind of food both by day and night without any rules of diet or regular hours for meals. He was quite happy with half rancid cheese and all kinds of milk dishes, brown bread, small beer, but most usually sour milk.

'"By living frugally and roughly, and without cares, in humble circumstances, he in this way prolonged his life."

'That's it, then. What do you think? Pretty interesting for nearly four hundred years ago.'

'He had a bloody horrible diet, didn't he? His hundred and fifty-four years must have seemed like eternity, having to eat all that rotting dairy food. But surely this story is not true? I mean, a hundred and fifty-four years? That's not possible, is it?'

'No, not possible,' I agreed. 'I reckon he was probably the spitting image of his father and people got them confused, so we're actually looking at the conjoined lives of two men. But who knows?

'I wonder what King Charles made of this report. If he was looking for hints for a long life he was out of luck. He had his head chopped off a few years later, so he didn't get too far along the road of life himself.'

I put the piece of paper back in the cabinet. 'Let's go down and meet Betty Fisk, our 101-year-old. We will see if she, too, has vigorous intestines, whatever that is supposed to mean.'

* * *

Betty was lying on the gurney awaiting us. She was slight, at 55 kilograms, with a BMI of 19, so she was at the low end of the healthy range. That could have been predicted: old overweight patients are not that common.

Her skin was mottled over her shins, possibly by some vascular insufficiency, but mild as they go. Otherwise, I could see nothing unusual. I nodded to Pat.

'You can begin.'

The scalpel slipped smoothly from sternum to pubic bone in one easy cut, the skin peeling cleanly apart. There was no subcutaneous fat. We were so used to seeing significant amounts of subcutaneous fat that its absence was notable.

The abdominal wall likewise sprung open as Pat slit the thin midline tissue. At a glance the intestines were smooth, glistening and neatly coiled in the cavity.

'They look "fleshy and vigorous" to me,' I said wryly. 'Just like Thomas Parr.'

The secateurs cut through the ribs, but the usual crunching sound was absent. The cartilages were soft and uncalcified. This, too, was unusual in the elderly and once again by coincidence matched William Harvey's ancient description.

The organ pluck of lungs, heart and aorta from the thorax, and separately of the abdominal organs, were both easily executed. Often, I had seen our assistants struggle in the depths of the chest to free up the pleural scars binding the lungs to the ribs. These are common and, as in Parr's ancient autopsy, are a sign of an old pleurisy. The assistants would often come out sweating from the physical effort of the removal.

But not this time. The organs were as sweetly smooth as a newborn babe.

The autopsy was quite singular in my experience. It proceeded like an anatomy demonstration, with every organ, vessel and tube in its place and almost willingly peeling open to show their beauty. The absence of fat was as notable internally as it had been in the abdominal skin.

'Look at her coronary arteries!' I had opened the three main vessels to the heart along their length, starting in the aorta and following them to their minute endings, into which even my delicate coronary artery scissors could no longer fit. The registrar craned over to see. 'They are perfect and soft. There is not a fleck of atheroma anywhere. And look how big they are! They would be more than twice the calibre we usually see. They are like drainpipes!'

'I suppose it shows that Betty would have had no problems with her cardiac blood supply?' The registrar was interested now and, despite his earlier misgivings, was fully engrossed in our investigation.

'Certainly. I have often wondered whether the calibre of your coronary arteries is the key factor in whether or not you get significant coronary artery disease. I have quite commonly seen these big hosepipes in the elderly, while in younger people with fatal ticker jobs the coronary arteries are often small calibre and gummed up with atheroma and crunchy with calcium.'

'It makes sense. A seventy per cent block of a five-millimetre diameter artery would still let through enough blood to keep you going, but the same obstruction in a one-millimetre diameter one will kill you straight off.'

'It does seem logical, but I don't think the pathologists have sorted this one out yet. The radiologists have good arterial calibre numbers from all their angiograms, but they are usually dealing with patients with diseased arteries to start with. We need to study the sizes in all ages of people who have died from other causes.'

Betty's heart was petite, at 279 grams, and was fit for purpose in every way. Her aorta was smooth and soft with none of the porridgey, sickly atheroma that so often decorates this structure today.

So it was with every organ. They were perfect. Even the lungs looked spongy and uniform, with only a few spots of carbon, from the odd wood fire no doubt. The elderly often lose the fabric of their lungs and develop age-related or senile emphysema. This is less serious than the smoking or other pulmonary disease-related emphysema but is the reason why the elderly often find themselves a tad short of breath while going up stairs.

Her brain was significant, too. I could see no sign of any age-related atrophy. This was not surprising. The Pol47 police report said that she was normally fully aware and able to care for herself without too much help. There was no suggestion of any trace of dementia.

'Well, well,' I said at the end of it all. 'This has been a surprise. There is absolutely nothing wrong with Betty at all.

My age is against me

I would classify her as being completely healthy, except for the undeniable fact that she is dead.'

'What will you tell the coroner is her cause of death, then?'

'That's difficult. We can use "frailty of old age" as an introductory one-liner, but usually they still want you to give some medical condition to back it up. It's nonsense, of course. Betty wasn't even remotely frail and was quite possibly healthier than many sixty-year-olds. There really is no medical term for dying of old age, although most folk do aspire to it, preferably in their sleep.

'I had better go and confess to the coroner that I was quite wrong.'

* * *

Aging is a complex issue, and exactly why it happens is still unknown. Betty was free of any pathology, and that is arguably why she lived so long. But that does not reveal the particular event that caused her to shut down all her normal systems that night and not any other.

Some have looked at genes, some at stress and environmental toxins. When I was a young medical student, we were told that cells can divide in two exactly 55 times, and when you reach that magic number, that's it: curtains for you. Then they found that the telomeres that tidily knot off the end of our chromosomes get shorter with each division, until they cannot be laced up anymore. That seemed to be the logical reason why there was a limit of 55 divisions built into our cells.

Now the scientists have discovered 'zombie' cells. It seems that instead of dying and disappearing, a lot of our cells become senescent with age. Like a grumpy old fella with gout, they hang around snapping and snarling, spreading their bad character and damaging everyone else. There are several possible medicines that can knock off these nuisance cells and stop them causing trouble, so maybe an anti-aging pill is on the horizon. I wouldn't hold my breath, though, for these so-called senolytic drugs, as these things are always a long time coming.

It is much more common for the elderly to die from precisely determinable reasons rather than that nebulous Xanadu of 'old age' for which we all hope. There is little doubt that old age can be seriously bad for your health. There are a horrible host of individual diseases, from dementia to dermatitis, osteoarthritis to osteoporosis, to be afflicted with, and the average 80-year-old has four or more of them.

One July evening I was returning from Wellington to Palmerston North by train. This is a convivial journey that leaves Wellington at 5 p.m. and usually arrives, after several stops, in Palmerston at 7.30 p.m. There is a buffet car, and I was sitting back with a glass of wine watching the darkened countryside flash past. I did not envy the motorists crawling along State Highway 1, dodging all those interminable orange roadwork cones.

My phone started buzzing in my pocket.

'Is that the pathologist on call?'

'I suppose I must be if you're calling me.' The wine was making me light-hearted.

'Good evening, doctor. CIB here. We have a suspicious death in Foxton we'd like you to have a look at. Are you available?'

'Good evening to you, too. Yes, although I am currently on the train up from Wellington. I only get in to Palmy about seven thirty.'

'Hold on, please. I'll give them a call and get back to you in a minute or two.'

I waited, sipping my wine contemplatively. There was nothing else I could do. The train sped on through the darkness.

'Doctor, whereabouts are you?'

'Just short of Paekakariki.'

'Excellent. Can you get off at Levin?'

'Yes, I can do that.'

'A car will meet you at Levin station and take you to the scene. It is on its way there now.'

At Levin, half a dozen of us climbed off in that desultory way folk do at their destination. A blast of icy air met us as we clambered down from the muggy carriage. A police officer stood on the platform, rubbing his hands against the cold.

'Dr Temple-Camp?'

I nodded and was soon strapped into a car beside the policeman, speeding north with heaters blasting, sirens wailing and lights flashing.

'What's the hurry?' I asked curiously. 'Surely they'll still be dead when we get there?'

The policeman smiled. 'The CIB said we must come as fast as possible, so I don't need a second invitation.'

'Why? What's up?'

'They can't go inside until you have looked at the scene, and they say they are all freezing outside.' He laughed. 'They've been there an hour or two already!'

The Final Diagnosis

We made good time and soon pulled up outside a small, nondescript but tidy-looking house. The lights were blazing within, though all was in darkness around. Parked in front was an unmarked police car. Its engine was running, and two officers were draped over the bonnet. They stood up as I got out of the car.

'Good evening,' I said. 'What on Earth are you doing?'

'We're trying to keep warm on the bonnet.' Apparently, the heaters inside their car did not work, but they would not go into the house for fear of contaminating the scene.

'What's happened here?'

'A 76-year-old widow, Evelyn Revell, lives here alone.' The officer's teeth were chattering. I could feel mine weren't too far off doing the same. 'The neighbour called and said she had popped around and Evelyn was dead, with blood everywhere. We turned the lights on inside. There's no evidence of a forced entry. That's about the sum of it.'

'Any medical history?'

The detective shrugged. 'Don't know of any. There isn't a GP in Foxton at the moment. That's a problem, too. Can you sign a life extinct certificate for us? We don't want to have to get the police surgeon, Jack Drummond, all the way over from Palmy.'

Evelyn's body lay on the kitchen floor. Her head was stuck to the floor in a pool of clotted blood. Dried blood was caked over both of her hands as well as smeared around her mouth.

She wore a heavy tartan skirt, and a blouse with an unbuttoned cardigan. There were red stains on the blouse, and suspicious dark patches spread across the cardigan and stained the pattern on the skirt. From this scene it was obvious there must be blood elsewhere in the house, I decided. I was right.

It was all in the bathroom. The floor was awash with watery blood, in which lay clumps of darker purple and black clots.

'She's lost most of her blood on the floor in here,' I said to the detectives. The bath had been run and enough blood was in there to make the water a light rose colour. There was no blood splatter flung higher than the floor, so a vigorous attack and a struggle were improbable. I opened the medicine cabinet.

There was a chaotic plethora of pills, no different from most such bathroom cabinets, including mine. I spotted celecoxib and ibuprofen and methotrexate, amongst others. She must have had arthritis, I thought.

I examined Evelyn's body as best I could, as she was on the floor and fully clothed.

'There are no evident injuries, and nothing that I have seen looks suspicious to me,' I told the CIB men and my personal policeman-chauffeur, who had joined us inside. 'This looks like a haematemesis or vomiting of blood. I am reasonably sure her death is natural.'

There was a palpable air of relief. We could all go home. No one wanted to investigate a homicide on that cold night.

I was driven back to Palmerston North by the policeman, albeit at a suitably sedate speed.

* * *

Evelyn was my first patient the next morning.

'I think she has had a gut bleed,' I told Pat as he started his evisceration.

I was right. As the abdominal wall was retracted, the stomach bulged into view, blue and distended with blood.

I laid her organs on the dissecting table face down and opened her oesophagus from larynx down to stomach. A large coagulum of blood flopped out of the stomach as I opened the organ along its curved edge. I swabbed the mucosa clean with a damp sponge.

A small gastric ulcer was present just next to the entrance into the duodenum. It may have been small, but it was lethal enough, with the wall of a large artery buried in its sloughy base. The inflammation of the ulcer had eaten away at the coating of the vessel until the blood pressure within burst through the weakened patch, and a cascade of blood hosed uncontrollably into her stomach.

'It must have eroded as she was running her bath. Her stomach would have distended quickly and whoops, up it all came. What a terrifying thing that would have been for her. Evelyn then ran to the kitchen, probably to phone for help. But it was already too late. Her bleed was torrential, and she would have soon fainted from blood loss and then died quickly of haemorrhagic shock.'

Pat shook his head sadly. 'Not much chance, then?'

I agreed. 'It must be one of the worst ways to go. All alone and your blood hosing everywhere in front of your eyes. I suppose it's a bit of a blessing that at least it was quick.'

'How long do you think she had it? Why didn't she have warning symptoms?' the registrar asked.

'It's a longstanding ulcer. You can feel the thick scarring that's grown up around the ulcer crater.' I was gently squeezing the wall of her stomach and could feel the hard edge of her healing fibrosis. 'Here, palpate it yourself.' I handed the sheet of tissue, opened like a wet flannel, to the registrar. Diagnosis in autopsies is as much about feeling as looking for disease.

'Mrs Revell suffered from rheumatoid arthritis.' My eyes went automatically to her gnarled knuckles and swollen joints. 'She took a variety of medicines and quite a few NSAIDs to damp down her pain. They are probably the cause of her ulcer, but Evelyn needed the pain relief from her joints, so it's a balance between treating the problem and avoiding the side effects of the treatment. That's the rub with so many of the medicines we all take.'

Two very different deaths: one unexplained in advanced old age, and one horrifically explicable but in one not quite as old.

We all must die of something, and do not have much choice over what is to be our personal cause of death. There can be no doubt which of these two would be preferable for me if I had a choice.

A man who reviews the old so as to find out the new is qualified to teach others.
— Confucius, *Analects* 2:4

* * *

'Good morning. Is that Mr Charles Chadwick? It's Dr Temple-Camp from the lab here.' There was a pause. 'Are you there?'

I sighed and repeated myself, but much more loudly. I was used to my patients being a little hard of hearing.

'Yes, yes. I can hear you. What's the matter?'

'I am phoning about your blood test and your next dose of warfarin.'

'Oh yes?'

Most of the living patients I talk to directly are elderly, and I really enjoy the banter while treating them.

Hold on! I hear you say. *How does a pathologist have live patients to talk to? I thought your patients were all cold as stone on that steel table downstairs.*

While that is true of most pathologists, I am lucky to also be part of a daily roster for helping patients find the precise dose of rat poison they need to keep their blood from clotting. Each day of the week, hundreds of patients haul themselves along to our venesection centres to have a blood test to help us get their dose of warfarin just right. They come from early in the morning, often travelling great distances, hours and hours return from Pongaroa and Eketahuna and Hunterville and Tangimoana, and everywhere in between.

What's this dosing all about?

Warfarin is a great poison invented for killing rats. But by happy chance it also happens to be brilliant at stopping strokes in patients with atrial fibrillation, and pulmonary embolism in those with deep vein thrombosis. It is so good that hundreds of thousands of lives have been saved by it, and they say that nearly one person in ten over the age of 80 is now on it.

Some days, as I labour through dozens of patients, it feels like there must be a lot more people than that. The good thing is, though, that give or take a few big bleeds in an unlucky few, most people have no side effects from this brilliant drug.

They say some get black hairy tongues, some lose a bit of hair and others feel the cold quite badly, but I have never come across anyone who has said any of these things has happened to them. Most of these patients are elderly and they come from a resilient generation not much given to complaining, so maybe they just keep schtum about their minor afflictions.

Our problem is that there is no one-size-fits-all warfarin dose, as everyone's blood is different. Each individual's dose can and often does change frequently. It depends on how much you drink, whether you are eating a lot of broccoli or spinach, and just about everything else you might eat or do. My job is to check how 'thin' your blood is and change the amount you take so that we hit the Goldilocks spot: the dose that is not too much and not too little but is just right for you.

Humans are much trickier to treat than the rat, whose dose is easy. With rats you have only to give the little bastards 'a whole heap' to chew on and they will conveniently chomp away and then head off to bleed to death somewhere else, hopefully a good distance away. But we can't have our patients bleeding out like rodents on our watch, so the lab endlessly gets them back to collect repeated blood samples to make sure their blood has not become too thin.

That is why I was on the phone to Charles Chadwick.

'I am a bit puzzled at what we have here,' I explained. 'According to the form, you are taking five milligrams of warfarin each day. Is that correct?'

'Yes, doctor. Five milligrams each morning, before breakfast,' Mr Chadwick confirmed.

He had passed my first test. Charles was cognitive, competent and alert.

Most of the snafus we come across are because our patient is confused. Sometimes it is the forgetfulness of old age, but more often it is because of the 'polypharmacy' to which almost every older person in the developed world is subject. It seems the elderly today take piles of pills of every shape, size, colour and hue. Each 15-minute appointment with an overwhelmed, harassed, time-poor GP can easily add yet another one to the mix. Only rarely, it seems, is one stopped.

So, we all get confused and mix up doses and days and duration. How could we not? But your warfarin dose is very sensitive, especially when new pills are added.

'It says here that I am to advise you of your ongoing dose today, Mr Chadwick,' I went on. 'Also, that the lab service is advising you what dose to take. Are you quite sure your GP or someone else isn't dosing you?'

'That's correct, doctor. You have been doing it.' My elderly patients are all so very polite. That seems to be a generational thing.

'And it says here you have been taking warfarin for years?'

That too was confirmed.

'The problem, Mr Chadwick, is that we have never seen or heard of you before. You have never had a clotting blood test before to check how thin your blood is, and we have never suggested a dose to you before. Also, you have never had a warfarin prescription from any pharmacy hereabouts either. How do you explain that?'

There was a silence.

'Mr Chadwick. Your blood result is 3.1. That means your blood is more than three times thinner than normal blood from a clotting point of view, so you are certainly taking warfarin. Where are you getting it from? Who is dosing you?'

'It's my wife's warfarin, Doctor.'

My age is against me

It was my turn for silence as I thought about this.

'Your wife's? How do you mean?'

'We got mixed up. We both had prescriptions to pick up last month on the same day. We got them mixed up.'

I was flabbergasted. 'How did you do that?'

'The chemist puts them into blister packs for us, because we are both on so many medications it is hard to keep a track of what to take and when. He makes us both one, but we've been using each other's packs.'

'When did you discover this? How long have you been doing this?'

'We found out two weeks ago.'

'So you stopped taking your wife's medicine a fortnight ago, then?'

'No, doctor. We decided we should just continue with each other's pills because you had told Milly to come in for her blood test today. We thought it best to continue as we were, so I could take the test for her instead.'

I burst out laughing — I just couldn't help it. This was priceless. It was so naively well-meaning and so ridiculous that it ignited my sense of humour. Yet it seemed to have had no bad effects, for both Charles and Milly were apparently quite well on each other's medicines.

'Well, it's not usually recommended to swap medicines with anyone else. I think you both need to get back onto your usual pills and we'll take it from there. Oh, and let your doctor know as soon as you can. He will want to have a think about all this, too.'

Many of the elderly rely on their spouses to keep the clock ticking and get their pills in the right time and sequence. Usually this works well, until it doesn't, as the Chadwicks found out. These days we text the warfarin dose to the patient's phone and that works really well for everyone.

In the pre–cell phone days we relied on the landline, and that could be a problem. Late one night we had to send the police and an ambulance to a remote farmhouse way beyond Dannevirke to rush the wife to hospital as her blood test showed she had an international normalised ratio (INR) of 13. That meant her blood was thirteen times thinner than normal, and she was in clear and present danger of joining the rodents in a sudden massive and terminal bleed.

She and her husband had taken their phone off the hook as they did not want to be disturbed while they watched a movie on television. The police later gave them quite a well-deserved bollocking.

The most poignantly difficult dose we had to telephone through was to an elderly couple who lived out Feilding way. The husband was on warfarin because he had suffered a few strokes. He was quite hard of hearing. His wife was a lovely lady who had sadly lost both arms. Together they got by fine in life, however, supporting each other in all the necessaries.

He could hold the phone but couldn't hear, and his wife could not hold the receiver. They got around this by him holding the phone to his wife's ear for her to hear his INR level, the new warfarin dose and when we wanted him to come back for a retest. She would shout this information to him as we gave it.

There were two problems. He could not remember what she said for more than a few seconds, so had to write it down. To do this he had to put the phone down. Added to this, he could not hear her clearly, so everything had to be shouted repeatedly to him. The operation needed much juggling of

My age is against me

phone and pen for us to be successful. Then there were the times that his ballpoint pen would not work properly …

They were a lovely couple, and I was saddened when he died, and our weekly banter disappeared. I think it does a pathologist good to have some contact with living people and experience some of their myriad of problems.

I feel sympathy for my GP friends who tell me that the gobs of issues they daily deal with are like running a marathon through treacle. I wouldn't want too much exposure to all of that, but a little daily dose of my older patients is brilliant, just to push the questing scientist in me to one side and remind me that I, too, am growing old.

When you are old and grey and full of sleep,
And nodding by the fire, take down this book,
And slowly read, and dream of the soft look
Your eyes once had, and of their shadows deep.
— WB Yeats, 'When You Are Old', 1893

CHAPTER 13

'It looks like we've made the wrong diagnosis'

We all suffer from the tyranny of domestic chores, but some we dislike more than others. Cleaning out a soot- and grease-hardened dirty oven is one of the worst. I am very bad at cleaning up after roasting a couple of ducks; I usually just give the inside a desultory wipe with a damp cloth, though I know this is as pointless as tinkering with the chairs on the *Titanic*. I always put it off until it is really far too late to be done without an industrial level of effort.

Katharine was an active, 52-year-old receptionist, and the time to clean out her oven had come round at last. She pulled on a pair of heavy kitchen gloves to protect her hands and sprayed a commercial oven-cleaning gel over the crusty surface. This type of gel is the answer, because it contains caustic soda, which liquifies the crud and peels it away. It's great for blocked drains, too, for the same reason.

As its name suggests, caustic soda or sodium hydroxide is dangerous stuff. If even a drop gets on your skin, you can get awful chemical burns, which is why the manufacturers tell you to be careful and wear gloves while using it.

'It looks like we've made the wrong diagnosis'

'I sprayed on the cleaner, then I stepped back from the open oven,' Katharine told us, 'but the bloody dog was lying there. She must have come into the kitchen to see if I was doing something with food, and she just flopped down there behind me. I got such a fright that I became unbalanced and threw myself to one side. My right arm went through the open oven door and grazed the wall. Mostly the cleaner went on my glove, but I think there was a bit that went on my forearm.'

'Did you graze or break the skin at all?'

Katharine shook her head emphatically. 'Definitely not. There was nothing to see, so I just ignored it. It was only later, about four hours later, that I noticed there was a patch of skin that had gone black.'

She did not have any pain, however, and it was four days later when Katharine finally went to see her doctor. By then it was a shallow ulcer.

He was reassuring. 'You've got some infection in the wound. I've taken a swab to see what we grow, and I'll give you a script for an antibiotic. Are you OK for painkillers?'

The microbiologists grew nothing from the swab of pus from the wound — no staphylococci or streptococci or any other of the suspects from the multitude of bugs that swarm all around, looking for their opportunity to get into us and breed. Katharine stoically bore the pustular emblem of her brush with the cleaner on her arm as multiple courses of antibiotics, cleansing applications and dressings by rosters of district nurses were tried and failed. She is a tough lady and just kept going as best she could.

Finally, her doctor decided that the stubborn lesion had defeated them all, and his treatment suggestions had run dry.

'I am referring you up to Palmerston North Hospital to see the surgeons. I think our best option may now be to cut it out and get rid of it surgically.'

The surgeons agreed, and Katharine came in for her first clean-up of the wound.

'I'll scrape out all the pus and yucky stuff until there is only clean, bleeding tissue. It'll leave a bit of a gap on your arm, but I'll slap a skin graft over the top and she'll be good as gold,' Mike Young reassured her.

The scraped-out tissue came to the lab, and I set about seeing what was afoot.

'It's an abscess,' I said to Mike, as I was looking down the microscope at it. 'It's just pus, granulation tissue and some scarring. Nothing out of the ordinary. Certainly no tuberculosis or fungal infections or cancer to worry about.'

'Odd, though.' Mike looked at me pensively. 'Every culture has been sterile. So what the hell is causing it?'

The skin graft failed. It dehisced from the arm like a tin roof in a tornado. And the pus was soon back, purulent and evil, messily rotting around the ulcer.

'Bugger!' Mike was not impressed. No surgeon likes to see his beautiful work break down. 'I'll have to do it again.'

But first we had a conversation. 'Is it at all possible Katharine is doing it to herself?' Mike asked.

'You mean self-inflicted? A factitial dermatitis?'

Doctors train to have definite diagnoses for their patients so they have some reasonable idea of what to do to treat them. When something just doesn't add up to a textbook diagnosis, we have trouble handling the uncertainty. Too often, and often too quickly, we begin to think about psychosomatic

'It looks like we've made the wrong diagnosis'

causes. That is a polite and fancy way of saying, 'It is all in your head.'

Although the presence of Katharine's abscess was undeniably not imaginary, there are a sad subgroup of people who come in with strange skin lesions that are self-inflicted. This is the intriguing and rare 'I did it to myself' group of patients.

They won't admit it, of course. All sorts of things are used to damage the skin, from fingernails to chemicals to burning cigarette ends. No one knows why they do it, other than the psychiatric boffins who talk of the afflicted patients' emotional and psychological needs, which is out of my league. It is important to get the diagnosis right, because these folk need psychological help; medical and surgical treatment of the injuries alone just doesn't cut it.

There are a number of variations to this theme. When I was a senior registrar, I went to sit in on a dermatology clinic with the professor, Norma Saxe. A 15-year-old girl called Ruth was our patient, and she was accompanied by her mother. Mum answered the questions and interrupted and did much of the talking. I was difficult to get Ruth to engage, which was noticeably odd.

'Her hair keeps falling out. I just don't know what to do next. I've tried all the different shampoos and conditioners. Vitamins, too. It's cost me a fortune!'

I studied Ruth with interest as Norma tried to divert the questions from mum to daughter. Ruth was a pretty girl with a fine corona of fuzzy, whitish-blonde hair circling her scalp, all about 2 to 3 millimetres in length.

The dermatology registrar did a punch biopsy of the centre and another of the side of the scalp so we could look at her hair follicle roots and find the cause of the problem.

The Final Diagnosis

'It's trichotillomania, isn't it?' Professor Saxe and I were together microscopically examining the shafts of Ruth's hair.

'Yes,' I agreed. 'It's quite unequivocal.' The broken and twisted hair shafts, with lumps of melanin pigment extruding into the dermis, was not a subtle or difficult diagnosis.

'I knew it was that as soon as I saw her mother.' Norma looked smug. 'There's some oddity to their relationship there.'

Maybe she was right, but once more we are in the realms of psychology, so I really couldn't say. Trichotillomania is compulsive hair-pulling, and it is a strange condition in which I have always been interested. It was similar to the pterotillomania that afflicted a feather-plucking macaw that I looked after for a few months when I was a teenager. I have also heard that cats sometimes have it, when they over-groom themselves to baldness. People are said to experience momentary pleasure as the hair pops out, but who can tell if that is what cats and parrots feel, too?

Anyway, as Katharine's wound had grown no bacteria, fungi or viruses, it was inevitable that the thought would pop up that this might be self-inflicted. But I shrugged in answer to Mike's question. I have always regarded this as a diagnosis of the destitute, though I, too, have suggested it a couple of times over the years.

'What about a spider bite?' Kirsty, a young registrar, asked. 'There were some really toxic ones about when I worked in Perth.'

'Necrotising arachnidism?' I nodded. 'You hear a lot about whitetails in New Zealand, but they're harmless, and their bites don't cause ulcers like Katharine has got.'

'What about the katipō, then? They're venomous, aren't they?'

'It looks like we've made the wrong diagnosis'

'They sure are, but it's a neurotoxin — it doesn't do this. No, not spiders.' I shook my head firmly. 'They've got a bad name that they don't deserve, and if it wasn't for them, we would be knee-deep in mosquitoes. I wish people would stop killing them for nothing. No, we are not going to start blaming spiders for Katharine's arm.'

'Well, I am going to debride all her dead tissue again and put on another skin graft. This time I am putting her arm in a cast, so she can't get at it. Then we will see what happens.' Mike was still suspicious of deliberate interference.

The new tissue specimen he cleared out was still full of pus and dead dermis and fat. It was also still as sterile as the moon. Not a bug grew from anything, despite our best efforts to nurture something, *anything* into the light of day.

We hoped for the best and waited six weeks to give the skin graft some dark peace and quiet to take beneath the plaster cast. The day of unveiling came at last, and we found the graft had rotted away and was a grey film floating in a sea of pus. Yet still we could grow nothing from that barren soup.

'Not self-inflicted, then?' I said to Mike. 'What's next, do you think?'

Mike looked at me morosely, shaking his head. 'Maybe she stuck a knitting needle down the back of the cast to get at it?'

'Not impossible, but unlikely. If Katharine did do that, she would have inoculated bacteria into the wound, and we would have found that there. I mean, a knitting needle is not exactly sterile, is it?'

'True enough,' Mike conceded. 'I had better get her to a dermatologist and see if the skin boys have any ideas.'

The Final Diagnosis

Mike Leibowitz was a very astute and experienced dermatologist, who left his Wellington practice to come up to Palmy and help us out for a couple of days a fortnight. He was onto it straight away.

'You've got pyoderma gangrenosum! It's not a typical one but I am quite certain of the diagnosis,' he told Katharine.

'What's that?' Katharine asked. It was quite a mouthful to say, never mind getting your brain around it.

'No one really knows the cause. The ulcers are usually on the legs, but sometimes like yours come up at a different place, especially places you have injured in some way before. The good news is, we can treat you with steroids and that'll clear it up.'

Back in the hospital we heard about Katharine's new diagnosis.

'That would explain what has happened and why all the bacterial cultures are sterile. The microscopy of pyoderma is identical to an abscess, so that all fits very well,' I said thoughtfully, casting my mind over our specimens.

'It's a bit embarrassing to have missed it, isn't it?' Kirsty said.

I sighed, but it was a fair question. 'It is always embarrassing to be wrong. We have gone through the usual saga to get to this diagnosis. Half of all cases of pyoderma are misdiagnosed for long periods before the penny drops. Most are called abscesses, but a self-inflicted factitial dermatitis is also a very common misdiagnosis. We're just about average in performance. Hopefully we'll do better with the next patient we get.'

'What's the cause of pyoderma?' Kirsty asked.

'My old professor always said it was a vasculitis — that an injury changed the blood vessels in some way and the body

'It looks like we've made the wrong diagnosis'

then attacked the walls of the capillaries and the neutrophils poured out to make pus. Lots of us have thought so, too, but there are all sorts of other fancy biochemical explanations these days. It's just another thing we don't really know.'

Thirty years later, sadly Katharine's ulcer has never gone away. Multitudes of treatments and enough pills to fill the back of a ute, and the ulcer still persists to this day. Whatever happened to Katharine's damaged blood vessels all those decades ago became permanent and has so far defied our efforts to heal it. For certain it was never self-inflicted. Katharine remains optimistic and even cheerful in the face of this adversity, a tribute to human resilience.

* * *

Katharine's misdiagnosis was not my first and it will not be my last. Though not common, they are what I dread and feel really bad about. The correct pathological diagnosis is the cornerstone of modern medicine.

When I was a young pathology registrar in my first year of training, I heard a story illustrating how critically important our histological diagnoses of cancer really are. Professor Uys, Head of Pathology at the university, leaned forward one morning at the shiny yellow-wood tea table, smiled at us youngsters, and told the tale.

'If you are ever in doubt how important your diagnosis is, you have only to read up on the case that Professor Symmers reported in the *British Medical Journal* back in 1955.' I would have been one year old then, so of course I hadn't read it, but the point of that story, which has aged year by year like a fine wine alongside me, has never gone away.

Prof Uys told us of a young, newly qualified general surgeon who was operating in the theatre. Last on his list was a young man with a strange swelling of his thigh. It was thought to be a tumour or perhaps a tuberculoma. Tuberculosis was much more common back then, and it was not unusual for TB to present at odd sites as a tumorous mass, mimicking cancer.

The surgeon palpated the mass while the young man was lying on the table waiting for the anaesthetist to put him under.

'I think this may be a cyst and not a solid tumour,' he said, looking up uncertainly. 'Could it be a hydatid cyst, I wonder?'

He decided to put a needle into the mass and see if he could aspirate any fluid and deduce from its appearance what he was dealing with. He held out his upturned palm while looking down at his patient.

'Syringe with a twelve-gauge needle please, Sister.'

The theatre sister had anticipated his need, as they always miraculously seemed able to do, and she firmly but carefully placed the glass syringe and needle into his hand. He pushed the needle deeply into the lesion and drew back on the plunger. Yellow pus smoothly slid into the chamber until it was full. A small spurt of fresh blood trickled in right at the end.

The young surgeon passed the full syringe to the sister. He was still looking down, studying the puncture site where blood and pus were oozing out onto the drapes.

'Can you send that to the laboratory for microbiology? I think it may be an abscess.'

Unfortunately, the sister was looking the other way and did not see him passing the syringe, needle first, towards

'It looks like we've made the wrong diagnosis'

her. He stuck the needle through her theatre gown and into her right breast. She screamed and jerked away but it was too late.

'Terribly sorry about that, sister.' That was the best the young surgeon could do, though to be fair he immediately cleaned and dressed the puncture site. In those far-off days that was about all you really had to offer.

The pathologist later examined the specimen and found that it was indeed pus, and that bacterial clusters of gram-positive cocci were present.

'This is a staphylococcal abscess,' he reported to the still-embarrassed surgeon. 'I am culturing the bacteria on a blood agar plate to confirm its identity, but I am quite sure of the diagnosis.'

A few days later, the theatre sister took the surgeon aside in the theatre and confided, 'I think something may be rather the matter in my breast.'

He was horrified to find her breast had become hot, swollen and red. It was also extremely tender to his touch. There was an abscess in there, and it was centred precisely on the hapless surgeon's puncture mark.

He became decisive. He would fix what he had started, and now. That is what surgeons do.

'You have developed an abscess. I will need to drain it forthwith.'

The anaesthetist was summoned, and the theatre sister was taken into her own theatre, where the surgeon scrubbed up for action.

It all went smoothly. The taut skin of the breast peeled open when the scalpel was pressed down, and pus and blood shot out in a jet under the pressure within. This slowed down to a trickle, then the surgeon probed deeply into the breast tissue with his fingers, breaking down the locules and being rewarded with fresh expressions of blood, pus and dead tissue. Eventually only fresh blood was running, and the toilet was complete.

'Gauze,' the surgeon ordered, and a roll of a long ribbon of gauze soaked in soft yellow paraffin was placed smartly onto his gloved palm. He unrolled the end and took it in a pair of forceps, the point of which he pushed into the furthest depths of the cavity he had made.

He left the head of the gauze behind on withdrawing the forceps, then proceeded to pack the rest of the cavity with the roll until it was filled. Only the tail protruded through the skin to provide a ready port of drainage for any new pus that might form.

'Remove the gauze wick by one inch per day,' he said. That should allow a period of drainage followed by healing from within, as the gauze was incrementally withdrawn, and the cavity healed and obliterated itself.

All went according to plan and the breast healed up well. This was expected, as the sister was a young and vigorous woman and she had received the most professional and careful wound-care to be had anywhere.

However, some months later she once again pulled the young surgeon aside and took him into her confidence.

'I think I may have grown a lump in my breast. Would you mind having a look at it for me?'

He obliged, and was horrified to feel a hard, craggy mass in her breast. It was close to but somewhat above the healed scar of his previous exploration, but he was sure there was something ominous growing there. It felt like a cancer.

'It looks like we've made the wrong diagnosis'

The operating theatre was arranged again, and once more the sister lay draped and anaesthetised, with the surgeon scrubbed and scalpel poised over her scarred breast.

The breast was confidently opened, and he began a dissection around the hardened tumour. Eventually he worked it free, and it lay firm and white in the steel kidney bowl the assisting nurse had obligingly held out.

The surgeon and anaesthetist both eyed the offending tissue. Then they looked at each other.

'What do you think? Is it a cancer?' quizzed the anaesthetist.

The surgeon shrugged. He did not know. He picked it up and fingered it thoughtfully, then suddenly reached a decision. The scalpel flashed, and the tumour was split in two.

He picked it up and squeezed it. Cords of yellowish material shot out of tunnels hidden within. The surgeon let out a triumphant exclamation.

'A-ha! Did you see that? That's comedo necrosis!'

The theatre staff looked at him quizzically. The expression meant nothing to them.

'It's the necrosis you often get with a scirrhous carcinoma. That unquestionably makes this a malignant tumour!' He considered the idea briefly and decided, 'We will proceed to a radical mastectomy and a dissection of her axillary lymph nodes.'

No one demurred, and the mastectomy proceeded to its successful completion. The excised breast with the covering of scarred skin from the previous abscess surgery, together with all the lymph glands and fat from her right axilla, were placed in a bucket of formalin and sent off for the pathologist

The Final Diagnosis

to examine. The lump of scirrhous carcinoma diagnosed by the surgeon was placed in a second jar and off that went to the lab, too.

The young surgeon was shocked by a call from the pathologist a few days later.

'I am afraid there is no evidence of cancer anywhere in the breast or in the eighteen lymph nodes we have found from within the axilla. The separate "tumour" you initially removed is much more interesting. It is not a cancer at all, though.'

'But what about the comedo necrosis I saw? That surely must mean it's a cancer?'

'It's an oleogranuloma, I'm afraid. The "necrosis" you saw were in fact cords of unabsorbed paraffin wax. The surrounding tissue is a granulomatous inflammation and scarring in response to the paraffin wax that has remained within the breast from the gauze you previously inserted.'

'My God, what have I done?' The surgeon looked stricken, as well he might.

'Well, a mastectomy probably was not necessary. It's a pity you did not have a biopsy diagnosis before operating. Next time we would be happy to do a frozen section for you at the outset.'

The crestfallen young surgeon slowly and thoughtfully went on his way down the long corridor. He had a difficult conversation ahead with the theatre sister.

'What did she say? I bet she was ropable at the news. I mean, a mastectomy! That's a really big thing to do for a benign lesion.' I was young and inexperienced, but the enormity of this faux pas was obvious to me even back then.

'Oh no, it all ended very happily.' Professor Uys beamed at us all. This was the part of the story he obviously enjoyed.

'It looks like we've made the wrong diagnosis'

'The surgeon proposed marriage to the young woman, and she accepted. I believe the marriage was a great success, too.' He shook his head, grinning.

'There are two lessons to learn from this story, really. The first is always make sure you have a proven pathological diagnosis of cancer before carrying out a radical treatment.'

We nodded and looked expectantly at the professor.

'What's the second?' one of us prompted.

He chuckled as he spoke. 'The second is that just maybe you can afford to make one such mistake with a breast in your career, but only if you are able to marry your mistake forthwith. And, of course, if she will accept you. Most of us have no such option available, so make sure you get your diagnoses right the first time.'

I now know he was not serious about the marriage proposal, but the importance of having the correct diagnosis still rings true more than half a century later. In modern-day parlance it is 'mission critical'. No surgeon today would ever do any major procedure without a confidently confirmed diagnosis from the pathologists.

* * *

A pathologist creates their experience over decades by learning from unusual cases such as that of the hapless theatre nurse. I missed Katharine's pyoderma gangrenosum, but with the addition of that sobering experience to my knowledge base I hope I will not miss the next case I see.

It is a great feeling when you have an odd or rare case and can say, 'I know what this is! I have seen this condition before.' I was recently reminded of the theatre sister's needled breast and her paraffin granuloma when I had a call from a forensic pathologist named Amy.

'Can I come to show you a strange case that's puzzling me?'

'Sure. What's the story?'

'The patient is a 46-year-old man, a sudden death. The cause of death is not a problem, but he has a most strange-looking tumour on his penis. I've never seen anything like it before.'

The photographs of the lesion were very odd, just as Amy had said. The shaft of the penis was lumpy and irregularly swollen by a poorly demarcated, distorted excrescence.

I knew exactly what this was, for I had seen this condition before, as well as knowing the story of the theatre sister. There is some truth in the wise old saying 'There is nothing new under the sun.'

I suppose a sarcoma, a lymphoma or some other form of cancer would be a possible diagnosis, but in the penis, those are as rare as a blue dick on a pig. One look at the slide under the microscope was enough to confirm the diagnosis. There were clear, rounded globules embedded in the scar tissue, and multinucleate giant cells clung greedily around their circumference.

'It's an oleogranuloma.'

'A what?'

'An oleogranuloma. He's injected Vaseline into his penis, and the paraffin component cannot be absorbed or broken down by the body, so it becomes a granulomatous scar. And that always looks like a tumour.' It was precisely the same body reaction to soft paraffin products as the theatre sister's breast 'cancer' had been, nearly three-quarters of a century before.

'It looks like we've made the wrong diagnosis'

'But who did that to him? Why?'

'He most probably injected it into himself or maybe got a mate to do it. The "why?" is a lot more difficult to answer.' I considered. 'Basically, it's to increase the size of the penis. Just as some women feel a need to have their breasts enlarged to be more attractive, so some men think enlarging their penis size is a great idea. Only it's not.'

Inserting all sorts of things into your penis, from glass to gold and precious gems and pieces of ivory, has been around for thousands of years, including an endorsement in the *Kama Sutra*, so it is not a new idea.

'I have seen a case of an injected penis once before,' I explained, 'though that patient was vehemently in denial. I am not sure his urologist quite believed us either. It's common in prison populations, particularly in Eastern Europe. They call it "Jailhouse Rock" in Hungary, where they reckon one in six of their male muster have had it done.

'Apparently, their results are pretty shabby, with lots of infections and other complications from secretly doing it in a grubby cell. Most prisoners say their sex life is much worse afterwards.'

Prisoners have a complicated social existence, and most who have it done do so on the recommendation of other inmates, even though the results are so dreadful. I suspect there is an element of cocking a snook at authority as well, since these injections are against the prison rules.

Sheer boredom no doubt plays a part, too. I can easily imagine someone thinking, 'I'm not doing anything much on Wednesday, so maybe I'll inject my cock with Vaseline, just to pass the time.'

The Final Diagnosis

* * *

'This is a truly enormous bleed, so the cause of death is not in doubt.'

I had the brain on the mortuary dissecting board, and had just sliced it in half across the middle of the two hemispheres. The right side was swollen and bulging, causing an unnaturally asymmetric appearance. I had already pointed out this obvious abnormality to the registrar when the skull cap was first lifted, exposing the brain.

'This haemorrhage is the grandaddy of them all, measuring ten by six by six centimetres. That hardly leaves the brain much room inside the skull. The clot is centred around his middle cerebral artery. I suppose it will be from a ruptured berry aneurysm as usual. What's a berry aneurysm?' I threw the question to the registrar as I traced the artery concealed like a drain in the groove of the Sylvian fissure.

'It's a congenital aneurysm which looks like a berry on the vine. It's a common cause of intracerebral bleeds.'

'That's right. They're very common — maybe even one person in twenty has one, or even lots. Like your home plumbing, your blood vessels leak at the joints, usually where two artery branches join up. Fortunately, most are very small, and they never bleed. We just carry them unknowingly to our death bed.'

There was nothing clever about this diagnosis. We already knew he had been found unrousable in bed at home and had been brought in by ambulance, unconscious, with a Glasgow Coma Scale result of seven. That's pretty bad, and usually needs aggressive surgery for the patient to have any hope of survival.

'It looks like we've made the wrong diagnosis'

An emergency CT scan had clearly showed the ugly bleed. Sadly, David Whale had died in ICU before anything much more could be done. The cause of death was evident, so for once the autopsy was not being done to discover that. David's family had asked that I do the autopsy, which is very unusual, but they had their reasons and so I agreed.

Two months earlier, David had been in a collision with a truck. It could have been worse, but he was restrained and had got away with multiple lacerations to his face from glass and a superficial graze to his left eye. He was conscious and coherent in ED, with no signs of any significant injury. David couldn't recall the accident, but that is not so unusual. It was not a bad outcome for car versus truck.

A precautionary CT scan was urgently performed, which confirmed he had no obvious internal injuries.

'Dad was wheeled out into the corridor, as he seemed OK,' David's son Daniel told me. 'We stayed with him all the time, but they were too busy to look at him again. We hung around and then they said he seemed fine so we could take him home.'

David remained in bed for a couple of weeks. 'I could see he wasn't himself and slept a lot. Then he recovered and was up and about as usual. He even went back to work.'

There was one worrying problem. The duty radiologist looking at the CT scan on the night of the accident had spotted something unusual. There was a 2.8-centimetre abnormality in the left lung, with some surrounding atelectasis or collapse. She thought this was nothing to do with the trauma of the accident; a tumour was probable, but whether it was benign or malignant was not obvious. There was an enlarged lymph gland in the mediastinal chest cavity, too, which was somewhat ominous, as lung cancers usually spread first to these nodes.

As the lung tumour had nothing to do with that night's trauma, David was referred to the Respiratory Outpatient Clinic for a formal investigation for lung cancer, once he had recovered. He was awaiting a biopsy of the lung tumour when his fatal cerebral haemorrhage hit.

The family accepted the natural nature of the final cerebral catastrophe, but they really wanted to know whether David did have a lung cancer. That was my main task in this autopsy, but I could not resist a look at the brain pathology, too. You just never know what you'll find when you look for yourself.

I looked up quizzically from my dissection when my attention was attracted by a low whistle of surprise.

'Hey doc, look at this, will you!' Pat was cleaning the inside of David's skull for my inspection.

I could not credit what I saw. There was a massive ring fracture of the base of the skull. The break was not a hairline crack but was a good 2 centimetres across. It was still in its normal position and bone had not been driven up into the skull cavity. That was fortunate, as that would definitely have killed David immediately.

'Where in God's name has that come from?' I looked at Pat, perplexed. 'That's not the place for a physical assault. Has he had a massive fall that no one saw, perhaps? It's hard to imagine a deep fracture like this in an ordinary domestic injury.'

This did not make sense. A fractured skull was certainly not the work of a berry aneurysm. I re-examined David's head carefully. Hidden behind his left ear was bruised tissue.

'It looks like we've made the wrong diagnosis'

'This is old bruising by the looks of it, and it has tracked here from the fracture. For God's sake, he was at his GP for a check-up that same morning before his bleed and was passed as fit then. I would guess this fracture is weeks old at least. The fracture and this bruising surely must have happened in the collision with the truck.'

I looked again at the CT scan report from the night of the accident: 'No calvarium or skull base fracture.' It was not visible, which was not surprising. This is perhaps a hard site to see on an X-ray, and the ring fracture was not displaced out of its normal position.

'What does it mean? Do you think it caused that haemorrhage?'

'No.' My mind was running through all the possibilities. 'They aren't related. The haemorrhage is a naturally ruptured berry aneurysm. The fracture is well away from the haemorrhage. The odds are it is from his accident.

'But the accident can't be considered a minor one anymore — it was pretty damn serious. He must have been unconscious with this sort of fracture. I am just surprised that he seemed quite OK when he reached ED. I would have predicted he would have been facing months of concussion, at the very least. It's very odd.' I shook my head in amazement. 'Let's get on with the autopsy. We've got a lung cancer to nail down.'

That was the next surprise. There was no cancer.

I diligently sliced open every single bronchial branch and there was no tumour, benign or malignant.

'It's not here,' I said firmly, looking up. 'The entire lobe is solid, but that is an advanced pneumonia, not a cancer.'

The Final Diagnosis

This was a surprise, too. 'David should have been as sick as a dog with this extent of pneumonia. But there's no history of that at all. Just his sudden collapse.'

I called the Whale family to find out how David had been.

'He was fine. He was a bit up and down after the accident but getting better. He had gone back to work, you know,' his wife told me. 'He'd mowed the lawns the night before his collapse, and then sat down and had a beer. No, he was OK.'

That was extraordinary to me. It seemed nothing had fazed David, neither a fractured skull nor an advanced pneumonia. He must have been a tough hombre.

The surprises were not over yet. The histology of the brain tissue changed everything again. There was no berry aneurysm to be seen, but his blood vessels were in trouble. There was a septic vasculitis, with white blood cells attacking and destroying the vessel walls. The walls were pink with fibrinoid necrosis, which basically means the inflammation had rotted them away. Blood had burst through the destroyed coat and that was the cause of his haemorrhage.

'What on Earth has caused this?' I was bemused at how David kept throwing up confounding issues when his was a straightforward death.

David's lung was as I had thought, and was obliterated by a necrotising pneumonia. There was no cancer there.

In working out a cause of death, you should pull all information and findings into a single story. You can die with several different things going on, but it is messy if they do not fit closely together. What, then, could be David's unifying story?

The best, and perhaps only, reasonable fit is that it all came about because of the motor accident. David fractured

'It looks like we've made the wrong diagnosis'

the base of his skull and was knocked unconscious for a spell at the scene, which explains him not remembering it. While unconscious, he had aspirated some infected material into his left lung, and that was the lesion seen on the CT scan that night.

The lung aspiration had continued to fester during his recuperation and had extended into a necrotising pneumonia. Bacterial organisms had broken through from this into his bloodstream and had seeded into the vessels of the brain. Usually with bugs in the blood you would be really crook, but David seemed to have evaded that one, too. He was always so well as not to excite any concerns.

David's death was unexpected and there is a significant possibility that it is due to the complications of his accident.

'Could we have saved him?' his son Daniel asked me. The answer is that there is no answer to this question, but it is possible that an early recognition of his pneumonia may well have led to a different and successful treatment, but the cards did not fall that way. The infected and inflamed blood vessels of his brain were where his fatal problem lay, and when they burst, they have written *finis* to this script.

> *... a man whose blood*
> *Is very snow-broth; one who never feels*
> *The wanton stings and motions of the sense*
> — William Shakespeare, *Measure for Measure*,
> Act I Scene IV, 1604

CHAPTER 14

Semper ad meliora — always towards better things

Death is what pathologists are known for. It is an inevitable date for all of us and may even be the apotheosis of our lives. The science-fiction writer David Gerrold has a droll but accurate view of it all: 'Life is hard. Then you die. Then they throw dirt in your face. Then the worms eat you. Be grateful it happens in that order.'

The 'if' of death is certain, the 'when' is unknown, but it is the 'why' that really gets people's interest.

The investigation of the cause of death for me is the highlight of pathology. It is a bringing together of so much that is fascinating: the circumstances in which the body was found, the background of the dead person whose turn has come unexpectedly, the concealed stories the police have gathered — all are naturally engrossing, but the best part is yet to come. That 'best part' is the careful autopsy with everything examined, photographed, dissected and its significance pondered to bring forth the person's final story.

The scientific method underpins every aspect, from

Semper ad meliora — always towards better things

observing the injuries or diseased organs to making assumptions and deductions about how they arose, and then testing the conclusions reached. It feels like successfully finishing the last clue in a tricky crossword puzzle or line in an advanced sudoku.

The most intriguing part with suspicious deaths is checking back to see if the story you have put together makes sense. To see how this is done, we must go back to what my old forensic pathology lecturer Kevin Lee taught us so long ago.

'Put yourself in the mind of the murderer and think what he would have done at the scene and why. Then look at all the evidence and see if your theory fits the observed evidence or not. There is little point in suggesting a scenario that any rational person would look at and say, "Nah! Never happened,"' he told us.

'Most folk are simple creatures, and they behave exactly as you would expect in any given situation. If they don't—' Kevin would shake his head here and grin at us, 'then you have a problem, don't you? Because you'll have a wild card on your hands, and they're unpredictable.'

I always try to carry out the Kevin Lee reality check before reaching a final decision. I remember Kevin telling me of a memorable case involving a murder — a brutal stabbing in an Australian city — that demonstrated this procedure perfectly.

The police had found the body of a woman stabbed multiple times, lying on her kitchen floor. Kevin had a bit of a look around and a ponder, then he asked the police what they wanted to know.

The detective smiled, apparently humouring Kevin. 'So, who did it then, doc?'

The Final Diagnosis

Kevin told him what he thought had happened. 'The murderer was a man six foot two or three tall, who was known to the victim. He has killed her with a nine-inch-long carving knife that he took out of her kitchen drawer.

'He has then left the house by the front door, and has reached up and put the knife in the spouting above the veranda outside the front door.'

The bemused detectives had a ladder brought in and placed up against the spouting. A bloodied carving knife with an ivory handle lay gummed to the floor of the spouting with dried blood.

'How did you figure that out?' I asked Kevin. I was impressed. His level of detective work was at least on a par with Sherlock Holmes at his best!

'It's all reasonably straightforward.' Kevin always said that, even when it did not seem to be so to any of us. 'The amount of blood in the kitchen showed she had clearly bled out all over the floor, so obviously it hadn't happened somewhere else in the house.

'It was obvious from what I could see even without an autopsy that she had been stabbed many times by a broad-bladed knife, like a carving knife. They are usually nine inches long.

'The knife drawer in the kitchen was closed, and even though I did not go through it, a betting man would be safe putting money on there being a carving fork in there but no companion knife. Why would that be? The murderer surely must have picked up the knife here, because no one comes visiting carrying a nine-inch carving knife in their hands, do they? It doesn't fit easily into your pocket for starters, and it's a bit conspicuous.

'There was no evidence of breaking and entering. No sign of a struggle, rape or robbery, so it's logical that she let the murderer in the front door because she knew him.

'The front doorway opened onto the street, which, while not hectic, was reasonably busy with passersby, both pedestrian and the usual traffic. There were other ways out of the house, but they all led into neighbouring houses, so were probably not the first exit of choice for someone wanting to escape from a murder scene.'

'And the knife in the spouting? That's pretty specific.'

Kevin nodded. 'Get into his mind and think of what you'd have done. You have just completed stabbing someone multiple times, and you walk out onto a busyish road with a large knife, dripping blood, still clutched in your hand.

'The knife must still be in your hand, because we know you didn't leave it behind in the kitchen, did you? It's far too big to hide by putting it into your pocket.

'The road's busy. Someone will see you with it for certain and then be able to identify you. You're very conspicuous holding that knife.

'You stop and look around you. What the hell should you do?

'You look up. There is the spouting. That's a good place to hide it.

'As you are six foot three, you do not need a ladder. You are able to just stretch up and pop it over the top into the pipe. So you do exactly that.

'I was lucky this time,' admitted Kevin. 'When I looked up, I could also see a tiny speck of blood on the edge of the spouting where he had brushed it with his hand, so I knew the knife was in there.'

The Final Diagnosis

I have always tried to do the same mental transference and put myself both at the scene and in the mind of all my cases, so I can see if all the evidential ducks line up and the cause of death makes sense. I do it for all unnatural deaths, not only the murders, though I have to confess never with the same panache that Kevin Lee brought to his case.

The real joy is when the case all becomes clear, and I reach that a-ha! moment when I can tell the tale of the deceased with complete confidence that this is logically what happened.

I have shown how several of my cases turned out applying this method. Let us now have a look at a famous historical suspicious death and see how we get on using Kevin's pathological approach.

* * *

I went to Wellington a few years ago to see the Van Gogh Alive exhibition, though it was his death rather than his life and paintings that caught my attention. I was surprised to read there that Vincent van Gogh had died a full two days after attempting suicide by shooting himself. I knew that he had committed suicide, and I had always thought with his history of cutting off his ear that he must be a victim of depression. That is the sort of narrative that most people have heard.

On reading this, my pathologist's antenna went up immediately, however. How on Earth did he take two days to die? That sounds very odd for a suicide. What were the circumstances? How was the death investigated? Did his bullet miss? How?

Semper ad meliora — always towards better things

I decided to research his story, and the whole scenario seems to me not to be as it has conventionally been presented. I will explain why by looking at what we know of his death from a modern-day pathologist's perspective.

Vincent van Gogh's background history was certainly unusual. He had earlier cut off his ear in a rage, precipitated by a fight with fellow artist Paul Gauguin. Gauguin apparently did not want to share accommodation with Van Gogh, which is not too surprising given his subsequent behaviour. Amputating an ear is a rather excessive reaction to a squabble with a mate. He also presented the severed organ to a friendly prostitute called Rachel as a sign of his affection, which is not exactly the conventional way to a girl's heart, you would have thought.

Vincent realised all was not well with his mental health. He had prevailed on his older brother to pay for him to spend time in an asylum near Saint-Rémy a year before his death. While there, his progress was patchy, but he recovered reasonably well, though he thought the other inmates were a bad influence on his mental state. He therefore discharged himself.

He next headed off to Auvers-sur-Oise, a pretty area that was something of an artists' gathering spot in northern France, to continue his painting. He put up at the Auberge Ravoux, a local inn where other artists were also in residence.

He painted a number of pictures there and took time to write to friends, saying, 'Then I felt I had better try a change, and for that matter, the pleasure of seeing my brother, his family and my painter friends again has done me a lot of good, and I am feeling completely calm and normal.' To his mother and sister, he wrote of his majestic painting of the

The Final Diagnosis

wheatfields far up in the hills: 'I am in a mood of almost too much calm, just the mood for painting this.'

There were darker letters, too. Clearly Vincent was a man in torment and prone to mood swings, and it is hard for us to fathom his mind through the small instalments in his letters. His brother Theo suggested that he should consult his doctor, Paul Gachet, about his ill health.

Dr Gachet was a homeopath and an amateur artist, as well as being a friend to many other artists. Vincent was not impressed by him at first, writing to Theo: 'I think we must not count on Dr Gachet at all. First of all, he is sicker than I am, I think, or shall we say just as much, so that's that.'

Many patients have probably had similar thoughts about their doctors, I am sure, but Vincent did change his mind over time, and even painted the good doctor's picture, twice. In these paintings, Gachet is holding a foxglove, the source of digitalis. Some have wondered if Gachet might have been treating Vincent with digitalis and overdid the dose, as this substance causes xanthopsia or colour disturbances in your vision, and may have been the inspiration for those yellow swirls he painted so vividly in his amazing picture *The Starry Night*.

As pathologists these days, in investigating suspicious deaths we are expected to collect blood, urine and stomach contents, as well as various organ tissues to perform toxicology tests on. That was not so in 1890, so we can only guess at what, if anything, was in Van Gogh's blood. What we might have found is rich in possibilities, and Dr Gachet's possible overdosing with digitalis is but one aspect.

Van Gogh's favourite tipple was absinthe, 'the green fairy'. Absinthe is an interesting spirit that hails originally

Semper ad meliora — always towards better things

from Switzerland, and was immensely popular with painters, writers and other creative types back in the late nineteenth century. A significant component of it is the wormwood plant, *Artemesia absinthium*, which contains psychedelic chemicals called thujones that can cause both psychosis and seizures. The liquor was banned because of these chemicals in parts of Europe and the United States for nearly a hundred years.

How much absinthe he drank around the time of death is unknown, but he was also known to refresh himself with the turpentine he carried as part of his painting kit. He also generally put copious amounts of camphor on his pillows and mattress to help him sleep. Camphor is toxic, causing irritability and fits if it gets into the body in significant amounts.

Finally, Vincent was in the habit of sucking on his brush handles. Whether by habit, from deep artistic thought or because he had pica (a condition whereby people compulsively eat substances that are not food), as has been suggested, I do not know, but many of his paints contained lead pigment. Lead is a long-term neurotoxin, and the historical poisoning of artists is a well-known danger.

None of this toxicology is available to assist us in our investigation today, but we do have Vincent's last draft letter to Theo, written the day he was shot, and found on his body. It is a bit rambling but to me is not a suicide note like others I have seen. The letter seems more concerned about art dealers and their vulturine financial exploitation of dead artists' works — probably as intense a topic amongst artists back then as it is now. It is notable that Van Gogh sold only one painting while alive, *The Red Vineyard*, for 400 francs, the modern-day equivalent of NZ$2600.

The Final Diagnosis

That's a long way short of, for instance, the foxglove-adorned painting of Dr Gachet, which is reckoned today to have a value of about NZ$180 million! Imagine being worth so much more dead than alive!

So much for his mental health background; what do we believe happened on that Sunday morning, 27 July 1890? What we do know is based mainly on second-hand eyewitness accounts, mostly given decades later, once Van Gogh had become posthumously famous. We have seen from the earlier discussion of the Olivia Hope and Ben Smart murders the poor value of any eyewitness evidence, particularly when it is given so much later, in a blaze of publicity. We must bear that in mind in this investigation, too.

The conventional story is that he went up in the wheatfields to paint. The sombre *Wheatfield with Crows* is often represented as his last work, but the actual picture on which he was working was never found. Very curiously, his paint box and other apparel also vanished. We must conclude it was either hidden away or was stolen.

Dusk fell and Vincent had not returned to the inn, which was very unusual, as he had been out since just after breakfast. He crept back very late, at about 9 p.m., clutching his stomach as he climbed the stairs to his bedroom, and lay groaning on his bed.

Arthur Ravoux, the master of the house, went up to Van Gogh's room and asked him if he was ill. Vincent pulled up his shirt to show a gunshot wound to his upper abdomen, below the heart. The innkeeper sent for Dr Gachet, who dressed the wound but said it was hopeless. Ravoux, good host that he was, sat up with Vincent throughout that night.

Semper ad meliora — always towards better things

The local gendarmes arrived the next morning and asked Vincent, 'Did you intend to commit suicide?'

Vincent replied, 'I think so.'

This is a strange and rather equivocal sort of answer, and I do not think that this comment, even if true, resolves what happened.

Vincent van Gogh died at 1.30 a.m. on the morning of Tuesday, 29 July 1890 — 29 hours after he had first staggered back to the inn.

On reflection, the site of the entrance wound is immediately suspicious to me. It is a most improbable spot for a potential suicide to choose to shoot themselves. Death would be anything but certain, as it is easy to miss all the vital organs, as indeed happened to Vincent. No one can seriously believe he was shot precisely 29 hours earlier, moments before he dragged himself back into the inn. He certainly would have been shot significantly earlier on that Sunday, and therefore survived a good while after.

To shoot oneself in the midriff involves awkwardly holding a revolver reversed, with fingers of the right hand around the butt, and a thumb inside the guard to pull the trigger. Revolvers are heavy, so the barrel would have to be held in the left hand. A bit of experimentation shows this is a most unnatural position, and one I think is highly improbable in an attempted suicide.

The limited reliable information about the wound is pathologically significant only in what it does not say. There were no mentions of powder burns on his left hand or sprayed across the skin around the entry point. The cartridges of those days were dirty, and more than half of the powder would be hurled unburnt onto hands and skin if the gun

The Final Diagnosis

was close enough to the point of firing. In a suicide, the gun obviously must be close to the body, and powder burns would be inevitable. Conversely, a shot from a distance — as in a murder — would create a completely clean entry wound.

Forensic expert Dr Vincent DiMaio published a brilliant forensic pathology article looking into the effect of shots fired from the same 7-millimetre calibre Lefaucheaux model revolver allegedly used in the shooting. He found that it was 'not probable for Vincent van Gogh to shoot himself without a described powder burn'. The shot therefore must have been fired from a distance.

It looks like someone else shot Vincent, and that he has then concealed this fact for some reason. Guns were not readily available in Europe in the 1890s, and certainly not to the likes of the chronically hard-up and mentally fragile Vincent van Gogh. So, from where did the offending weapon come? And who fired it?

A compelling exposé of the murder hypothesis was published by Pulitzer Prize-winning writers Steven Naifeh and Gregory White Smith in their 976-page book *Van Gogh: The Life*. They ferreted out the existence of a group of well-to-do teenagers in the neighbourhood. One of them, 16-year-old René Secrétan, liked to dress in cowboy clothes modelled on 'Buffalo Bill' Cody, who he had seen in a show in Paris the year before. René was able to source an unreliable revolver with live ammunition as an accoutrement for his costume, apparently from none other than innkeeper Arthur Ravoux.

This gang of teenagers made a sport of bullying the shambling, mumbling Dutchman Van Gogh, at times salting his drink, spicing up his brush handles with hot pepper and once putting a snake in his box of paints. Many years later Secrétan, now a retired successful banker, admitted the boys bullied Van Gogh. He also said of his revolver, 'It worked when it worked', and rather tellingly implicates himself by saying that it was 'fate' that it chose to work on the day it shot Van Gogh.

Secrétan denied any direct involvement in Van Gogh's death, though, and was anxious to point out he had an alibi, as he had left town for Paris before the shooting. This unplanned early departure was very unusual, as it was still only mid-summer, and the middle of his holiday break. One wonders what precipitated his premature return. Could it perhaps be a case of discretion being the better part of valour, and that putting some distance between himself and unfolding events was perhaps prudent?

I am speculating, but it would be remarkable if Van Gogh did not on occasion lose his rag with his teenage tormenters. That may have happened on this Sunday and brought about some unfortunate horseplay in response, leading to an accidental discharge of the revolver.

Van Gogh decided to keep quiet about what happened between them, either because of his own guilty contribution to the fracas or because of an aberration of his mercurial state of mind. Possibly both reasons contributed, which explains his strange statement to the investigating gendarmes: 'Do not accuse anyone. It is I who wanted to kill myself.'

The innkeeper Ravoux also later openly said it was suicide, too, but as the alleged supplier of the offending revolver to Secrétan, he possibly had a very good reason for the death not to be too closely scrutinised.

Van Gogh's death remains highly contentious and unresolved, with most art experts strongly advocating for the long-held view of the unrecognised but brilliant artist taking his own life in despair. This is not surprising, as the Van Gogh brand has considerable intellectual property invested in this compelling suicidal characterisation of his death.

This armchair investigation of Vincent's death is an interesting exercise and one that is difficult to resolve now, though DiMaio suggested an exhumation and autopsy to start with. An autopsy might unlock the puzzle, although the most revealing remaining question to me is one I have not yet seen discussed: did the bullet pass through his clothing or not?

If it did not hole his clothing, that would suggest a suicide to me. Forensic pathologists believe it is generally more plausible that a suicide would bare their skin before firing a bullet. Why is that? It is due to one of those ironic twists in our human nature, where first of all you wouldn't want to ruin your clothes with a hole, and secondly you wouldn't want to put even a minor deflecting barrier between the bullet and yourself.

For me, his clothes not having a bullet hole would clinch the cause of death as suicide. I cannot visualise any reasonable scenario where Vincent, or indeed anyone at all, might have lifted his shirt to present his naked midriff for an impending gunshot assault.

Although it is still possible to argue that he may have shot himself through his clothing, I think that the combination of his clothing being both bullet-holed as well as unstained by a powder burn would indicate a distant shot, and prove we are looking at a murder. Alas, the condition of Vincent's clothing is lost to us forever and cannot now help our investigation.

Those are the facts as far as we know them today. Suicide

or murder? I personally think there is a reasonably strong circumstantial case for murder, but I am also sure that even an average defence lawyer would get an acquittal for René Secrétan.

What would you tell the coroner?

* * *

Pathologists deal in real things. Bodies, organs, specimens, blood — those are all the physical subjects of my stories. But is there more?

'Do you think the bodies of the people you autopsy have a soul?'

It is a deep question I am frequently asked, and the short answer is yes.

The first dead body I ever saw was as a 19-year-old medical student, on the first day I entered the Dissection Hall in the Anatomy Department, in July 1973. I perched on a hard stool along with five other nervous students arranged around an embalmed body lying on a gurney. We looked at each other but avoided staring down at the 50-year-old African male lying naked between us. The smell of the embalming fluid is a strong memory of that first day.

This time the previous year I had been a prefect at school, wearing a straw boater, khaki shorts and a shirt with a stripy tie. Now I was sitting by a dead man and truly on my way to becoming a doctor.

Once we had been into that hall a few times, the novelty wore off, and I found myself thinking more of the person I was dissecting rather than of my inner turmoil of thoughts.

'Who were they?' We did not know and were never told.

The Final Diagnosis

'How did they come to be here?' Also a mystery.

'Where were their family? Did they know their loved one was here and what we were doing?' No one knew.

'What did they die of?' We were young and knew nought of pathology, so we were studying their anatomy only, and we never saw or had pointed out to us the cause of their death.

They were destined therefore to remain forever strangers to us, despite a very intimate knowledge of every fibre and nerve of their bodies.

I often thought about these questions and others during the long year we shared so intimately with these people. I felt I knew them well and developed something of a sense of who they had been, what they had meant to people and how they might have experienced life.

This is a long-winded way of saying that I thought there was 'something' there. We say 'something' when we are embarrassed by using the word 'soul'. This is partly because we do not want people to think that we might believe in God in preference to the prosaic logic and reason that now prevail in the twenty-first century.

The soul is the immaterial essence of life. It activates life and makes us real as humans. In a way, it means to our living, cognitive existence what the Higgs bosun or 'God particle' means to the Big Bang and to the creation of the solid, purely physical part of our being.

Unlike the Higgs bosun, the soul cannot be detected or measured, so it perforce must rest in the twilight world of the unproven and not sit in the bright, sunlit pastures of science.

Yet I did sense a soul in him, my first ever dead body, and many a time I have felt the same feeling of that 'something' in the bodies of my patients. I feel their sadness and sometimes despair, and it seems more real to me than merely the usual compassion I or indeed anyone might feel towards another human being beset by the gravest misfortune of their lives.

I do not know why I am always asked this question about the soul, because I cannot answer it. That is because I do not know the answer for a scientific fact.

I tell people what I think, when I am asked, but I hope I am not arrogant enough to confuse genuine knowledge with my opinion. Such a confusion is a surprisingly common failing in pathology, as it most probably is in most professions.

For example, in the Privy Council hearing of the Lundy appeal, Professor Bernard Knight told the court he had done 25,000 autopsies and that 'gastric emptying is of little use' in determining the time of death.

Professor Knight was giving his opinion on a dynamic process occurring in the living based on his postmortem observations. Did he actually know the precise interval between the last meal and the death of any of these 25,000 people? I would think it very unlikely, and if not, then what he said is not scientific knowledge, it is only his opinion.

Professor David Silk, on the other hand, contradicts Professor Knight and says gastric emptying is a physiologically predictable process, and he can measure it in living patients using a sophisticated test meal. He says that 90 per cent of a meal remains in the normal living stomach after one hour, based on thousands of patients he has tested. Professor Silk's observation is reproducible and is therefore true scientific knowledge.

I have an opinion that the dead do have a soul, but this is not the same as having provable knowledge that there is

The Final Diagnosis

such a thing. This opinion is an act of faith. As a scientist I shouldn't be answering questions of faith with any sort of authority. In fact, no one should, because you just cannot create a scientific fact merely by having an opinion.

If we could measure the presence of a soul in a repeatable way, it would become a fact about which I could talk with authority. But we can't measure the soul. Or can we? Does the soul have a measurable colour or temperature or weight that will convince the sceptical scientists?

Dr Duncan MacDougall believed the soul must have weight, and when it left the body at death, he should therefore be able to measure this loss. Back in 1901 in Haversham, Massachusetts, he set out to do exactly that.

Dr MacDougall was a graduate of the Boston Medical School, described by *The New York Times* as a 'reputable physician'. As well as being a poet he was a careful scientist, and his experiment was well constructed for the turn of the nineteenth century.

He began his experiment on 10 April 1901. Wilbur and Orville Wright were then still only tinkering with their flying contraption in their garage, and it would be nearly four years before they got it to take off on a beach in Kittyhawk for mankind's first controlled flight. We must therefore look at what Dr MacDougall did and what happened through the lens of this earlier time and not ours.

Dr MacDougall set up a bed for his dying patients, 'arranged on a light framework built upon a delicate, balanced platform on a Fairbanks scale'. This was an industrial scale used to weigh bolts of imported silk, which was accurate down to two-tenths of an ounce or 5.67 grams. Any urine or stool inadvertently passed at death would remain in the bed and would make no difference to the overall weight.

'I thought it best to select a patient dying with a disease that produces great exhaustion. The death would occur with little or no muscular movement. In such a case the beam would be more perfectly at balance and any loss occurring readily noted.'

The problem was, where to find a supply of such patients who might readily agree to be his ghostly guinea pigs? As it happened, there was a possible supply of patients whose deaths were reasonably predictable from the Cullis Consumptives Home for those terminally ill with tuberculosis, which was also in Haversham. Tuberculosis was quite widespread in those days, and it killed about 25 per cent of its victims. Thousands of these had been cared for in the Cullis Home, which was faith-based and hoped for a cure through the power of prayer. It was an easy matter to find a few willing subjects amongst the dying.

'My first subject was a man dying of tuberculosis,' Dr MacDougall said. He sat with two other doctors and the patient waiting for the moment of death to come, which took three hours and forty minutes.

Dr MacDougall found in the four patients he conducted this experiment on that the weight of the body decreased by between three-eighths and three-quarters of an ounce at the precise moment of death. This three-quarters of an ounce captured the public imagination, and became the 21 grams that popular culture has assigned to his findings ever since.

He repeated the whole shenanigan with 15 dogs that he euthanised. There was no such drop in weight in the hapless hounds, which is what he expected, since dogs were believed not to have a soul. I am sure my two Labradors would not go along with that observation, although it is a fact they would sell any soul they might possess for half a biscuit!

So perhaps there is a measurable soul after all? His findings and experiment have been widely rejected and criticised for all sorts of reasons, of which none of the scientific counterarguments stand up to scrutiny.

That is not the scientific way. In science, if an observation is made it should be repeated and shown to be a constant or at least a consistent finding by lots of others. Then if this phenomenon does exist, we could propose a theory to explain what we have seen and continue to test the hypothesis.

None of this has happened, almost certainly due to ethical considerations. I understand the hesitancy, yet if it were possible to do it, it would be great, if only to set our curiosity at rest.

I thought the loss he saw might be due to air exhaled out at death as breathing stops. I experimented breathing fully in and then out on our mortuary scale, which is accurate to 0.1 gram, and it made not the slightest difference to my weight. It therefore cannot be the expulsion of air in the proverbial death rattle that causes the loss.

I thought I was onto a possible explanation when I read in *New Scientist* that you weigh different amounts by day and night. You are heavier at midnight than midday, due to the additive gravitational pull of the mass of the Earth added to that of the sun. Mike Follows, a physicist and researcher into superfluids and dark-matter detection, writes, 'Celestial mechanics are complex', but that 'crunching the numbers, the weight of someone living on the equator would increase by about 0.1% when on the dark side of Earth compared with the lit side'. He continues: 'If you are at the same latitude as the UK, the diurnal variation would be down to about twenty grams.'

Bingo! I thought. Might it account for the missing 21 grams if MacDougall happened to do his weighing at the opposite ends of the day?

It seemed very unlikely, but you never know unless you check. Once I re-read Dr MacDougall's account, I saw his patients were being continuously weighed throughout the period of their dying, and the fall was seen only at the very moment of death. Although difference by day and night was a tempting explanation that, alas, could not therefore be the cause.

In short, I have no plausible scientific explanation for the loss of weight, but I remain intrigued to know the cause of what Dr MacDougall recorded. I also mischievously sometimes imagine what would be the result if Dr MacDougall's observations were proved correct. We live in a secular society, which mirrors the Western world at large. Would we think differently if we suspected or knew we had a soul? Would there be a renewed interest in religion? In spiritualism? Do atheists also lose weight on death, or do they have no weight to their souls, like MacDougall's hapless hounds? What about souls in different religions? Do Christian and Buddhist souls both weigh the same?

There are so many questions to be answered about science, about humankind, about pathology and even about our souls. I only wish that we could all know more.

The Final Diagnosis

He who knows and knows he knows,
He is a wise man, seek him.
He who knows and knows not that he knows,
He is asleep, wake him.
He who knows not and knows he knows not,
He is a child, teach him.
He who knows not and knows not that he knows not,
He is a fool, shun him.

— Persian proverb, origin unknown